# INDUSTRIAL RELATIONS
# A MARXIST INTRODUCTION

# INDUSTRIAL RELATIONS

*A Marxist Introduction*

RICHARD HYMAN

MACMILLAN

First edition 1975
Reprinted 1977, 1978, 1979, 1981, 1982, 1983, 1984, 1986, 1989, 1990

Published by
THE MACMILLAN PRESS LTD
Houndmills, Basingstoke, Hampshire RG21 2XS
and London
Companies and representatives
throughout the world

Printed in Hong Kong

ISBN 0–333–18666–4 (hardcover)
ISBN 0–333–18667–2 (paperback)

for judy: partner and comrade

# Contents

# Preface

Research and analysis in industrial relations usually start from the assumption that stable and orderly relationships between employers and workers are normal and self-evidently desirable. Much of the literature is explicitly designed to advise managers how to maintain a tractable labour force. The Marxist focus on class struggle and workers' self-activity is therefore alien to the most commonly disseminated perspectives on industrial relations. Understandably, the very concept of 'industrial relations' is regarded with suspicion by Marxists: 'the consecrated euphemism for the permanent conflict, now acute, now subdued, between capital and labour' (Miliband 1969 : 80).* This has not inhibited some Marxists from criticising the mystification and apologetics displayed by much of the literature. But the critics themselves tend to accept their opponents' battleground, by confronting particular aspects of the current orthodoxy in a piecemeal and negative manner. None has attempted to set out an integrated alternative approach, rooted in more general Marxist theory.

This then is the aim of the present book. The intention is to sketch an approach which grasps 'industrial relations' as an element in a *totality* of social relations of production. Because of the focus on theory, the development of a framework for analysis, no attempt is made to provide a comprehensive survey of the empirical detail of industrial relations or the views of other writers – though the text deals partially with both.

My intellectual debts are twofold. Whatever understanding of Marxism I can claim I owe to the writings of Marx and Engels

* References and quotations in the text give author and date of publication, together (where appropriate) with the page(s) cited. Details of publication are given in the Bibliography.

themselves, of Lenin, Luxemburg, Trotsky, Lukacs, Gramsci and a host of others; to discussions with many fine comrades in the course of a number of years in the socialist movement; and to the lessons of workers themselves engaged in struggle. Most that I know about British industrial relations I have learned from teachers, colleagues, students and trade unionists. Since in this book I focus on many points of mutual disagreement, it is appropriate to record how much I owe to Hugh Clegg, whose compendious knowledge and unrelenting critical eye have done much over the years to sharpen my own presentation of controversial interpretations. In writing this particular book I have benefited from the criticisms of a number of colleagues, many of whom are unsympathetic to its basic argument.

In seeking to develop a Marxist perspective for the introductory reader I have been faced by two problems which I cannot claim to have resolved satisfactorily. The first is that Marxism is far from monolithic : but most of the differences of interpretation and subtleties of analysis have had to be neglected here. The second is conceptual. The categories which form the normal framework of academic analysis and everyday discourse (and not merely in industrial relations) are often superficial, and fail to permit adequate analysis of key social processes and relationships. For this reason, Marxists have developed concepts and terminology which are often strange and even uncomprehensible to the uninitiated. Because of the introductory level of this book I have attempted to employ everyday language as far as possible; and for this reason, some Marxists may accuse me of oversimplification. The Guide to Further Reading at the end of the book points to more varied and more developed Marxist treatment of many of the issues covered in the text.

May this book soon become redundant : first by stimulating more, and better, Marxist scholarship in industrial relations; second, and far more important, by the *abolition* of 'industrial relations' as it exists today through working-class struggle.

R.H.

*Coventry, February 1975*

# Introduction

Until quite recently, industrial relations was[1] usually regarded as one of the least exciting areas of social analysis. It normally took some major breakdown between employers and unions – and these were far from common – before press and television showed much interest in the processes of collective bargaining. Leaving aside those professionally involved in industrial relations, serious students of the subject were few and far between, and often regarded with some puzzlement by their academic colleagues.

In the last few years this situation has been transformed – for reasons some of which are discussed later. Whereas practitioners of industrial relations used to regret the neglect of their activities in the media, today they are more likely to complain of excessive attention. Relations between unions, employers and the state have been elevated to the status of a central social and political issue. University departments of industrial relations have burgeoned. In such courses as sociology and economics – at degree, diploma and even GCE level – growing attention is given to the subject. This book is intended to provide a short and readable introduction to industrial relations for the increasing numbers of such students. At the same time it is designed with the general reader in mind – and in particular for those whose activities in factory, shop or office provide the matter which others analyse and investigate.

The aim of the book is explicitly *theoretical*. Perhaps this calls for an explanation, for 'theory' is something of a dirty word in this country. The English, wrote Tawney, 'are incurious as to

[1] Should it be 'industrial relations were'? It is doubtless grammatically odd, but when the concept 'industrial relations' is used to designate the area of study it is normally treated as singular rather than plural.

theory, take fundamentals for granted, and are more interested in the state of the roads than in their place on the map' (1961 : 9). Theory is seen as something indulged in by people in armchairs or in ivory towers, a luxury which practical men cannot afford. Yet a theory is not something divorced from and opposed to action; without theory men *cannot* act, for a theory is a way of seeing, of understanding, and of planning. The real world is so complex, it comprises so many phenomena, relations and events that we can make sense of it only by focusing on some aspects and ignoring others. We generalise from those elements of social life with which we are familiar, and seek to interpret and explain the unfamiliar in the light of these generalisations. We make predictions about the future course of events, and in the light of these we choose one course of action rather than another. In every case we are organising and selecting on the basis of some principles, some analytical framework : and it is precisely this which is meant by theory. Those who glory in their pragmatism and insist that they are immune from theory are simply unaware of their own preconceptions and presuppositions. They employ random hunches; their stock of ideas and beliefs, because commonplace, are not critically scrutinised but are viewed as 'mere common sense'.[2] Yet taken-for-granted assumptions are not always the best basis for action, particularly in a world which is constantly changing and where traditional ideas are therefore rendered obsolescent. By contrast, explicit theoretical discussion and argument which seeks to locate individual happenings in their broader context can inform and illuminate action : it is thus a highly *practical* activity.

Suspicion of open theorising is particularly common in industrial relations. Few managers see any point in analysis which does not offer an obvious and immediate pay-off. Trade unionists, whatever their differences on other questions, for the most part agree on this point. 'Indifference towards all theory', wrote Engels a century ago, 'is one of the main reasons why the English working-class movement crawls along so slowly in spite of the splendid organisation of the individual unions' (1958 : 652). The

[2] Keynes's comment is often quoted: 'practical men, who believe themselves to be quite exempt from any intellectual influences, are usually the slaves of some defunct economist' (1936 : 383).

same is largely true today; and the consequences, as is argued below, can be extremely harmful for trade unionism.

Even among academic analysts of industrial relations there is considerable reluctance to concentrate explicitly on the discussion of theory. The literature provides a great wealth of empirical detail on trade unions, employers' organisations, bargaining systems, processes of wage determination and so on; but so complex is the picture that emerges that any purely empirical or descriptive account of British industrial relations is altogether perplexing to the student. Most of the theoretical argument which does occur is focused on limited areas of the field: the effect of payment systems on the pattern of disputes, for example, or the determinants of union growth. Attempts to develop an integrated and comprehensive theoretical framework for the analysis of industrial relations as a whole are however comparatively rare. Essays in general industrial relations theory, when such *are* made, almost invariably centre around the notion of an industrial relations system – which has enjoyed something of a vogue in the last few years. This book is written in the conviction that this dominant theoretical approach is not particularly illuminating, and indeed distorts or conceals important aspects of industrial relations; and that a more satisfactory theoretical framework can be constructed. The book therefore begins with a fairly generalised theoretical discussion, which sets the context for the more specific analysis of subsequent chapters.

The approach adopted is explicitly Marxist. This description calls for some elaboration. The use made of the notion of Marxism is, often, on the one hand loose and vacuous or on the other narrow and dogmatic. In the half-century up to his death in 1885, Marx wrote voluminously in his attempt to provide a comprehensive analysis and explanation of social and economic life. It was a monumental task, and Marx was able to complete only a fragment of his projected life's work. Nevertheless, the power and cogency of the theories which Marx did develop not only profoundly influenced succeeding generations of thinkers; more importantly, they moved men to action. Yet because Marxism became a movement, the label has often been divorced from the essence of Marx's approach to understanding society. At one extreme, purist sects or party functionaries have insisted on the exclusive truth of their own version of this or that 'sacred text'; at the other, many writers have made opportunistic use of the name to give their own ideas a radical image.

Out of this confusion, no authoritative definition of the meaning of Marxism is possible. Marx completed most of his writings over a century ago, and these cannot be applied mechanically to today's world; to adopt a Marxist approach is to apply a particular *perspective* to the understanding of this world. With the utmost brevity, this perspective could be summed up without too much distortion in just four words: *totality, change, contradiction* and *practice*. By totality is meant the fact that different social phenomena are interrelated, and that no area of social life can therefore be satisfactorily analysed in isolation. Marx argued, for example, that the way in which economic activity is organised in any society – its *relations of production* – will shape its political institutions, conventional modes of thought, family relationships and so on. Thus a society forms a *system*, with particular elements influencing others, and with the influence exerted by some institutions and processes being particularly strong.

The concept of system often gives rise to a misleading view of social reality. Many who write of a social system or an industrial relations system imply that the social relationships under discussion form a stable and integrated whole, which is resistant to fundamental structural change; often it is assumed that those involved in these relationships share common beliefs, values and objectives which reinforce social stability. Marxists insist, on the contrary, that any static model of the social and economic system involves a dangerous distortion. Social relationships are essentially dynamic: what exists at any point of time is the product of past actions and relationships and contains in turn the potential for future development. To do justice to this dynamic character, any valid social analysis must contain a *historical* dimension.

In explaining social change, the notion of contradiction is of vital importance. The Marxist conception of the social and economic system, far from regarding different processes and institutions as compatible and integrated, views these as pressing in *opposing* directions. Thus Marx argued that the growth of large-scale industrial production, directed by capitalists who hired labour by the hour or the day, was incompatible with traditional social and political institutions. These latter reflected the relationships prevailing in a feudal, largely rural, society in which market competition was rigorously circumscribed and rights and obligations were largely prescribed by custom; they were incompatible with the principle of buying in the cheapest and selling in the dearest markets, with the disregard of social obligations not explicitly undertaken as part of an economic contract, which underlie the dynamism of capitalist industry. The consequence was that, in one country after another, the economic developments which constituted the industrial revolution gave rise to an often violent process of social and political revolution. Yet incompatible social forces continued to operate : for example, economic activity both within the factory and in society at large became increasingly interdependent, at the same time as decisions on the organisation of production were made in a fragmented and unplanned way by independent entrepreneurs; and the result was the recurrent 'trade cycle' of boom and recession. It needs little ingenuity to recognise similar contradictory forces underlying industrial relations today; and the often intense social conflicts which occur are the natural outcome.

Against this background it is possible to appreciate the significance of perhaps the most crucial concept within the Marxist perspective : that of *practice*.[3] 'Men make their own history', wrote Marx, 'but they do not make it just as they please; they do not make it under circumstances chosen by themselves, but under circumstances directly encountered, given and transmitted by the past' (1958 : 247). Marx always stressed the extent to which the material features of social life, and in particular the structure of economic relationships, limit the possibilities available for the organisation of human existence. Hence he was critical of 'utopians' who devised blueprints for an ideal society, without considering how it might be constructed from the materials actually to hand. Yet Marx never suggested that material technology and the economic system mechanically determine the whole of social life, that men are the impotent playthings of impersonal forces. On the contrary : *men make their own history*. There exists an area of choice in the structure of social relationships, even if this

[3] The notion of *praxis*, which is only loosely translated as 'practice', is of key significance in Marxist theory but involves many complexities. It is unnecessary to pursue these here; for a sensitive discussion see Avineri 1968 : ch. 5.

choice can occur only within definite limits; moreover these limits tend to relax as the level of technical and economic development rises and productive potential expands. (Today, given new forms of social and industrial organisation, it could be possible to satisfy a wide range of social needs while making work itself more civilised : a point which is taken up in the final chapter.)

The existence of contradictory social forces provides the major opening through which men can make their own history. In the era of the industrial revolution the rising bourgeoisie, or capitalist class, was able to transform traditional society because the tide of economic and technological dynamism ran in its favour. Today, the social contradiction which offers the greatest potential for structural change is that between the interdependent, collective character of productive activity and the concentration of the ownership and control of economic resources in a small number of hands. Those who actually work together in the production of goods and services – as direct or indirect manual workers, as technicians, or in a range of other white-collar functions – suffer from this contradiction in a variety of ways which are discussed in the following chapter. In consequence, they have a clear interest in creating new structures of industrial and social management which reflect the social character of economic activity and replace the often anti-social forms of contemporary economic control. The spontaneous collaboration which modern production requires offers a basis for the collective intervention by workers to transform society; the crucial additional ingredient for such a transformation is conscious organisation in pursuit of this objective. How far existing patterns of industrial relations contribute to such consciousness and organisation is one of the major issues to be considered in this book.

There is no simple and clear-cut 'Marxist theory of industrial relations'. This book seeks to develop an analysis which is firmly rooted in the Marxist perspective, and is necessarily influenced by the attempts of others to apply this perspective to the field of industrial relations. But at the same time it stems from one individual's insights and interpretations at a particular point of time. In no way is this intended as a definitive statement or analysis; indeed, given what has been said already, such a notion would be absurd. Suggestions are therefore made for further reading, in which the reader can confront alternative interpretations, and also obtain more detailed empirical information than is possible within these pages. The book is designed, as its title indicates, to provide an introductory guide; it will have served its purpose if it helps the reader in making his or her[4] *own* judgements.

[4] There exists no stylistically elegant method of avoiding the appearance of sexism when the third person singular is used repeatedly. The reader is asked to excuse the fact that, in the pages that follow, the masculine alone is used at times.

# 1 What is Industrial Relations?

What is meant by the term 'industrial relations'? The subject has become an accepted area of academic study, with its own professors and university departments; and some clear definition of its scope and content might therefore be expected. Yet such definitions are surprisingly rare; and if those with unquestioned expertise in the field were to seek to specify its nature precisely, they would be likely to disagree in significant respects.

Most writers on industrial relations would agree on at least one point: not *all* social relations in industry fall within their province, hence the term is not to be interpreted too literally. Relations in industry clearly include a vast variety of routine personal interrelationships: the conversation or horseplay that takes place between workers during a tea-break, or the allocation of tasks by a supervisor to the members of his gang or team. But such everyday interaction would normally be regarded as too trivial and insignificant to be treated as part of industrial relations. At the other extreme, there is an area of social relations in industry which exerts a profound influence over all others: the decisions taken by employers and managers in opening or closing a workplace, determining the type and level of production, introducing particular forms of technology and work organisation, allocating a specific distribution of profits. Such decision-making processes are conventionally taken as given, as lying outside the field of industrial relations, although they determine much of the character of the actions and relationships which *are* recognised as the subject's central focus.

Most experts on industrial relations would treat it as virtually self-evident that certain kinds of relations in industry should be disregarded, and that they should concentrate their attention on, for example, the collective bargaining activities of trade unions.

But what principles explain this selectivity? This is a question which is rarely confronted explicitly. This in turn reflects the empiricism which, it was suggested earlier, is characteristic of much British writing on industrial relations: a reluctance to engage openly in theoretical discussion, an insistence on treating merely with 'facts' and 'practical problems'. Such empiricism, as was argued previously, is misplaced: theoretical assumptions are not excluded, they are merely hidden below the surface. Hence the industrial relations expert may claim, in effect, to know intuitively what is to be included within the subject and what excluded; but this merely entails that certain criteria of selection are applied which are not made explicit and are therefore shielded from criticism. Such a situation is unhealthy for the writer and unhelpful to the introductory student.

The empiricist approach is far from universal among writers in the field: a number have indeed pursued theoretical self-awareness, seeking an explicit theoretical foundation for their study. The best known of such writers is Dunlop, whose *Industrial Relations Systems* (1958) has attracted considerable attention in recent years. Dunlop's analytical focus is what he terms the *network of rules* which govern the workplace and the work community: the character of these rules and the manner in which they are formulated, administered and altered. Dunlop applies this focus to define more clearly the notion of a system of industrial relations, used loosely by previous authors: 'the full range of rule-making governing the work place is . . . central to an industrial-relations system' (p. 5). Dunlop's claim is to have given theoretical coherence to industrial relations by defining it in terms of the study of 'the rules of the system and their variation over time' (p. 383).

This analysis was subsequently developed by Flanders, who contributed much to the revival of explicit theoretical debate in British industrial relations. 'A system of industrial relations', he argues, 'is a system of rules'.

These rules appear in different guises: in legislation and in statutory orders; in trade union regulations; in collective agreements and in arbitration awards; in social conventions; in managerial decisions; and in accepted 'custom and practice'. This list is by no means exhaustive, but 'rules' is the only generic description that can be given to these various instruments of regulation. In other words, the subject deals with certain regulated or institutionalized relationships in industry.

'The study of industrial relations', Flanders concludes, 'may therefore be described as a study of the institutions of job regulation' (1965 : 10).

These analyses by Dunlop and Flanders are of great significance as pioneer attempts to give theoretical unity and precision to the study of industrial relations; and for this very reason they have proved highly influential. Much of what they write is unassailable. Rules of various kinds clearly do pervade the world of work and employment, and the institutions which devise and implement this network of rules are of central importance for the study of industrial relations. But to define the subject *exclusively* in terms of rules and regulation is far too restrictive, and has unfortunate evaluative overtones. The implication is that what industrial relations is all about is the maintenance of stability and regularity in industry. The focus is on how any conflict is contained and controlled, rather than on the processes through which disagreements and disputes are generated. From this perspective, the question whether the existing structure of ownership and control in industry is an inevitable source of conflict is dismissed as external to the study of industrial relations – which must be concerned solely with how employers, trade unions and other institutions cope with such conflict. Thus to accept the definition of industrial relations as job regulation is to share the traditional concern of conservative sociologists with the 'problem of order' : the interest is in how existing patterns of social relations are stabilised, rather than the significance in their own right of challenges to the prevailing social structure.

This conservative tendency is reinforced when the notion of an industrial relations system is used to suggest that processes are naturally at work to maintain stability and equilibrium; that the various institutions and procedures are compatible and well integrated; and that conflict is therefore largely self-correcting. Dunlop commits himself to this position, with the argument (which in turn reflects the direct influence of conservative sociological thought) that the beliefs and values of the participants in industrial relations are an automatic source of order. 'An industrial-relations system creates an ideology or a commonly shared body of ideas and beliefs regarding the interaction and roles of the actors which helps to bind the system together . . . The ideology of an industrial-relations system comes to bear a close relationship to the ideology of the particular industrial society of which it is a subsystem' (1958 : 383, 18). Yet if the system of industrial relations is so well integrated, and if the goals and values of the participants are so much in agreement, how is it that industrial conflict occurs at all? From a perspective which defines industrial relations solely in terms of job regulation, this question is unanswerable.

It follows that this approach to the subject, however influential, is one-sided and inadequate. The implications are twofold. First, the notion of an industrial relations system – as was suggested in the Introduction – is of analytical value only if it incorporates the existence of *contradictory* processes and forces, and hence treats instability and stability as of equal significance as 'system outcomes'. Second, and in consequence, the definition in terms of job regulation must be broadened to take account of the *sources* as well as the *consequences* of industrial conflict. The definition adopted in this book is as follows : industrial relations is the study of *processes of control over work relations;*[1] and among these processes, those involving collective worker organisation and action are of particular concern. At this stage, the implications of this redefinition may appear obscure; but its significance will emerge.

This abstract discussion of 'industrial relations systems' may seem academic, in the worst sense, to the uninitiated. What has all this got to do with the real world of shop stewards, personnel managers, union leaders, CBI spokesmen, and government ministers? To repeat the argument of the Introduction, the whole point of an explicit theoretical perspective is to provide a framework within which the complex detail of the real world can be organised and thus understood; and the remainder of this book attempts to demonstrate how, by defining industrial relations in

---

[1] This definition includes 'job regulation' within its scope. Regulation – 'control by rule' according to the Oxford dictionary – is merely one of many forms of control in industry.

terms of processes of control, the goal of understanding can be achieved.

For the moment, though, it is useful to consider how Dunlop seeks to link his notion of an industrial relations system to the real world. He makes the connection by characterising industrial relations as the interplay of three sets of actors within the system. These actors he defines as 'a hierarchy of managers and their representatives in supervision', 'a hierarchy of workers (non-managerial) and any spokesmen', and 'specialized governmental agencies . . . concerned with workers, enterprises, and their relationships' (1958 : 7). They interact, Dunlop argues, in a context set by technological, economic and political factors, in the light of their prevailing ideology.

While Dunlop's definition is in terms of managers and workers, it is significant that much of his detailed discussion relates primarily to the *organisations* which are involved in negotiations and are parties to collective agreements. In this respect he follows an approach which is traditional in academic industrial relations. Until very recently at least, most courses and textbooks focused almost exclusively on the *institutions* of industrial relations : companies and employers' associations, trade unions and multi-union federations, government departments. Such organisations are obviously of great importance and deserve close attention. Yet an institutional focus directs the student simply to the formal or official aspects of industrial relations : negotiating committees, bargaining and disputes procedures, collective agreements, union rulebooks, the machinery of government intervention. This creates a dangerous tendency to conceive the subject solely in terms of relationships between agencies and organisations, rather than between people. Such a mechanical and depersonalised approach to social analysis is often termed *reification* : in other words, treating abstract collective entities, which are the creations of human activity, as the active agencies in social relations and in consequence, devaluing the part played by human actors.

This tendency to reify industrial relations is closely linked to the theoretical approach just discussed. Flanders, it will be recalled, defines the subject as 'a study of the *institutions* of job regulation'. He bases this definition on the argument that 'personal, or in the language of sociology "unstructured", relationships have their importance for management and workers, but they lie outside the scope of a system of industrial relations' (1965 : 10). At first sight, this may seem uncontroversial. If a manager and a shop steward chat about the previous night's football match, this would seem irrelevant to most people's conception of industrial relations. Yet the attempt to draw a boundary between 'personal and unstructured' and 'impersonal and structured' relationships is not a satisfactory means of defining the subject matter of industrial relations. For in a crucial sense, *all* relations in industry are personal. Managers, union officials and civil servants are all people; they are not simply disembodied representatives of organisational interests. And conversely, most sociologists would question whether *any* social relations are wholly unstructured. By 'structure' – a notion surprisingly difficult to define – is normally meant the principles of organisation which appear to underlie a society, the patterning and regularities in social relationships and behaviour; and sociologists would normally start from the assumption that few social relations in industry are wholly random or arbitrary, or completely uninfluenced by the various institutions of the broader society.[2]

In considering whether a particular relationship is relevant to the study of industrial relations, the essential question is : *how far* does it influence or derive from other institutional regularities, or how far is it 'merely' personal? What is involved here is a distinction of degree rather than kind, and one which does not provide any clear-cut dividing line. For instance, workers in a paint shop may regularly grumble about inadequate ventilation in their workplace. During the tea-break one hot afternoon their complaints are heard by the shop steward on the neighbouring section, who takes up the issue with management and demands immediate improvements. Spurred to action, the painters walk out on strike. Or to take an example from a very different level of industrial relations, the President and General Secretary of a national union may develop an intense personal rivalry. This leads them both to adopt an inflexible position in negotiations, since each fears that any apparent weakness on his part will be

---

[2] For this very reason, even the trivial example of football gossip may be relevant for the analysis of industrial relations. If a manager and shop steward can engage in sociability of this kind, it is probably indicative of the nature of their relationship over serious issues.

exploited within the union to his discredit by the other. As a result, they find themselves leading a national strike which neither really desires. Both examples are hypothetical, but they indicate a very real point about industrial relations : that actions and relationships which are 'personal and unstructured' may lead by a natural progression to situations in which the formal institutions of the various parties are centrally involved. Any attempt to define the precise point of time at which a 'personal relationship' becomes an 'industrial relations situation' is almost inevitably artificial and anomalous.

In practice, most current students of the subject accept the force of this argument; the prevailing conception of the scope of industrial relations has broadened considerably during the past decade. A notable landmark in this process was the report of the Royal Commission on Trade Unions and Employers' Associations (Donovan 1968), which argued that 'Britain has two systems of industrial relations. The one is the formal system embodied in the official institutions. The other is the informal system created by the actual behaviour of trade unions and employers' associations, of managers, shop stewards and workers' (p. 12).[3] The report took as its starting point the fact that informal and only loosely structured relationships on the shop floor tended to qualify, supplement or indeed controvert the decisions taken within the official national institutions.[4] Contemporary academic discussion likewise reflects a growing awareness that many of the most important processes of control over work relations do not flow through official, institutionalised channels; and that to base the study of industrial relations on the formal procedures and organisations alone is to impose unacceptably narrow limits. Clegg's *System of Industrial Relations in Great Britain* (1970) exemplifies the current approach : the book begins with a discussion of the impact of informal work group relations, stres-

[3] The much-repeated notion of 'two systems' is unfortunately misleading; it implies the existence of two detached sets of processes and areas of activity. It is more appropriate to speak of *one* system of industrial relations with formal and informal aspects, which are in part complementary and in part contradictory.
[4] In the United States the formal institutions of collective bargaining exert far greater control than in many British industries over actual practice at shop-floor level; but here too, forms of evasion and resistance exist.

sing the importance of unofficial 'custom and practice' in controlling many aspects of the organisation of work and employment.
This represents a sharp contrast to the previous volume of the
same title (Flanders and Clegg 1954), which adopted an almost
exclusively institutional focus.

Trade unionism provides a good example of the way in which
a purely institutional perspective can be dangerous and misleading. It is very common to meet such statements as 'the union
has reached an agreement with the employers'; but what precisely
does this mean? A trade union is in many ways a very peculiar
kind of organisation. Its main work does not involve the production of identifiable goods or services, but rather the attempt to
influence the actions and decisions of *others*: employers and
legislators, for example. Only a fraction of union organisation
and activity is represented by full-time employees based on a union
office; trade unionism 'exists' wherever workers are unionised,
yet most members are engaged in identifiably trade union functions only infrequently. Hence a trade union is not a physical
entity in the same way that factories, hospitals or prisons are. So
what does it mean to say that 'the union' adopts a particular
policy or carries out a certain action? This is a clear instance of
what was earlier termed reification: treating an impersonal
abstraction as a social agent, when it is really only people who
act.

Sometimes the term 'the union' is used to refer to the various
workers who are members of the organisation in question. But
this is unsatisfactory, for it is not uncommon for policies to be
adopted or agreements signed without any involvement of the
mass of a union's membership, and perhaps without their knowledge. Conversely, the notion of 'the union' may be applied to the
actions or decisions of official union spokesmen, representatives
or leaders, or to membership activities which are initiated or
endorsed by them. But this too is unsatisfactory; for if a union is
not simply the sum of its members, neither is it merely the
property of its leaders. To identify a union with its officials is to
imply that the latter need not be differentiated from the membership as a whole. But on the contrary – to anticipate an argument
which is developed in Chapter 3 – the *situations* of union leaders
differ significantly from those of the members they represent; and
this leads in turn to differences in attitudes, interests, objectives,

and conceptions of what is good for the members and for 'the union'.[5]

Any analysis of industrial relations which takes as its starting point the trade unions and other formal institutions can scarcely avoid coming to grief over problems such as this. The approach adopted in this book is thus to focus not only on trade unions as organisations, but also on *workers* and their problems and aspirations. Those employed in industry or commerce or in public services naturally devise strategies to satisfy their aspirations or to redress their grievances, and such strategies involve in part the attempt to control the work relations in which they are involved. Official trade union action is at times central to such strategies. But the effects of trade union involvement in job control are often ambiguous, for reasons which are discussed later; so in some circumstances, workers may view the official union as irrelevant to their objectives or even as an obstacle.

If workers' grievances and aspirations are to form the starting point of industrial relations analysis, it is clearly necessary to investigate what these are. What do workers want? There is no simple answer to this question; and indeed, intense controversy surrounds the whole issue of what men and women expect from their employment, and what their work means to them.[6] Any attempt to survey attitudes to work would draw an immense variety of responses. Most of these would normally focus on aspects of the job other than the work tasks themselves. A typical employee would probably say that what he looks for in a job is a decent level of pay with increases at the going rate; reason-

[5] The perceptive reader may argue that precisely the same objections could be made to the use of abstractions like 'capital', 'management' or 'the state'; yet these are employed throughout this book. Two justifications may be offered. Firstly, management and state bureaucracies are explicitly *authoritarian* control structures where far greater uniformity of practice is imposed than is the case within trade unions. Secondly, conflicts of interest and objective among governmental and managerial bureaucrats are not of central relevance to the issues discussed in this book; nor are they normally salient for workers in industry, whose perspective forms its analytical starting point. (In Chapter 5 attention is called to the fact that such conflicts can on occasion be recognised and exploited by workers' representatives.)

[6] For a discussion of some of the issues involved see Fox 1971.

able working conditions; sociable mates and a chance to talk to them; a foreman who isn't a bastard . . . If asked to consider the job itself, most people would hope for work which is neither too exhausting physically or emotionally, nor so routine as to be monotonous; they would also seek some opportunity to control their own work, rather than being subject to constant instructions and supervision.

In almost every case, some work aspirations can be easily and clearly expressed, while others are confused and perhaps scarcely recognised in a conscious manner. The patterns of job expectations which people hold tend to be affected by the character of their occupation, their social background, and similar factors. Expectations are also shaped by broad societal influences. Where men and women are encouraged – by general cultural values and by costly and sophisticated means of mass persuasion (such as TV advertising) – to aspire to every latest consumer gimmick, it is not surprising that pay is often given top priority; that many workers seem less concerned with what happens to them during working hours than with what their job allows them to buy outside work. Moreover, most people before starting employment undergo a process of schooling which seems primarily designed to teach them that it is natural to obey orders from those in authority without question; while more diffuse pressures generate the widespread assumption that any job is likely to be fairly uninteresting and unpleasant. Thus it is not surprising that aspirations for creative work, and for control over work, tend to be below the surface of everyday job discussion. But even if suppressed, such aspirations nevertheless exist and can erupt to make their mark on the processes of industrial relations.[7]

To say that employees have certain expectations and aspirations, and that these necessarily affect industrial relations, is not to provide any concrete information about the character of industrial relations. To do this it is necessary to add information about the *context* of work and industry. Any succinct statement of this broader social and economic context involves selective emphasis on a few key characteristics. From a Marxist perspective, the crucial fact about the economies of Western Europe and North America – where most studies of industrial relations have had

[7] The relative significance of economic and non-economic motives as sources of industrial conflict is discussed in Hyman 1972: ch. 5.

their focus – is their *capitalist* character. This means that much
of the productive system is privately owned, with ownership concentrated in a very small number of hands;[8] that *profit* – the pursuit of economic returns to the owners – is the key influence on
company policy (whether or not top management actually
possesses a financial stake in the firm); and that control over
production is enforced *downwards* by the owners' managerial
agents and functionaries.[9] In most countries, it is true, the state
owns a growing sector of industry; but almost invariably, the
operation of this sector is modelled on private capitalism in
terms both of its hierarchy of control and of its respect for the
constraints of profit. (Arguably, in Eastern Europe – where state
ownership of industry is almost total – these same features of
capitalism are maintained. Possibly this could help explain many
aspects of *their* industrial relations. But this is too large an issue
to pursue here.)

A capitalist environment has consequences with important implications for the nature of industrial relations. Most fundamentally, work has the status of wage-labour. Jobs are located
within a labour *market*; the prospective worker must find an
employer willing to pay a wage or salary in return for the disposal of his skill, knowledge or physical strength. The capacity to
work is thus bought and sold, rather like fruit or vegetables
(though unlike fruit and vegetables, workers can band together
– and at times stand up and fight).

From the fact that labour is treated as a commodity stem many
of the fundamental conflicts in industry. The wages and conditions which the worker naturally seeks as a means to a decent
life are a *cost* to the employer, cutting into his profits, and he will
equally naturally resist pressure for improvements. (It is true that
employers normally recognise that certain minimum standards
of wages and conditions are necessary in order to recruit and
retain labour, and to sustain the 'morale' thought essential to

---

[8] In Britain, surveys have shown that only 4 per cent of the adult population hold shares in industrial or commercial companies, while 1 per cent
own 81 per cent of all privately-owned shares. Yet gross profits account
for roughly 20 per cent of the national income.

[9] Some writers have exaggerated the significance of the growth of professional management, arguing that this alters the capitalist character of
modern industry. For a discussion of such theories see Nichols 1969.

encourage hard work. But this normally gives employers only
a limited motive for generosity.) Because the employer must
regard labour as a cost to be minimised, it is in his interest to
retain a worker in employment only while it is profitable to do so.
This means that workers' jobs are always at the mercy of economic and technological vagaries. If there is a slump in demand
for the goods or services produced, or if new techniques are
devised which can allow them to be produced more cheaply
and profitably, men and women will find themselves unemployed.

Within capitalist industry, workers are treated less as men and
women with distinctive needs and aspirations than as dehuman-
ised 'factors of production'. Their upbringing and education is
often devoted primarily to rendering them in some narrow
respect *useful* to an employer. In the absence of an immediate
use they are declared redundant – useless, unwanted, surplus to
requirements. So long as they are employed it is their narrowly
defined sphere of usefulness which dominates their work experience. Utilitarian criteria may prescribe that they perform tasks
which are excessively strenuous or degrading – or so monoton-
ously repetitive as to eliminate any significant scope for intrinsic
enjoyment in work. The stunting consequences of the capitalist
pursuit of a narrowly defined goal of 'efficiency' were bitterly
exposed in the last century by Ruskin : 'We have much studied
and perfected, of late, the great civilized invention of the division
of labour; only we give it a false name. It is not, truly speaking,
the labour that is divided; but the men : divided into mere seg-
ments of men – broken into small fragments and crumbs of life
. . .' (Clark 1964 : 282–3). The same principle which breaks down
so much of work into routine and meaningless tasks requires that
management shall organise and coordinate these fragmented
activities into one collective effort, issuing orders and instructions and in the process eliminating any serious opportunity for
most employees to control their own work. Sociable relationships
between workers are likely to be tolerated only to the extent that
they do not obstruct the utilitarian priorities of profit. The same is
true of safeguards against accidents and industrial diseases : it is
estimated that work in British industry kills 3000 men and women
a year, and injures many thousands more; but measures which

might reduce this horrific toll are often strenuously resisted by
employers (Kinnersly 1973).

The capitalist structure of industry and of wage-labour is
closely connected with the pattern of class division in society.
Wealth is narrowly concentrated : 5 per cent of the population
owns well over half the wealth in Britain. Incomes are similarly
unequal. In 1974, half the adult employees in Britain earned
£37 a week or less before tax, and a quarter less than £27 – only
slightly above the officially defined 'poverty line' for an average
family. Women rank predominantly among the lowest paid – on
average they earn little more than half as much as men. Inequality is also obvious in the difference between manual and
non-manual earnings : men in the first category earned on average £42, those in the second £54; and the gap would be far
greater but for the fact that men in manual occupations work
on average eight hours a week longer than white-collar employees. Moreover, the latter group is far from homogenous :
routine clerical and technical staff receive little more, or even less,
than the average manual worker. It is the top managerial and
professional groups that enjoy five- and even six-figure salaries;
and to the same social group are paid sometimes even larger
*unearned* incomes.

Pay differentials run in close parallel with other inequalities
at work. The highest paid normally have pleasant working conditions, flexible working hours, long holidays, generous sickness
and pensions schemes, secure employment. The lower paid are
often particularly exposed to accident and disease and to insecurity of earnings and employment, have the longest standard
hours of work, often have to work shifts and unsociable hours,
and usually enjoy few 'fringe' benefits. They are also commonly
required to 'clock in' at work and are subject to a range of other
regulations and conditions which underline their inferior status.
The link between the hierarchies of pay and control is very close :
in general it is the occupations with the least formal autonomy,
in the most subordinate positions, which receive the lowest earnings. As the extent of control over subordinates increases, and the
closeness of direction from above diminishes, so income normally
rises. At the extreme, those rich enough to live comfortably on
their unearned income can choose work (if indeed they choose to
work at all) which is altogether free from subordination.

Economic inequalities pervade the rest of social life. The level
of income defines the general possibilities of a family's quality
of living, leading to material and cultural impoverishment or
enrichment. Health and life-expectation vary directly with income
and occupational status. The children of the rich enjoy educational privileges, and hence are well placed to enjoy the same
career success as their parents. The *political* influence wielded by
the wealthy and the industrially powerful is disproportionately
great, which helps explain the resistance of the structure of inequality pressure for reform, its self-perpetuating quality.[10] (This
point has implications for any appraisal of the role of the state in
capitalist society, and in particular the significance of state ownership and intervention in economic life : topics which are examined further in Chapter 5.)

Facts like these form the crucial background to the Marxist
argument that capitalist societies are class-divided. The bulk of
the population own no substantial property, and in order to earn
a living must sell their own capacity to work. The wage or
salary they receive is far less than the value of the wealth they
collectively produce. The surplus is taken by the small minority
who own the means of production; part is re-invested to provide
for future profits, part is used for personal gratification. The
control of this minority over the productive system necessarily
carries with it the control over those whom they employ. Hence
there exist two fundamental social groupings or classes. On the
one hand are those who work in a variety of manual occupations,
in clerical positions, as technicians, or in minor supervisory grades:
men and women who make an obvious contribution to production which is not adequately reflected in their pay and conditions.
(When Marxists use the notion of 'working class' they refer to
the whole of this category, not merely to manual workers and
their families.) On the other, there are those whose property
allows them to live from the labour of others; and the top levels of
managers who, whether or not they have a major stake as shareholders of the companies they control, pay themselves salaries
which far exceed any contribution they may make to the productive process. (There also exist marginal social groups which do
not fit into either category; but they do not complicate the

[10] This point is developed in more detail in Hyman 1974a. See also
Field 1974.

picture unduly.[11]) Between these two classes there exists a radical conflict of interests, which underlies everything that occurs in industrial relations.

In the eyes of the law – and of many apologists for the present economic system – such facts simply do not exist. Relations between employers and workers are governed by a contract of employment which is, in theory, freely agreed between the two parties. But the notion of a free contract between equals has little relevance to the real world. In practice, the ownership of capital represents concentrated economic power, a legal entitlement to dominate; hence the employer can virtually dictate the broad outlines of the employment contract. In the words of a classical economist, 'labour is often sold under special disadvantages, arising from the closely connected facts that labour power is "perishable", that the sellers of it are commonly poor and have no reserve fund, and that they cannot easily withhold it from the market' (Marshall 1920 : 567). The employment contract is indeed free in the sense that men and women are not forced to work at gun-point; but if the alternative to working on the employer's terms is poverty and starvation, this is no great consolation. It is true that the possession of scarce skills, or the existence of a tight labour market, may help to lessen the imbalance. Moreover, workers who band together in trade unions are far less vulnerable than isolated individuals. (For this very reason, the most significant area of industrial relations involves the *collective* relationships between workers and employers.) Sometimes, indeed, it is argued that the power of organised labour equals or even exceeds that of capital. But such a suggestion is fanciful. In the last analysis, an employer can threaten to shut up shop and take his capital elsewhere; but even though individual workers can move to a different labour market, a whole labour force has no such option. An employer, moreover, can count on decisive support from the state and from other dominant sections of society, in the event of any radical trade union

[11] Such extra-industrial groups as small farmers, independent professionals or small shop-keepers are marginal to the main class structure. Within industry, the position of middle management is ambivalent: some are close to, and may eventually expect to achieve, the decision-making powers of top management; others have little more independent authority than ordinary foremen.

challenge to his prerogatives. Such a challenge is inhibited, moreover, by a comprehensive network of ideological influences which reinforce the existing structure of society. Hence the characteristic form of the employment contract is one which underwrites the dominance of the employer, his right to exercise control over the worker during the production process.[12]

The unequal power in the formulation of the employment contract leads to a significant *asymmetry* in its content. The obligations undertaken by the employer are relatively precise and specific : he agrees to pay a specified wage or salary, possibly supplemented by various bonus elements; arrangements for holiday and sickness pay and any other fringe benefits are laid down; he is committed to observe the various legal regulations on conditions in factories, shops and offices. But he is required to do little in his relationship with employees which is not formally prescribed by law, in the individual contract of employment, or in a collective agreement.

The obligations on the worker, by contrast, are imprecise and elastic. In the normal situation, the employee does not agree to perform an exact amount of physical or intellectual work – no more and no less. In most cases this would be quite impossible : despite the widespread use of techniques of 'work measurement', much work simply cannot be precisely quantified. Moreover, no employer can exactly predict his workload or the labour available at any given point of time. He thus requires to be able to make flexible use of his labour force; and the contract of employment permits him to impose just such an open-ended commitment on his employees. Rather than agreeing to expend a given amount of effort, the employee *surrenders his capacity to work*; and it is the function of management, through its hierarchy of control, to transform this capacity into actual productive activity. The 'equality' of the employment relationship is one which gives the employer the right to issue orders, while imposing on the worker the duty to obey.

Yet workers are more than slaves : there are limits to their duty to obey, and to the employer's right to command. Industrial relations is not only about disputes, negotiations and agreements

[12] Many of these points are taken up in the following chapters. For a succinct analysis of the inequality of power in current industrial relations see Fox 1974 : ch. 1.

over pay and related conditions – important as these undoubtedly are. It is also about the nature of these limits and the way in which they are determined. The law imposes some constraints; the employer has a right only to issue 'reasonable' orders, and hence there are some instructions which an employee can legitimately disobey. The legal notion of an unreasonable order is however narrowly defined; and in practice, a far more important restriction on employer control is set by the point at which workers individually or collectively *refuse* to obey orders, and the employer is unable or unwilling to force the issue. This point of effective resistance is usually unclear and often unstable. An employer would not dream of ordering a skilled toolmaker to sweep the floor – or if he did, the response would be unprintable. But just how far outside his normal range of duties can a man expect, and be expected, to work during the course of his employment? The answer will vary between workplace and workplace, from job to job, and from time to time. The same is true of the level of effort that an employee can reasonably expect, and be expected, to put into his or her work. Reference is often made to the notion of an 'effort bargain' : a level of performance which is tacitly accepted by both employers and employees as a reasonable equivalent for a given rate of wages. But such understandings are always imprecise and fluid. Performance standards, production speeds, job allocations, and a whole complex of practices governing workers' relations with one another and with management : these are the outcome of a shifting set of traditions and understandings which are never identical in any two work situations. For while the powers of the employer are enormous, he is at the same time *dependent* on his labour force. Sociologists have argued that even such institutions as prisons or mental hospitals can function effectively only if the inmates are prepared to acquiesce and cooperate to some degree. In work organisations, the need for commitment and initiative on the part of ordinary employees is immensely greater. Constant supervision is impossible, and a disaffected labour force can easily sabotage production; while a manager or supervisor cannot rely on the same enforced and unquestioned discipline which is normal in a prison or army. The more technically sophisticated the work process, or the more strategic the functions of the labour force, the more vulnerable is the employer to hostile action by employees. Hence in every workplace there exists an invisible frontier of control, reducing some of the formal powers of the employer : a frontier which is defined and redefined in a *continuous* process of pressure and counterpressure, conflict and accommodation, overt and tacit struggle.

An unceasing *power struggle* is therefore a central feature of industrial relations. The notion of power is notorious among sociologists for the analytical and empirical problems associated with it.[13] In this book, the concept has a precise meaning : the ability of an individual or group to control his (their) physical and social environment; and, as part of this process, the ability to influence the decisions which are and are not taken by others. This ability, it is assumed here, is typically founded on a privileged access to or control over material and ideological resources. Ownership and control over the means of production clearly involves power, since it carries the ability to admit or exclude those who depend on employment for a living. The ability to call on certain generally accepted beliefs and values – the 'rights of management', for example, or the belief that 'there will always be masters and men' – is likewise a source of power, since it entails that certain challenges to managerial control are unlikely to occur. This indicates an important aspect of power : the ability to overcome opposition is one sign of power; but a more subtle yet perhaps even more significant form of power is the ability to preclude opposition from even arising – simply because, for example, those subject to a particular type of control do not question its legitimacy or can see no alternative.

Two aspects of power are often distinguished : what may be termed 'power for' and 'power over'. In the first case, it is possible to conceive power primarily as a resource used in the service of collective interests. A group of peasant farmers, for example, may band together to share the use of a tractor, to purchase seeds and fertiliser in bulk at a discount, to rationalise the shape of their plots and introduce some specialisation in what each grows, and to market their produce cooperatively. In this way they may be said to increase their power, both over the natural environment and over the market; all members of the group may produce and earn more : their increased power is used for the general benefit. But where relationships of conflict

[13] For a useful discussion of some of these problems see Lukes 1974.

exist, power is typically wielded by one individual or group *over* others. The power of management is founded, in effect, on the subjection of employees; and workers can assert their own control only *at the expense* of the employer. In capitalist society, because of the manifold conflicts of interest which exist, power relations are normally of this kind.[14] Even when individuals band together in order to increase their collective power ('power for'), this is normally directed towards a conflict relationship with a third party ('power over').[15] Trade union organisation is an obvious example : workers develop their collective power precisely in order to counteract the even greater power of the employer.

Because the interests of employers and employees conflict so radically and systematically, the power relationship between them is also necessarily conflictual. The frontier of control at any point of time represents a compromise unsatisfactory to *both* parties, and attempts to shift this frontier are only to be expected whenever either side feels that circumstances are in its favour. Conflict and change are thus inseparable from industrial relations.

Conflict in industry conventionally centres around the distribution of its product, the level of wages and salaries. The bulk of formal negotiations focuses on questions of payment, and this same preponderance is reflected in the statistics of issues involved in disputes. This is to be expected : as already suggested, strong social pressures encourage workers to express grievances and aspirations in economic terms, rather than as demands for control and creativity in work (though indeed, such demands *are* at times openly expressed). These pressures are reinforced by the institutional procedures of industrial relations : pay claims are readily negotiable, since they provide ample scope for bargaining and compromise; whereas non-wage demands often involve questions of principle on which compromise is far more difficult. Trade union negotiators, faced with the power of capital, are normally far happier pursuing demands which offer reasonable

[14] For this reason, the somewhat bizarre example of peasant farmers was given above; it is difficult to find a similar example within the mainstream of capitalist society.
[15] This is true in part even of the peasants' collective: in so far as their aim is to increase their market power, this is achieved at the expense of other participants in the market.

prospects of peaceful settlement; hence workers' own organisations reinforce the bias towards wage-consciousness.[16]

What influence can workers collectively exert over the level of
wages? Marx warned against exaggerating the economic impact
of trade unionism. Since man's ability to work is, in capitalism,
treated as a commodity, he argued that its price is set like that of
any other commodity by market forces: specifically, by the costs
of production.

> Wages will rise and fall according to the relation of supply
> and demand, according to the turn taken by the competition
> between the buyers of labour power, the capitalists, and the
> sellers of labour power, the workers. The fluctuations in wages
> correspond in general to the fluctuations in prices of com-
> modities. Within these fluctuations, however, the price of
> labour will be determined by the cost of production . . . What,
> then, is the cost of production of labour power? It is the cost
> required for maintaining the worker as a worker and of
> developing him into a worker (1958 : 88).

Marx denied, however, that there was any 'iron law of wages'
which would make trade union action futile.[17] The level of wages,
he insisted, was 'only settled by the continuous struggle between
capital and labour, the capitalist constantly tending to reduce
wages to their physical minimum, while the working man constantly presses in the opposite direction' (1958: 443). Trade
unionism provided some protection, and even a means of
advancement; yet at the same time, 'in its merely economic
action capital is the stronger side' (p. 444). Marx believed, moreover, that industrial development would increase the imbalance:
mechanisation would create a growing pool of unemployed,
undermining trade union strength.[18]

[16] For a detailed discussion of this bias see Hyman 1972 : ch. 5.

[17] The notion of an 'iron law', expounded by the German socialist
Lassalle, was strenuously criticised by Marx. Remarkably, some 'learned'
writers nevertheless attribute this absurd doctrine to him.

[18] A thesis at times asserted by Marx predicted the increasing 'immiseration' of the working class as capitalism developed; his meaning has since
been hotly debated. At times, Marx indeed foresaw an actual decline in
wages, since he assumed that the spread of mechanisation would continually expand the 'reserve army of unemployed'. On other occasions he

At first sight, contemporary wage bargaining is inexplicable in such terms. Yet Marxist analysis remains possible, once the *contextual* changes since Marx wrote are appreciated. The 'reserve army of unemployed', though historically a major source of weakness for the labour movement, has been of far less significance in the past three decades (for reasons discussed in a later chapter). Trade union organisation is thus immensely stronger and more extensive than when Marx wrote : in relation to the labour force, unionisation has probably increased more than ten times. The competition of worker against worker no longer forces down wages in the same way as in the nineteenth century; rather, forces of supply and demand are mediated by an overt *power* relationship between monopoly capital and the 'labour monopoly' of trade unionism. In addition, price inflation provides a basis for successful pressure for higher wages – though by the same token, significant increases in *real* wages are not easily achieved.

Also of key importance is a factor recognised by Marx, but not systematically analysed. 'In contradistinction . . . to the case of other commodities, there enters into the determination of the value of labour-power a historical and moral element' 1959 : 171). The maintenance of a worker and his or her family did not depend on the requirements of physical subsistence alone : 'besides this mere physical element, the value of labour is in every country determined by a *traditional standard of life*. It is not mere physical life, but it is the satisfaction of certain wants springing from the social conditions in which people are placed and reared up' (1958 : 442). Elsewhere Marx wrote that 'the rapid growth of productive capital brings about an equally rapid growth of wealth, luxury, social wants, social enjoyments . . . Our desires and pleasures spring from society; we measure them, therefore, by society and not by the objects that serve for their satisfaction. Because they are of a social nature, they are of a relative nature' (1958 : 94). This analysis (involving the notion which modern sociologists often term 'relative deprivation') is remarkably apposite in explaining trends in wages since Marx wrote. As the general level of production has increased, so con-

implied that greater productivity would permit *increased* wages, but that 'immiseration' would consist in the more *intensive* exploitation of their labour (a not inaccurate prediction). Sometimes he also suggested that other social changes might offset the 'law' of immiseration.

ventional definitions of a living wage have risen in step. Moreover, modern media of communication have ensured that workers today have a clear conception of the living styles of other social strata, and their ideas of tolerable standards are necessarily affected. Upward pressure on wages naturally results.

This same factor helps explain the differentials between the earnings of various occupational groups – differentials which show considerable historical stability, and are often a focus of industrial conflict. Marx noted that 'as the costs of producing labouring powers of different quality differ, so must differ the values of the labouring powers employed in different trades' (1958 : 426). Since Marx was interested in wages in general rather than in specific occupations, he did not pursue this question in detail; he assumed (like many modern economists) that differentials were largely attributable to differences in skill and hence in costs of training. However, variations in 'the traditional standard of life' clearly influence relative as well as absolute earnings levels. As was noted in the nineteenth century, 'customary standards of expenditure' are associated with different occupational strata; and these are, 'within a specific range of variation, tacitly recognised by both employers and employed' (Webb and Webb 1897 : 332). There exists, in effect, a social hierarchy of occupations, with widely accepted notions of the standard of living (and hence level of income) appropriate for each. Such ideologies of occupational worth, it has often been argued, exert a considerable influence on the processes of wage and salary determination (since they affect both what employees are prepared to accept, and what employers consider reasonable to concede). These legitimations of income differentials, in turn, mesh closely with the broad structure of class inequality and the distribution of social power which it incorporates. Processes of power, prestige and ideology thus interact intimately in the labour market.[19]

All this is to indicate that the labour market is more than a forum for narrowly economic processes of supply and demand : it involves relations of power and control. (This was apparent to Marx : he insisted that the market was a mechanism of power, but that the apparently 'impersonal' character of the price mechanism masked this fact.) For this reason, wage and salary

[19] This point is developed in greater detail in Hyman and Brough 1975.

negotiations can properly be comprehended within the analytical framework developed above.

## CONCLUSION

In defining the scope of industrial relations, it is necessary to define the subject more narrowly than the total network of social relationships in industry. But the popular definition in terms of 'institutions of job regulation' is unsatisfactory. First, it diverts attention from the structures of power and interests, and the economic, technological and political dynamics, of the broader society – factors which inevitably shape the character of relations between employers, workers and their organisations. Second, the emphasis on institutions carries with it a danger of reification : it becomes easy to ignore the real, active men and women whose activities *are* industrial relations. Third, the notion of regulation conceals the centrality of power, conflict and instability in the processes of industrial relations.

The definition adopted in this book – in terms of processes of control over work relations – avoids these difficulties. It provides a criterion for excluding 'merely personal' relationships in industry from the field of study, while including those informal processes of control which recent writers on industrial relations have felt obliged to take into account. It points to the fluidity of the *process* of control : a continuous and shifting relationship, which can never be effectively frozen in a formal rule. And finally, it helps indicate that the continuous relationship of conflict, whether open or concealed, stems from a conflict of interests in industry and society which is closely linked with the operation of contradictory tendencies in the capitalist economic system. These arguments explain the distinctive coverage of this book, which seeks to provide, not the narrow institutional analysis of 'job regulation' which can be found elsewhere, but a *political economy of industrial relations*.

# 2 Trade Union Structure

The main theme of the previous chapter indicates why *collective* action by employers is central to the study of industrial relations. The subject has been defined in terms of processes of control over work relations; but in seeking to exercise control over their jobs, their conditions of employment and their day-to-day work practices, workers inevitably come into conflict with the aims and interests of their employers. Because the economic power of capital – reinforced by a battery of legal sanctions – is so great, the amount of control which can be exercised by employees as individuals is extremely limited. Only when they band together in common action can they begin to make serious inroads into the dominance of the employer.

Trade union organisation is the most obvious foundation for such common action. Engels, Marx's lifelong collaborator, perceived the significance of the early forms of collective action by British workers in the 1840s.

> What gives these Unions and the strikes arising from them their real significance is this, that they are the first attempt of the workers to abolish competition. They imply the recognition of the fact that the supremacy of the bourgeoisie is based wholly upon the competition of the workers among themselves; i.e. upon their want of cohesion. And precisely because the Unions direct themselves against the vital nerve of the present social order, however one-sidedly, in however narrow a way, are they so dangerous to this social order. The working-men cannot attack the bourgeoisie, and with it the whole existing order of society, at any sorer point than this. If the competition of the workers among themselves is destroyed, if all determine not to

be further exploited by the bourgeoisie, the rule of property is
at an end (1952 : 218–9).

This possibility was as apparent to the defenders of the existing
social order as it was to Engels – and they responded accordingly.
The behaviour of powerful employers was often tyrannical in
the extreme, involving every possible effort to smash collective
organisation. Trade unionists, if discovered, were dismissed and
evicted from company-owned housing; activists were blacklisted
throughout whole districts; employees were forced to sign a 'docu-
ment' undertaking not to become a member of any union. Employers, wrote the Webbs, the early historians of British unionism,
'used their political and magisterial power against the men without scruple, inciting a willing Government to attack the work-
men's combinations by every possible perversion of the law, and
partiality in its administration' (1920 :165). For the first quarter
of the nineteenth century, the notorious Combination Acts outlawed virtually every aspect of union activity or organisation
(though how far these laws were actually used is a matter of dispute); and extensive use was made of spies and *agents provoca-
teurs*. The smell of repression is pungently captured in the manifesto issued by a noble coalowner in 1844 : 'Lord Londonderry
again warns all the shopkeepers and tradesmen in his town of
Seaham that if they still give credit to pitmen who hold off work,
and continue in the Union, such men will be marked by his agents
and overmen, and will never be employed in his collieries again,
and the shopkeepers may be assured that they will never have any
custom or dealings with them from Lord Londonderry's large
concerns that he can in any manner prevent.'[1]

Yet working men and women refused to be intimidated. Their
'periodical resistance . . . against the wages system', wrote Marx,
'and their periodical attempts at getting a rise of wages, are inseparable from the wages system, and dictated by the very fact
of labour being assimilated to commodities' (1958 : 441). Driven
by their conditions of labour to organise, they persisted with their
efforts to establish substantial unions with which employers were

[1] Quoted in Webb and Webb 1920: 166. For other accounts of the early
repression of trade unionism see Hammond and Hammond 1917; Engels
1952; Frow and Katanka 1971; and Aspinall 1949 (a collection of cor-
respondence between the Home Office and provincial spies and magi-
strates).

forced to come to terms. And having done so, the more enlightened managements soon recognised that unionism was in some respects far less threatening than had originally been supposed. (Why this is so is a major topic for discussion in later chapters.) Yet, to this day, hostility to trade unionism remains widespread. A recent study quotes an employer policy that 'every possible step is taken to ensure that staff do not reach the frame of mind which will make them think that membership of a union is appropriate', and describes the 'strategy of forcible opposition' which involves 'such tactics as : overlooking union members for promotion and pay rises, transferring active unionists from department to department, threatening to discontinue any "extras" presently being paid above the union rate, sending management officials to union recruitment meetings to note the names of those employees attending, and dismissing leading union members' (Bain 1970 : 132–3). While these examples relate to white-collar unions, most manual workers' organisations could describe experiences of the same strategy. Victimisation and blacklisting of union militants is still a common practice in much of British industry. And the most cursory knowledge of labour history will show that the courts have posed a persistent threat to trade unionism – both through anti-union legislation (the Industrial Relations Act of 1971–4 being the most recent example) and through judicial decisions which reflect the judges' own class prejudice (recent cases limiting the right to picket, including the gaoling of the Shrewsbury pickets, exemplify this tendency). In addition, there exist today far more effective means than ever before of mass persuasion and ideological manipulation; and for two decades or more there has occurred a constant campaign, sometimes subtle but often blatant, to discredit trade unionism.

All these sources of resistance entail that trade union organisation is rarely established without a struggle. In some situations the obstacles are particularly severe : for example, it tends to be particularly difficult to organise in workplaces which are small or isolated; in industries with a casual labour force; among unskilled, white-collar and female workers. Hence there exist considerable variations in patterns of organisation. Virtually 100 per cent unionisation has been achieved in some traditional sectors of industry – mining, railways, the docks – as well as in such modern areas as car assembly. In such cases, solid organisation is often reinforced by the 'closed shop' – which is sometimes officially approved by the employer but more normally tacitly accepted. In the public sector union membership is high, even among non-manual employees, because labour political pressure has forced local authorities and the government to recognise and encourage unionism. But there are also areas of employment in which organisation is extremely weak – most notably, perhaps, some service industries in the private sector.

Despite these obstacles, union membership in Britain has shown a persistent tendency to increase. Sometimes the growth has been explosive (as around 1890, after 1910, and during both world wars), sometimes more sluggish, and at times there have been set-backs. The worst relapse was during the two decades of mass unemployment between the wars, when deteriorating conditions and employer hostility caused the loss of almost half the peak membership recorded in 1920. Since the 1960s, the rate of growth has been significant if unspectacular. The total number of union members in Britain reached 10 million for the first time ever in 1964; by the end of 1973 this had risen to a record $11\frac{1}{2}$ million. This represented almost exactly 50 per cent of the labour force unionised – again a record. The growth in organisation in the last few years is specially significant for two reasons. Firstly, the post-war period has shown a sharp decline in employment in a number of industries which were traditional strongholds of unionism, and a growth in the labour force in precisely those areas which have proved difficult to organise. Secondly, the growth has not been checked by a level of unemployment considerably above the post-war norm – whereas historically, unemployment has usually led to a fall in union membership. The pressures towards collective action (which include the experience of wage restraint in a period of rapidly rising prices, the intensification of work demands in many areas of employment, and consciousness of job insecurity) are clearly proving stronger than the traditional obstacles.

The basic rationale of trade unionism is summed up in the familiar motto : unity is strength. The power of a collectivity is qualitatively different from the mere sum of the strengths of its members as isolated individuals. But on what basis do employees band together collectively? Trade unions are not *class* organisations, uniting all those who work for a living; workers combine along narrower lines of common identification and common interests (though sectional organisation, as is argued later, may nevertheless in certain situations form the basis of a broader class movement). The principles which underlie the patterns of union organisation – the criteria of inclusion and exclusion, the lines of demarcation and division – are commonly referred to as the *structure* of trade unionism. The concept of trade union structure thus has a rather special meaning : it refers, not to the internal organisational relations of individual unions but of the movement as a whole; as far as individual unions are concerned it indicates what has been termed their 'external shape'.

Structural divisions of some kind are a universal feature of trade unionism. In many European countries (as in other parts of the world) unions are split along lines of political or religious identification, and compete for the support of the same groups of workers. In Japan, and in some other Asian and African nations, there are many unions catering solely for the employees of a single company. Unions in Britain avoid differentiations of these kinds. The same is true of the USA. As in Britain, American unionism has long historical roots, having developed out of the spontaneous occupational organisation of skilled workers. But unlike their British counterparts, the American unions gained little significant foothold in modern mass-production industries. This was due in part to the bitter anti-unionism of the major employers, who encouraged spurious 'company unions' and used brutality and intimidation against *bona fide* trade unionists. In part also it reflected narrow craft-consciousness of the American Federation of Labor (AFL), which was unsuccessfully challenged towards the end of the nineteenth century by the Knights of Labor, and in the early years of the present century by the Industrial Workers of the World. Only in the 1930s were sustained attempts made to unionise in large-scale manufacturing industry, with the formation of organising committees on an industrial basis; but conflict between traditional supporters of organisation by craft and more radical advocates of organisation by industry led to a split, with the creation of industrial unions combined into a Congress of Industrial Organizations (CIO). Aided by the union recognition provisions of the National Labor Relations Act of 1935, the new bodies enjoyed a mushroom growth and soon exceeded the AFL in importance. In

1955 a reconciliation was effected, establishing the present AFL–CIO.

Today the AFL–CIO represents roughly three-quarters of American trade unionists. But it does not include the two largest unions, with a combined membership of over three million : the International Brotherhood of Teamsters, expelled in 1957 for 'racketeering', and the United Auto Workers, which seceded in 1968 in protest against its conservative policies; and a number of important white-collar and public employee associations are not affiliated. The largest affiliated unions are, in order of size, the United Steel Workers; International Brotherhood of Electrical Workers; International Association of Machinists; United Brotherhood of Carpenters and Joiners; Retail Clerks' International Association; Labourers' International Union; Amalgamated Meat Cutters; Hotel and Restaurant Employees; State, County and Municipal Employees; Service Employees' International Union; and Communication Workers of America. These eleven unions, each with over 400,000 members, share just under half the total membership of the AFL–CIO.

In general the structure of American unionism is simpler than in Britain, partly because the legally enforced system of 'bargaining units' prevents the representation of workers within a single plant by competing unions. Nevertheless the opposition between craft and industrial principles, and the survival of rivalries between organisations which date from the separate existence of AFL and CIO, constitute complicating factors.

American union membership, after a period of post-war stagnation, has expanded significantly since the early 1960s. In 1972 American unions had a combined membership of 23 million; excluding Canadian members (who account for the term 'International' in many unions' titles) this represented 24 per cent of the labour force, or 30 per cent of non-agricultural employment.. The level of unionisation is thus only approximately half that in Britain. This is largely attributable to far weaker organisation among white-collar workers (who are a far larger proportion of the labour force than in Britain) and public employees; and this in turn is partly attributable to legal obstacles and often intense employer opposition.

British unions, like American, are unusual in possessing a single central organisation, the Trades Union Congress (TUC), encompassing the main organisations of both manual and white-collar workers. In 1974 every major union was affiliated, giving a total membership of 10 million.[2] British unions are however almost unique in the diversity of principles underlying their organisation; their structure is famous – or notorious – for its complexity.

TABLE 1 Membership of the largest British Unions – end 1973 (,000)*

| | |
|---|---|
| Transport and General Workers' Union (TGWU) | 1785 |
| Amalgamated Union of Engineering Workers (AUEW) | 1375 |
| General and Municipal Workers' Union (GMWU) | 864 |
| National and Local Government Officers' Association (NALGO) | 518 |
| National Union of Public Employees (NUPE) | 470 |
| Electrical Electronic Telecommunication and Plumbing Union (EETPU) | 420 |
| Union of Shop, Distributive and Allied Workers (USDAW) | 326 |
| Association of Scientific, Technical and Managerial Staffs (ASTMS) | 316 |
| National Union of Mineworkers (NUM) | 261 |
| Union of Construction Allied Trades and Technicians (UCATT) | 257 |
| National Union of Teachers (NUT) | 250 |
| Civil and Public Services Association (CPSA) | 216 |

*TUC affiliation figures.

It has long been common to argue that British unions fall into three main categories. First, the craft unions : organisations of skilled tradesmen, perhaps straddling several industries. Second, industrial unions, recruiting every grade of labour in a single industry. Third, general unions, organising regardless of occupation or industry. These three categories certainly reflect fairly accurately the origins and early aspirations of many unions, and may still be enshrined in their official ideologies; but they are far too simplistic to do justice to the complexity of current reality. There are no pure industrial unions, in the sense of organisations which recruit within only one industry and have exclusive jurisdiction over every occupational group. There are very few pure craft unions; those societies which confine their membership to apprenticed craftsmen are small in numbers and usually limited in influence. And no union has aspirations as ecumenical as the notion of general unionism often implies. The picture is further

[2] The number of unions affiliated was however only 108, out of a total of 495 unions recorded at the end of 1973; but the outsiders were overwhelmingly tiny. Of the 495 unions in 1973 253 had under 1000 members; their combined membership was well under 1 per cent of the national total.

complicated, moreover, by the growth of white-collar unionism :
while some salaried employees are members of predominantly
manual unions, a far larger number are separately organised, and
membership has been expanding rapidly in recent years.

While the number of unions is considerable, over three-
quarters of their total membership is represented by two dozen
organisations; the largest dozen contain almost two-thirds of all
British trade unionists. A brief survey of the coverage of these
twelve unions, whose membership is listed in Table 1, shows
clearly how complicated the structure of union organisation is.[3]

The TGWU, the country's largest union, approximates to an
industrial union in such sectors as oil-refining, flour-milling and
the docks – though in each case it has to share the field with
other organisations. It is almost – though not quite – the un-
rivalled occupational union for road transport drivers across the
whole range of industries. It is also characteristically 'general' in
that it has some membership among production workers (and in
many cases among white-collar staff) in the majority of manufacturing industries. The GMWU is almost as extensive in its
range of membership; at the same time it is a quasi-industrial
union in the gas industry.

The AUEW is an amalgamation of four organisations which
remain far from fully integrated; it operates, in effect, as a federation of largely autonomous sections. The largest, the Engineering Section, is the old Amalgamated Engineering Union (AEU).
Within the engineering industry (or range of industries) it can best
be described as a semi-general union (though in competition with
the general unions proper). The old AEU contained all grades
of manual workers, as well as some supervisors; the amalgamations have brought in foundrymen and a large number of
white-collar staff – in particular in the technical grades. The
union also has strong organisation among maintenance craftsmen
in a variety of other industries. The EETPU shows some simi-
larities. In electrical engineering it is a general union for production workers; in construction, it covers electrical contractors and
plumbers; it organises maintenance electricians and their mates
across a range of industries; and it is an aspiring industrial union
for electricity supply.

[3] The coverage of the major unions is discussed in greater detail in
Clegg 1970.

NALGO can best be described as a multi-occupational white-collar union for local government. It covers every category from clerks to chief officers, with little serious competition from other organisations. In addition, it includes staff from some public utilities (usually where these were at one stage municipally owned). NUPE is to some extent its manual counterpart, which sometimes claims to represent an industrial union for local government. However, it has to compete with both general unions; and while it contains a small white-collar membership, it does not attempt to encroach on the preserves of NALGO. NUPE also has a considerable membership in the health service, though here it faces even greater competition from rival unions.

USDAW is an aspiring industrial union for the retail trades. But it contains few of the transport workers in distribution, and even among the sales staff its organisation is weak outside the Cooperative sector. Its membership does however extend into manufacturing industry, and in particular food processing, where it is comparable to a general union. The NUM is the closest British approximation to a pure industrial union. But its organis-ation does not extend to the supervisory grades, and among other white-collar staff it has only limited membership. UCATT is an aspiring industrial union in construction, though primarily con-fined to the woodworking and bricklaying crafts; like the AUEW and EETPU it organises maintenance craftsmen in a range of industries; while its woodworking membership gives it a signifi-cant status in furniture and shipbuilding.

The three remaining unions all cover white-collar employees. ASTMS has shown the most dramatic expansion of any British union in recent years. Its strongest base is among supervisors and technicians in engineering; but it has spread to a range of service industries, and aspires to the status of a general union for mana-gerial and technical staff. The NUT is the dominant union for primary and secondary schoolteachers, though it faces com-petition from a number of smaller organisations, particularly among male teachers and at secondary level. It cannot be regar-ded as even an aspiring industrial union for education, in that it does not attempt to organise manual employees or in higher education. The CPSA, finally, is a broad white-collar occu-pational union for the civil service. Unlike NALGO, which it resembles in some respects, it does not recruit above a relatively low level in the management hierarchy. Senior civil servants are covered by a number of smaller, sectional associations. CPSA membership extends to staff of some nationalised industries which were once directly integrated in the civil service.

Such details, brief as they are, suffice to show the inadequacy of any simple craft/industrial/general classification of union structure. But the mere description of the membership composition of the major unions contributes nothing to the *understanding* of the pattern : it merely presents a picture of extreme confusion. Is it possible to make sense of this variety, to give meaning to the confusion?

Union structure becomes comprehensible only if viewed in its historical dimension. Union structure is not a fixed phenomenon but a *process*, the historical outcome of the interdependent but *not purposefully integrated* strategies of a variety of fragmented employee groups. Throughout the process of structural development, two contradictory forces have operated : on the one hand towards breadth, unity and solidarity; on the other towards parochialism, sectionalism and exclusiveness. The one tendency encourages unionism which is open and expansive; the other, unionism which is closed and restrictive. But the two extremes of open and closed unions are abstractions, scarcely ever met in pure form in the real world. The tension between unifying and divisive pressures is in practice almost universal, within individual unions as well as between them : and this gives union structure at any point of time a dynamic character.

The theoretical maximum unity of trade unionism would be represented by a single organisation covering the whole working class – the 'One Big Union' which was once the dream of some socialist activists. In practice, there has never been any serious prospect of achieving such a goal. Nevertheless, the notion of working-class unity is more than a wild fantasy. The notion of the working-class – as was explained in the previous chapter – denotes the basic similarity of situation of *all* who lack ownership and control over the means of production, who are forced to sell their working capacity in the labour market, who are subordinated to a hierarchy of managerial control. All who are in this situation – that is, most white-collar as well as manual employees – suffer many *common* grievances in terms of insecurity of employment, lack of autonomy in work, dissatisfaction with pay and conditions, and so on (though of course the form and extent of these grievances varies). There is thus, objectively, a common relationship of opposition and antagonism to capital, and to the owners of capital and their functionaries. (It is indeed precisely this relationship of opposition which gives the notion of a working class its coherence and meaning.) This objective community of interest is the source of the unifying tendencies in trade unionism : the extension of organisational boundaries; re-cruitment of non-unionised workers; mutual support and solid-arity; amalgamation, federation, and the creation of such all-embracing bodies as the TUC. It is this common situation and common interest which gives the notion of a *labour move-ment* its meaning and its appeal.

Yet the notion of class – like any collective concept involving a high level of generality – is an abstraction, a means of indicat-ing the structural foundations which underlie the surface reality of social and economic relations. But *consciousness* of class iden-tity is often far removed from the everyday processes of industrial relations. While class opposition forms the basis of work relations in capitalist society, this is overlaid and often concealed by the immense variety of specific work contexts and work relations. There is a natural tendency for those involved to be conscious primarily of their immediate work milieu, their everyday experi-ences, their direct and personal relationships. Thus men and women normally identify themselves first and foremost as mem-bers of a specific occupational group, employees of a given firm, or workers in a particular industry – rather than in class terms. It follows that their overriding concern tends to be with the narrow area of interests and loyalties that lie closest to hand; and hence in many situations they may be more conscious of those interests which divide them from other groups of workers than of those that unite them. These inhibitions against class conscious-ness in everyday industrial relations, it must be added, do not merely arise spontaneously; they are encouraged by an array of powerful ideological pressures.

When workers organise in trade unions, these divisive tenden-cies are naturally expressed in their organisational boundaries, shaping the lines of demarcation. The very name *trade* union implies sectionalism : the inward-looking unity of those with a common craft or skill; and the broadening of organisation beyond the narrow limits of a specific occupational group has normally required an identifiable motive force beyond the simple fact of membership of the wider working class. An example is provided by the attempts to create a broader 'Union of Trades' in the 1820s and 1830s – a movement culminating in the Grand National Consolidated Trades Union of 1834, commonly associated with the name of the early socialist Robert Owen.[4] This movement may be seen as a response to such developments as the growth of large-scale capitalist employment in the cotton industry, or the rise of large contractors in place of the traditional small masters in the building industry. Despite the pretensions of some of its leaders, the Grand National made little serious attempt to constitute a class union, recruiting the unskilled and unorganised; and even the degree of broader unity which was achieved proved fragile and short-lived.

The development of trade union structure in Britain represents, in effect, the history of the variety of forces which have driven the boundaries of common organisation beyond their 'natural' narrow limits; and also of the strength of resistance to ambitious strategies of unity. It is the history of the expansion of the coverage of particular unions from an initial, usually reasonably clearly defined basis of membership, in both horizontal and vertical directions: moving across industries to recruit occupational groups similar to those already in membership; and taking in new occupational groups in the industries already covered. It is a process which has involved occasional bursts of rapid organisational innovation, more protracted periods of gradual progression, and some instances of retrenchment or even retreat.

The earliest unions (many dating back to the eighteenth century) were local craft societies or 'trade clubs'. Often they emerged spontaneously from the informal 'occupational community' of a craft group – being established, for example, at a

[4] Owen was a utopian socialist: that is, he devised blueprints for an ideal society but had little serious conception of how they might be implemented. His interest in trade unionism was short-lived; and the movements associated with his name in fact owed more to such lesser-known activists as the cotton spinner, John Doherty. Moreover, Owen's reputation as a socialist pioneer is exaggerated: he was less significant a theorist than were such men as James Smith and James Morrison, for a time associated with him.

public house where local carpenters tended naturally to congregate to 'talk shop'.[5] *Sociability* was often a primary purpose of such societies (in many cases, the rules prescribed the amount to be spent on drink at each meeting); in addition, an important function was the provision of *friendly benefits* (for sickness, accidents, unemployment, loss of tools, death, and possibly retirement). By contrast, the direct industrial relations activities of such early unions were often of lesser importance. The trades in which they were established operated on the basis of a network of rules prescribed by custom and often dating back to medieval times. The craft societies developed an industrial relations role primarily as *defenders* of traditional working rules and practices against either employers (who in some trades sought to introduce new methods of capitalist 'rationalisation') or the encroachments of other groups of workers. It was rare for them to undertake serious initiatives to change conditions : the main example was the occasional 'wage movement' launched in periods of rising prices; and here the main objective was to protect customary living standards.

Many of these early trade societies were short-lived : they rarely accumulated substantial funds, and might be broken by a single serious conflict with a major employer. But others proved more resilient, and some were able to wield considerable power. Effective craft unionism was founded on the principle of *unilateral control*. The union reserved to itself alone the right to determine the rules of the trade (usually relying on its interpretation of traditional practice) and the rates of pay, and to enforce these through its own members. The means were simple : members of the society would shun employment by masters who failed to observe union conditions; or if their employer flouted union rules, they would leave and seek work elsewhere. What made this possible was the existence of a monopoly of labour supply : the union controlled entry to the trade through rigorous apprenticeship rules, and jealously enforced the demarcation of its own area of work. Members unable to find work on union conditions could be supported on the benefit funds, and if necessary paid to 'tramp' to other areas in search of a job. Most employers were small, and it was therefore a feasible proposition to

[5] The names of many public houses indicate their traditional association with specific skilled occupations.

withdraw all union members permanently from the shop of a recalcitrant master. And because small masters had themselves often begun as ordinary craftsmen, and were nurtured in the customs of the trade, they were normally content to acquiesce in observing union conditions.

Two developments served to undermine the effectiveness of the traditional craft societies. One was the emergence in many trades of large employers, committed to the new capitalist principles of efficiency and innovation, and willing to override traditional practices where these stood in the way of higher profits. The other was the development of a national labour market, particularly with the rapid spread of railways in the 1840s, eroding the basis of any purely local control of labour supply. These developments stimulated the consolidation of trade unionism on a national basis, with a co-ordination of trade policies and standardisation of benefit rules. The process was pioneered by the Amalgamated Society of Engineers (ASE), formed in 1851, and followed in the succeeding decades by various other 'new model' craft amalgamations.[6] The key principles underlying these national craft amalgamations were the centralisation of financial control, and the cultivation of new standards of efficiency in administration (which necessitated the employment of a full-time general secretary). Often the new amalgamations deliberately shunned the alcoholic camaraderie of the old trade clubs. At the same time, their leaders sought an accommodation with the changing power structure on the employers' side. On fundamental issues such as apprenticeship and demarcation, which were seen as the very foundations of the craft, the principle of unilateral control remained the rule; but on questions of wages and hours they were more ready to negotiate and compromise.

The extension of craft unionism from its local origins to a national basis was obviously a form of increased unity. But this unity meant principally the consolidation of sectionalism. The 'new model' involved no significant relaxation of the vertical boundaries of union organisation : other crafts were often viewed suspiciously, as potential rivals in demarcation conflicts; the

[6] Recent historians have disputed how new the organisational principles of these unions in fact were, and how extensively they served as a model. But the name has stuck.

lower-skilled were a possible threat to the craftsmen's job monopoly, and possible competitors for a share in what was often thought of as a fixed 'wages fund'. Hence craft unionism remained for the most part firmly *closed* in a vertical direction : it monopolised various islands of advantageous conditions, secured partly *at the expense* of the broader working class.[7] There was no serious motive to transcend this sectionalism, for the mid-Victorian era provided a seeming vindication of the principle of craft exclusiveness. Industrial development proceeded smoothly (after the traumatic changes of the early nineteenth century, when many traditional crafts were undermined); and British capitalism established its dominance in the world markets. Most sections of the working class gained some material benefits from this period of increasing prosperity; but the 'aristocrats of labour' in their craft societies were unquestionably the most favoured.

The advantages of closed unionism – for those *within* its boundaries – proved highly attractive to the more privileged groups of workers in industries without an apprenticeship system controlling job entry. In cotton-spinning or iron- and steel-making, for example, there existed a clear hierarchy of occupations. The ability to perform the most skilled or responsible jobs, as spinners or as puddlers and melters, came through general experience rather than specific training; and workers attained these top jobs through promotion on the basis of seniority. In both industries, the minority of workers in the key occupations formed exclusive unions; at times they sought, moreover, to inhibit the lower-status majority from establishing their own collective organisation. Such exclusiveness had an evident pay-off : the key groups were able to secure differentials above the lower-paid which were at times even larger than those existing in craft industries. A similar situation tended to exist in coalmining, where the face-workers normally dominated the unions – even though other workers were

---

[7] This does not mean that there was no consciousness of broader common interests. In 1859–60, for example, the ASE made donations totalling £3,000 to the London building unions locked out by their employers – an unprecedented display of solidarity. In the 1860s, several of the leaders of craft societies participated in the International Working Men's Association, in which Marx himself played a key role. Their political involvements in the 1860s also showed a less exclusive orientation: though their predominant aim would seem to have been to win the upper strata of the working class a place 'within the pale of the constitution'.

not necessarily excluded altogether. Sectionalism was encouraged in all three industries by a tradition of sub-contracting : the privileged groups receiving from the employer an output-linked rate out of which they themselves paid the wages of the subordinate grades who worked as their assistants.

In other industries, the material basis of this form of sectionalism was far less. For example, in cotton-weaving (which was largely segregated geographically from the spinning districts) the bulk of the labour force were production workers without important internal differentiations; there was no clear hierarchy of skill or status, and the only occupational groups with anything resembling a craft tradition were ancillary to the main production process. Closed unionism was not therefore a serious proposition; on the contrary, effective control over wages and working conditions demanded united action across a broad front. Hence an open form of unionism was the logical requirement; and it was on this basis that weaving organisation developed from the 1850s.[8]

Since the end of the nineteenth century there has been a tendency towards the increasing openness of union organisation, as some of the traditional bases of closed unionism were eroded. Two developments were of crucial importance. First, the general economic climate altered. The 'great depression' which commenced in the mid-1870s caused substantial unemployment in a number of craft societies, and shook their faith in the constant bounty of British capitalism. Foreign competition spurred employers to cut labour costs, and in particular stimulated an attempt to overturn traditional craft controls. The ability of privileged groups of workers, acting independently of (and perhaps in opposition to) others in their industry, to deal effectively with such challenges was put in doubt. The second development threatened a more insidious erosion of craft unionism : the invention of new technologies which could enable semi-skilled labour to perform much of the work previously the preserve of apprenticed craftsmen. If such labour was unorganised, and could be employed at little more than labouring rates, the incentive to employers to displace craft skills would be further enhanced.

[8] Turner (1962) describes and analyses the development of textile trade unionism, and draws more general conclusions concerning the significance of 'closed' and 'open' organisation.

These general pressures combined with specific problems in individual industries to encourage the reduction of union exclusiveness. In coalmining, attempts had been made since the first half of the century to establish effective unionism which could confront the power of the large mineowners, acting in concert on an area basis. Such organisation was usually short-lived, unable to survive the strains of frequent periods of recession (when employers sought to cut costs through drastic wage reductions). It became clear that strong unionism required the organisation of *all* underground workers, linked on a national basis so that one area under particular pressure could be supported by the others. On this basis was formed in 1889 the Miners' Federation of Great Britain, the precursor of the present NUM. The logic of inclusiveness led later to the recruitment of manual workers on the surface also. This open orientation was doubtless encouraged by the physical location of the coalminers, living for the most part in tight-knit and often isolated pit villages.

In iron and steel, the position of exclusive unionism was undermined by the success of the lower-paid and subordinate groups in establishing their own separate union. The latter, the Steel Smelters, pursued an independent policy often in direct opposition to the older Iron and Steel Workers, and secured a membership several times larger than the latter. The conflict was eventually resolved by the amalgamation of 1917 which created the existing Iron and Steel Trades' Confederation. In cotton, the spinners had previously forestalled the possibility of such a development by permitting – or even compelling – their subordinates, the piecers, to join their own union. The piecers were accorded few rights or benefits, but were effectively prevented from establishing an independent organisation.

An example of the dramatic impact of technical change on union structure is provided by the footwear industry. The position of skilled hand-workers in the boot and shoe trade – who in the first half of the nineteenth century supported a powerful craft organisation – was rapidly undermined by the growth of mechanised factory production. The craftsmen could neither resist the changes, nor compel the new grades of worker to accept their own domination; and their society was displaced by a new, open union of boot and shoe workers. In printing, by contrast,

the craft unions were able to survive unscathed the major technological development of the late nineteenth century : the replace-
ment of hand-composing by linotype machines. Though the skill
content of the compositor's work was reduced, the traditional
craft controls (including apprenticeship regulations) were applied
to the new work, and the structure of craft exclusiveness was
preserved. In engineering, developments fell between these two
extremes. By the end of the nineteenth century, technical changes
had reduced the status of apprenticeship as the sole means of
entry to the trade : the ASE had been obliged to accept as
craftsmen those workers who had 'progressed' from semi-skilled
work to the ability to earn the skilled rate. More radical technical
changes around 1890 provoked pressure for a substantial recast-
ing of the membership basis of the ASE, to take in all machine-
workers. But the impact of new technology was uneven, and
most craftsmen felt that its challenge could be contained through
the traditional exclusive methods. Even after the traumatic
defeat of the ASE in the lockout of 1897–8, little was done to
open up its recruitment.

In these examples of reducing exclusiveness, recruitment was
opened in a *vertical* direction : the trend in iron and steel or
coalmining was towards industrial unionism. (In neither case,
though, was recruitment fully inclusive within the industry. The
tendency was to exclude labourers – who were often seen as tran-
sitory employees, not really committed to the industry, and in
any case lacking unionist strength; maintenance workers – who
were often already organised by craft societies; and clerical and
supervisory staff – who at the time were often few in number,
and regarded as intimately connected with the employer.) Yet
if industrial-type unions were vertically open, they were normally
horizontally closed – not attempting to organise outside the
boundaries of their own industry. And this characteristic could
generate its own form of parochialism, of insensitivity to the
broader interests and problems of the class.

In this respect, paradoxically, the closed craft unions were in
some cases better placed to adopt a broad perspective. For though
vertically closed and exclusive, they were often horizontally open.
The Carpenters and Joiners, for example, defined their interests
in terms of skilled woodworkers in construction, shipbuilding and
furniture making, and in smaller pockets in other industries. The

ASE viewed the apprentice fitter as a man qualified to maintain machinery in any industry; the shipbuilding fitter had an interest in the conditions of a maintenance worker in a chemical plant, for he might at some time seek employment there. Hence the member of such a union was unlikely to define his interests as a member of 'his' industry, in common with those of his employer, and in opposition to the interests of workers in other industries; whereas there was a tendency to precisely such an approach inherent in the structure of unionism in the steel industry.

The co-existence of craft and industrial-type unions – the one vertically closed but often horizontally open, the other the reverse – created a pattern of union structure which was not excessively complex. The main source of the confusion of contemporary British union structure is the development of unions which were *both* horizontally *and* vertically open: the 'new unions' of the late 1880s, many of which formed the basis of the general unions of today.

The historical significance of the upsurge of 'new unionism' has often been exaggerated, and there is a tendency today to play down its importance. Yet there can be no question that the movement of 1888–90, and the similar eruption a quarter-century later, caused the most radical alteration in union structure and the most explosive lasting extension of union coverage of any period of labour history. By accident or design, several of the new unions were expansionist in a manner which was wholly unprecedented.

There were three main reasons for this expansionism: this readiness to spread organisation wholesale (though haphazardly). The first stemmed from the scarcely questioned tendency in Victorian times to classify the working class rigidly into two groups. The skilled artisan, with his long craft training, was regarded as a type apart, solid, respectable, his material advantages and social standing resting on his special scarcity value in the labour market. All other types of worker were conventionally viewed as unskilled, unqualified, easily replaceable by his employer and with few ties to the employment in which he found himself at any given point of time. This simple dichotomy was highly misleading: across most industries, the bulk of non-craft workers performed a range of tasks requiring different degrees of experi-

ence and expertise, in many cases carrying out vital functions in
the production process. Yet non-craft workers themselves – outside occupations such as cotton-spinning or engine-driving, where
a clear promotion hierarchy existed – tended to accept the conventional classification, regarding themselves as undifferentiated
'general labourers'. This meant that sectional consciousness was
not strongly developed among gasworkers, dockers, or process
workers in most factory industries; and in consequence the unions
which sprang up in these industries were vertically open, recruiting every grade of non-craft labour.

These unions were in many cases horizontally open because
their members were often occupationally mobile. Many gasworkers, who were laid off in the summer when demand for gas
was low, found jobs in the brickyards which were then at their
peak of production. Hence the gasworkers' unions naturally
recruited brickmakers, and men and women in any other industry in which their members might be employed seasonally. Fear
of blacklegging during strikes also encouraged horizontal expansion; as Will Thorne, secretary of the main gasworkers' union,
put it : 'if we should confine ourselves to one particular industry,
such as gasworks alone, and if those other people in various parts
of the country are let go unorganised, then, if we had a dispute
with any of the gas companies, these men would be brought up
to be put in our places'.[9] A similar fear inspired the main dockers'
union to recruit extensively, even attempting to organise farm
labourers. The horizontal spread of unionism across industries
was also natural when workers of one category came into regular
contact with others in the course of their everyday employment.
Thus in South Wales and the Bristol Channel ports, organisation
spread rapidly from dockers to carters and other road transport
workers, and from them into flour mills, tin-plate works and
other factories to and from which they made deliveries.

A third source of expansionism was the political orientation of
many of the leaders of the new unions. Men like Thorne, or Tom
Mann and Ben Tillett of the Dockers' Union, were socialists who
thought naturally in terms of the common interests of the whole
working class. (Mann was typical of the small group of socialist
craft unionists who criticised the exclusiveness of their own

[9] Quoted in Hobsbawm 1964: 181. Hobsbawm provides an important
discussion of the sources of openness in the new unionism.

societies, and worked to organise the lower-skilled.) The parallel may be made with the development of trade unionism in many of the countries of continental Europe. Union organisation was often preceded, and directly stimulated, by the growth of a substantial socialist movement; and one consequence was the inhibition of occupational sectionalism.

This convergence of the anti-sectional spirit of many leaders and activists with ordinary members' self-conception of their own interests thus encouraged the double openness – both vertical and horizontal – of the new unions. Yet there were limits to the 'general' character of these organisations. Some stuck fairly closely to their initial recruitment base; and even the most expansionist tempered any aspiration to become all-embracing 'class unions' with a respect for existing strongholds of unionisation. While recruiting virtually every grade of manual (though rarely white-collar) occupation in a few industries, neither the gasworkers' nor dockers' unions seriously contemplated encroaching on the preserves of the craft societies, or into such industries as cotton, coalmining, or the railways (except in cases where some labouring occupations were spurned by the established industrial-type unions). Thus even the most expansionist of the new unions were essentially *residual* in their recruitment patterns, filling the numerous and often complicated gaps left by the earlier structure of trade unionism. Moreover, the dynamism of their open orientation tended to ebb. Once groups of non-craft workers established effective organisation they tended to become conscious of possessing sectional interests, and of their ability to pursue these sectionally. The most effective strategy could then appear to be the creation of a stronghold of unionism isolated from the broader labour market : excluding the alternative labour force seemed easier than organising it. Hence where dockers succeeded in enforcing a closed shop, excluding outsiders from the waterfront, their concern with conditions in other industries tended to diminish. In extreme cases, the growth of sectional consciousness led to breakaways by industrial or occupational groups which felt best able to further their special interests in isolation. The concern for class organisation on the part of socialist leaders also weakened. Recruitment among the unorganised demanded time and energy which were fully committed to servicing the *existing* membership : if the union could function effectively within its existing area of organisation, ideology alone proved a weak stimulus to further expansion.

The last half-century has thus tended to be a period of the consolidation of British union structure. The growth of white-collar organisation has formed the one significant element of innovation, and has brought new structural complexities and problems. Even among purely white-collar unions themselves there exists a variety of organisational forms : single- or multi-industry, single- or multi-occupation. The involvement of predominantly manual unions not only adds to the structural confusion, but multiplies the possibilities of competition and conflict. (This can be particularly acute where such unions fear the erosion of their traditional manual membership base by technical and occupational changes; the incentive becomes strong to recruit salaried staff, even if these have been largely ignored in the past. The recent dispute over organisation rights in the steel industry is a clear example of such problems.)

The remaining developments in this period represent the structural effects of the competition or convergence of existing, established unions; in many cases they reflect the organisational preoccupations of trade union leadership. The central trend is pinpointed by Clegg, who writes that 'the structural history of British trade unions during the present century records long periods of rigidity interspersed with bursts of amalgamation' (1970 : 55). The significance of this factor in recent years is shown by trends in the number of recorded unions. From the late nineteenth century until 1920 the number fluctuated between 1200 and 1400; most changes reflected the formation and dissolution of unions, many of which had only an ephemeral existence. By 1940 the number had fallen to 1000; but much of the reduction may be attributed to the casualties of mass unemployment. But since the outbreak of war, though union membership has almost doubled, the number of unions has more than halved : a process almost wholly attributable to amalgamation.

Just as the recruitment strategies of unions can be more or less open or closed, in both vertical and horizontal directions, so the patterns of amalgamation reveal similar variations. In a few cases, amalgamations of unions with similar principles of organisation have simplified trade union structure. Thus the main metal-working crafts in shipbuilding – boilermakers, shipwrights and blacksmiths – have merged; while the National Graphical Association has united most of the printing crafts, previously divided both occupationally and geographically. (In both cases, changes in technology and in employer structure and policy helped stimulate a reduction in union sectionalism.) But more often, amalgamation has tended to add further complexity of union organisation, at times creating new hybrid structural forms. Such an example can also be found in printing : the Society of Graphical and Allied Trades (SOGAT). Its main origins lie in an amalgamation of unions of papermill workers and printing warehousemen – who shared a common link in respectively producing, and receiving and storing, the industry's main raw material. But the warehousemen's union also recruited women who worked as assistants to skilled bookbinders; and this led eventually to conflict with the craft union of the latter. So intense did the conflict become that only one solution seemed possible : a further amalgamation. Hence SOGAT is at one and the same time a 'labourers' union' in the warehouse and publication departments of newspaper and magazine printing; a craft-dominated union in bookbinding; and an industrial-type union in papermaking. An amalgamation which would have added logic to this structure – with the main non-craft union in the central production departments in printing, the National Society of Operative Printers and Assistants (NATSOPA), was initiated in 1966; but the two organisations soon drew apart (though a re-amalgamation remains possible).

Because of their greater size and variety of interests, the development of the largest unions displays an even greater complexity. Occupational mobility among members, diversification of activities on the part of employers, and changes in work processes, have all stimulated expansion or amalgamation in a bewildering variety of directions. Thus the TGWU derives from the amalgamation in 1921 of almost twenty unions of dockers and road transport workers. Its relatively small stake among 'general workers' was boosted by amalgamation in 1929 with the Workers' Union, which possessed an unusually diverse membership and was particularly strong in engineering. Subsequent changes in industrial structure have transformed the pattern of the union's membership composition. The importance of transport has declined substantially, while that of engineering and other manufacturing industries has greatly increased. In particular, the TGWU now organises the majority of workers in the motor industry (its position being boosted by a recent amalgamation with the National Union of Vehicle Builders – itself a former craft union in the carriage trade, which adapted successfully to the advent of the motor car). The union also has a rapidly-growing white-collar section. The attractiveness of the TGWU as an amalgamation partner is enhanced by its system of semi-autonomous 'trade groups', which permits an organisation like the NUVB to retain some of its independent identity. On the same basis, its white-collar section can also present an independent appearance; it is even able to employ a distinctive title, the Association of Clerical, Technical and Supervisory Staffs.

The other main general union, the GMWU, was created in 1924 by the amalgamation of the old gasworkers' union with another, largely northern-based union of lower-skilled workers and with a municipal employees' organisation. Its relative stagnation in membership, in a period when the TGWU has expanded rapidly, reflects – quite apart from any lesser efficiency in exploiting opportunities for growth – the GMWU's limited foothold in expanding industries and occupations, and its inability to accommodate flexibly to potential amalgamation partners. USDAW – which to some extent represents a third general union – also owes this characteristic to amalgamation. Its main component was formed by the merger, in 1920, of a union of Co-operative employees with an organisation of warehousemen and general workers, which had grown from nothing to a substantial membership in the previous decade. A third union of shopworkers came in to form the present USDAW in 1946.

The main engineering union derives from the amalgamation in 1920 between the ASE and a number of smaller craft and other occupational societies. The traditional rigid craft control of the ASE had already been undermined by the introduction of new machine tools and new grades of labour to operate them. By the end of the 1914–18 war, production work in most large engineering factories had lost its craft character : apprenticed labour was virtually confined to maintenance, machine-setting, and the toolroom. But the ASE was slow to alter its recruitment policy: only after the 1920 amalgamation was membership opened to all male engineering workers, and it was another two decades before women were admitted. By then, the general unions were firmly entrenched among engineering production workers (both men and women), and obstructed the objective long cherished by the most far-sighted activists in the ASE: its transformation into an all-embracing industrial union within the metal-working industries. In a muted form, this aspiration has however survived, and underlies the recent amalgamations which created the present AUEW: incorporating the Foundry Workers, the Constructional Engineers and the Draughtsmen's and Allied Technicians' Association (now the Technical Administrative and Supervisory Section of the AUEW). The logic of this latter merger was reinforced by such technical developments as the introduction of numerically-controlled machine tools, blurring the boundary between manual and technical skills.

Another interesting example of expansion from an original narrow base is provided by ASTMS, which was initially a union of engineering foremen. Its expansion vertically into a wide range of technical and managerial grades – which brought it into conflict with the Draughtsmen – was aided by an amalgamation with the Association of Scientific Workers. The merger brought a significant membership outside the engineering and related industries (for example, among technicians in universities and the health service), and encouraged a policy of horizontal expansionism. Recruitment in new sectors of industry has encouraged further amalgamations, for instance drawing in several organisations of insurance workers.

A significant aspect of the recent spate of mergers is the scope presented for *choice* in the direction of trade union structural development. For half a century, the opportunity for expansionist unions to open up new areas of recruitment (at least among manual workers) has been limited. Once a union has established its title to organise a particular industry or occupation, any attempt by another union to venture into its preserves is deprecated; and by the 1920s, claims had been staked to most sectors of the labour force. Aggrieved member unions can appeal to the TUC, which since its 1939 Congress at Bridlington has possessed codified rules governing rights of organisation. Increasingly, then, the main way of broadening a union's recruitment base has been through amalgamation. In consequence, two or more organisations may compete to merge with the same prospective partner – offering quite different structural possibilities. The Draughtsmen might have amalgamated with ASTMS to create a multi-industry 'general union' of technicians; instead, the merger into the AUEW created a vertically open but horizontally more closed organisation, a choice based in part on an appeal to the principle of industrial unionism. This same principle was clearly rejected by the Vehicle Builders and the Operative Plasterers, which might have merged respectively into the AUEW and with the unions which joined to form UCATT, but which instead entered the TGWU. The formation of the EETPU created a particularly bizarre structural hybrid. The Electricians, a former craft union which had opened its membership downwards, possessed a membership pattern which would have complemented that of the AEU; the Plumbers, organising mainly in construction and in shipbuilding, might reasonably have participated in the craft amalgamations in either industry. Seeking a further merger, the EETPU has now made approaches to the AUEW, GMWU and UCATT.

Amalgamation decisions at times flow logically from the pattern of a union's existing membership, the coverage of the partner being industrially or occupationally complementary. But at other times, such decisions appear primarily to reflect the internal politics of trade union leadership. Those with the greatest ability to initiate or veto organisational change have necessarily a vested interest in the type of decision which is taken. Not surprisingly, the evidence indicates that many union leaders will strive to facilitate mergers which enhance their own influence and standing within the broader movement, or advance their career interests, and to frustrate those which threaten the contrary. Hence questions of union structure and union government clearly interact. A given structural pattern of union organisation affects the nature of the control which workers can exercise in industrial relations; yet to explain this pattern it is necessary to raise the question : who wields control *within* trade unions? This is one of the central issues of the chapter which follows.

Having considered the nature of British trade union structure, and some of its historical sources, it is necessary to examine briefly the key consequences of this structure. The complexity of the pattern of British trade unionism gives rise to regular criticism, both within and without the trade union movement itself. The presuppositions of such criticism tend however to reflect a variety of conflicting beliefs about the proper functions of trade unionism, and in particular about the appropriate direction for the application of control in industrial relations.

The most popular type of criticism is frankly managerial in orientation. It is argued that multi-unionism – the coverage of the employees of a single enterprise or industry by a number of unions – is a source of demarcation conflicts, encourages competitive militancy by trade unions, and prevents co-ordinated trade union discipline. Such critics often call for the re-organisation of union structure along industrial lines, at times drawing an idealised picture of the system operating in Scandinavia and West Germany.

There are three main weaknesses in this line of argument. First, the consequences of multi-unionism are overstated. Contrary to popular imagination, demarcation disputes are rare (causing only 2 per cent of recorded stoppages in recent years); moreover the sectional antagonisms which they reflect can find expression even within a single union. Nor is there much evidence that inter-union rivalry leads typically to increased militancy; indeed there is some evidence to the contrary. The second objection is that multi-unionism cannot practically be transformed into industrial unionism in Britain. Most of the major unions straddle a number of industries, and cannot be expected to agree to their own dismemberment; yet without this, a continuation of the process of amalgamation will necessarily give rise to new structural complexities. On these essentially pragmatic grounds, the Donovan Commission rejected the idea of industrial unionism, and submitted proposals for the 'rationalisation' of union structure which were modest in the extreme. Finally, the premise of this criticism cannot be allowed to pass unchallenged. The presupposition is essentially that trade unionism is (or should be) a source of orderly industrial relations, a means of control not so much *by* as *over* the labour force. (The objections to this conception of trade unionism – which to some extent make explicit the ideological assumptions implicit in the view of industrial relations as 'job regulation' – are discussed further in the next chapter.) The fact that multi-unionism may cause certain problems for managerial control should not be accepted as a valid basis for criticism of union structure; for if this were an appropriate criterion, it might be argued that managerial control could best be increased by abolishing trade unionism altogether!

Paradoxically, the goal of industrial unionism has historically been espoused from a radically different perspective. In the first decades of this century, it was common for revolutionary socialists to criticise the divisiveness of a trade union movement, fragmented among a multiplicity of sectional organisations and often dominated by a spirit of craft unionism. This sectionalism was seen as a source of weakness, which condemned trade unionism to a defensive posture and prevented any serious challenge to capitalist priorities in the organisation of work. Industrial unions were seen at one and the same time as a means of uniting workers in different occupations, skilled and unskilled, and also as potential vehicles of *workers' control*. Covering the whole of an industry, so it was assumed, each union would be in a position to devise an integrated set of policies reflecting workers' own interests and ultimately to take over the direction from capitalist management.[10]

The revolutionary conception of industrial unionism is open to the same practical objection as was mentioned earlier : it takes no adequate account of the institutional obstacles to the wholesale structural reconstruction of trade unionism. In Britain, industrial unionists divided themselves between those who sought their objective through amalgamation of existing unions, and those who aimed to create new unions in opposition to the latter. Yet, although the amalgamation movement did achieve important successes, these brought the goal of industrial unionism little closer – indeed the mergers which consolidated the two big general unions created an impregnable obstacle to this goal; and the policy of rival unionism was a disaster. Perhaps the most fundamental criticism to be made of the revolutionary conception of industrial unionism is its tendency to exaggerate the importance

[10] This analysis was central to the theories of the American Socialist Labour Party. Popularised in Britain by James Connolly, they were to prove highly influential in the shop stewards' movement of the 1914–18 war.

of formal union structure. The existence of sectional organisations is a consequence rather than a cause of sectionalism within
the working class (though at times it can certainly *reinforce* sectional consciousness). Industrial unionist blueprints proposed, in
effect, a purely *administrative* solution to fundamental problems
of ideology and class consciousness : 'they sought for a fusion of
officialdom as a means to the fusion of the rank and file' (Murphy
1972 : 18). In practice, such organisational reforms can have
only a subsidiary role in any process of broadening consciousness
and transcending sectionalism.

A third criticism of trade union structure focuses on the weaknesses which ensue in terms of control by and for workers in the
day-to-day processes of industrial relations. The structure and
coverage of British unionism, as has been seen, reflect the vagaries
of historical development rather than any co-ordinated strategy.
Where deliberate planning has impinged on this process, the
decisions have often reflected relatively narrow organisational
considerations. When the TUC examines general problems of
trade union structure (as occurs from time to time) a key consideration is inevitably the fear of giving offence to any established unions, which are normally highly jealous of their sectional
autonomy.

The consequence of sectional autonomy is however that unions
pursue divergent – and on occasion, mutually neutralising – policies; the potential control which could potentially be wielded by
trade unionism as a *class* movement is undermined. Some of the
most obviously deleterious consequences of policy fragmentation
can indeed be contained by such means as bilateral union contacts, industry federations, and the interventions of the TUC,
which have spread considerably in recent years. But such forms
of coordination as do exist contain checks and balances so powerful that the *positive* application of combined union power, particularly in an innovatory direction, is seriously inhibited.[11]

The structure of contemporary trade unionism is also in part

[11] Paradoxically, this weakness of central coordination is an obstacle to
the incorporation of British unionism: even when the TUC endorses
government policies which imply restraint over union action (as, for
example, in incomes policies) it lacks the power to compel the cooperation
of individual unions. The absence of 'power for' thus excludes the operation of 'power over'.

responsible for the existence of major gaps in unionisation. As was seen at the outset of this chapter, union coverage is extremely uneven. In the private sector there exist many areas of very weak organisation, including in particular small competitive employers and such services as shops, hotels and restaurants; and such groups as women and black workers, who tend to be disproportionately concentrated in such employment. Even expansionist unions tend to be less than impressive in the attempts made to recruit membership in 'difficult' sectors of employment, unless there are clear prospects of a pay-off in terms of their existing organisational interests. Yet the dangers are obvious. In some countries – notably the USA – it is often argued that there exist two, largely distinct, labour markets. In large, monopolistic, profitable companies the strongest union organisation is normally to be found; and the unions have established relatively favourable wages, conditions, and stability of employment. In small, competitive, less profitable firms, by contrast, unionism tends to be weak, wages very low, employment particularly insecure. Critics can thus argue, with some plausibility, that unions represent a relatively privileged minority of the working class, little interested in the conditions of the majority. Such an analysis is far less readily applicable in Britain : trade union coverage is considerably more extensive than in America, and 'dual labour market' theories are much less relevant. Nevertheless, when every other employee is non-unionised, and many of these endure conditions of employment far below the average, there are no grounds for complacency.

Trade union structure, as was argued earlier, is constantly developing. One of the crucial stimulants of change is the role of capital itself. Changes in technology and in the structure of occupations make traditional trade union forms obsolescent. Old skills are displaced and new ones created; traditionally clear-cut boundaries, like that between manual and non-manual employment, become blurred. The ownership of capital becomes more concentrated, and the economy becomes increasingly dominated by 'conglomerates' (often foreign-owned) with interests in a range of industries. Inevitably, such developments demand changes in the internal relationships of the working class. Concurrently, government initiatives in respect of economic management, incomes controls, and trade union legislation, tend to make *class* interests increasingly salient. These new problems (whose sources are analysed in later chapters) have already given rise to significant structural adaptations in British trade unionism – reflected, for example, in the amalgamations of recent years and the growing role of the TUC. It is reasonable to expect that in future years, capital itself (assisted by the state) will continue to undermine traditional trade union sectionalisms. Yet the process must be expected to remain gradual and tentative : labour history demonstrates only too clearly the strength of organisational inertia. Nor can it be seriously suggested that the sources of sectional organisation and consciousness could ever be wholly transcended.

CONCLUSION

The grievances and deprivations inevitably created by work relations in capitalist society cause a persistent tendency for employees to organise in increasing numbers in trade unions. But the forms of workers' solidarity indicate contradictory elements in their consciousness : there exist strong pressures on the one hand towards sectionalism, on the other towards broader unity; and these find their organisational expression in the complex patterns of trade union structure.

To an important extent, current union boundaries are a reflection of *past* experience of common interests and common action. 'The character of organisations', as Turner has commented, 'is very much a product of their ancestry and the circumstances of their early growth ... British trade unions, more than those of most countries perhaps, are historical deposits and repositories of history' (1962 : 14). Established institutions become a focus of loyalty in their own right, and sustain powerful vested interests in the perpetuation of traditional forms and practices. Thus the structure of trade unionism is in many respects ill-adapted to the realities of contemporary industry or to workers' own consciousness of their problems and interests; yet it constrains the manner of their response to these problems, and to this extent is an important obstacle to the capacity of the labour movement to exert positive control over industrial relations. Yet recent experience also shows that traditional organisational forms are not immutable : current trends in capitalism undermine some of the old sectionalisms, and contain pressures towards new forms of solidarity. Trade union structure is adapting to these pressures; but the process of adaptation occurs neither simply nor mechanically.

# 3 Union Policy and Union Democracy

The central argument so far can be briefly summarised : the study of industrial relations is in essence a study of processes of control over work relations. The employment relationship – which is encapsulated in the terms of the 'free' contract of employment – gives overriding authority in day-to-day work relations to the employer and to his or her managerial agents. The concentrated economic power of capital, buttresed by the various sanctions of the law, lies at the root of this right of managerial initiative through which the employer commands while workers are expected to obey. Hence there exists a 'natural' structure of one-way control over production and thus over the work activities of ordinary employees.

Yet the experience of work inevitably generates informal processes of resistance, of refusal to display obedience and diligence beyond certain limits, of insistence on priorities opposed to those of the employer. Through trade unionism, a formal basis is consolidated for a countervailing structure of control, which restricts and in some respects neutralises the dominance of the employer. A trade union is, first and foremost, an agency and a medium of power. Its central purpose is to permit workers to exert, collectively, the control over their conditions of employment which they cannot hope to possess as individuals; and to do so largely by compelling the employer to take account, in policy- and decision-making, of interests and priorities contrary to his own. As the vehicle of workers' interests *against* those of the employer, the union is involved in *external* relationships of control. (Such relationships are essentially two-way; as unions seek to affect the decisions of employers and governments they are themselves subject to influence and pressure from a range of external agencies.) But at the same time, processes of control pervade the *internal* relationships of the union, the interaction and interdependence of ordinary members, lay activists, local officials and national leaders. The problem of internal control, and the links between this problem and the external functions of trade unionism, represent the main focus of this chapter.

A trade union exemplifies the interconnection between the two types of power distinguished previously : 'power for' and 'power over'. A union can wield effective job control only if, and to the extent that, it can mobilise disciplined collective action on the part of its members. Such collective discipline is in turn dependent on members' willingness to subordinate, where necessary, their own immediate wishes or interests to common rules and collective decisions. Why should employees wish to limit their autonomy in this way? The rationale is obvious : concerted action requires, by definition, that all adhere to a common decision; and the gains in control attainable only through collective strength are expected to outweigh, at least over the long run, any possible costs in the loss of individual independence. Indeed this independence is in reality illusory, for the isolated employee can have no genuine autonomy; without collective support he is inevitably exposed to the arbitrary power of the employer.[1] In short, then, it is only through the power *over* its members which is vested in the trade union that it is able to exert power *for* them.

Yet if workers create collective organisations in which they invest an area of control over their own actions, how can they

[1] It is however possible for individuals to gain some of the benefits of collective organisation without bearing any of the costs; it is common, for example, for negotiated wage increases to be paid to all employees of a firm or industry, whether or not they are union members. (In the language of economists, many of the benefits of unionisation are 'public goods'.) From the perspective of narrow individualism, it is therefore rational for the worker *not* to submit to common rules and decisions; for his own abstention is too insignificant to have a measurable effect on the collective strength, so he still reaps the advantages. But if others followed this example, the strength of the organisation would soon be undermined, and *all* would suffer. To maintain collective solidarity it is therefore usually necessary to apply (or at least threaten) a measure of coercion against individuals who might follow a strategy of short-sighted selfishness.

ensure that this control is used in their own collective interests – rather than to serve the ends of those in charge of the union organisation, or even some external interest? Fear of the subversion of collective organisation cannot be dismissed as fanciful. It is a commonplace of social analysis that formal organisations develop an independence of identity which makes them something more than merely the sum of their members; and that the policies and purposes pursued in the name of an organisation cannot therefore be simplistically identified with the wishes of the membership. This insight – already touched on in Chapter 1 – is made pointedly by Ross :

> As an institution expands in strength and status, it outgrows its formal purpose. It experiences its own needs, develops its own ambitions, and faces its own problems. These become differentiated from the needs, ambitions, and problems of its rank and file. The trade union is no exception. It is the beginning of wisdom in the study of industrial relations to understand that the union, as an organization, is not identical with its members, as individuals . . . Experienced employer representatives are accustomed to emphasize the distinction between the union and its members (1948 : 23).

Hence the danger of equating 'the union' with the members individually – or even collectively.

It is equally dangerous, however, to suggest that institutions as such possess needs, ambitions and problems. This is to commit the offence of reification : by attributing human characteristics to impersonal abstractions, the agency of real individuals is obscured. Organisations do not perform actions or take decisions : rather, certain people decide and act in the name of organisations. The notion of 'institutional' needs or interests makes sense only if interpreted as a metaphor for the considerations and priorities motivating those with power within organisations. To get beneath the blank abstraction of such labels as 'the union' it is therefore necessary to ask a series of highly specific questions. What decisions are taken? What relationships between those in different positions inside a union – and also those *outside* it – lead to these decisions? What alternatives are considered in the decision-making process – and hence what lines of action are excluded from the realm of serious possibility? And through what processes and by what criteria is this prior framework of decision-taking created?

It is impossible, in the present context, even to attempt to provide detailed answers to these questions. Indeed, some are probably in principle unanswerable. (How, for example, can a solid empirical foundation be given to an explanation of why a particular decision was *not* taken and perhaps not even contemplated? Some sociological studies of decision-making processes simply exclude 'non-decisions' of this kind, and in the process trivialise what they describe.)[2] It is nevertheless possible to indicate some of the pressures and constraints which determine the content of trade union decision-making and non-decision-making.

The two-way power relationship which is central to the trade union function forms the ever-present context of the internal control processes within trade unionism. Trade unions are in the business of control: wrestling away from management an area of control over employment and over work itself, imposing priorities which reflect employee interests; and for that very reason they may disrupt the normal workings of a capitalist economic system. Those whose business it is to keep the system functioning – whether at the level of the individual firm or the overall economy – cannot be expected to observe such efforts passively. They will naturally seek to influence the way in which trade unionists interpret their objectives, and the strategies and tactics which they adopt in their pursuit. And here, the implications should be obvious of the comment by Ross that 'experienced employer representatives are accustomed to emphasize the distinction between the union and its members' : this suggests that those with social power which is potentially threatened by trade unionism may use this power in an attempt to turn the unions' organisational control *against* the interests of their members. This seeming paradox is well expressed by Anderson :

> It is a rule in a capitalist society that any institution or reform created *for* or *by* the working class can by *that very token* be converted into a weapon *against* it – and it is a further rule that the dominant class exerts a constant pressure towards this end . . . The working class is only concretely free when it can

[2] For a lucid discussion of the importance of such factors in any serious analysis of power relationships see Lukes 1974.

fight against the system which exploits and oppresses it. It is only in its collective institutions that it can do so : its unity is its strength, and hence its freedom. But precisely because this unity requires disciplined organization, it becomes the natural objective of capitalism to appropriate it for the stabilization of the system (1967 : 276).

It is indeed a commonplace of industrial relations that unions can readily be transformed, at least partially, into an agency of control *over* their members to the advantage of external interests (that is, the power *over* the membership which is the prerequisite of concerted action is divorced from its explicit purpose as a means of control *for* these same members). A commentator on the situation in the United States, for example, has noted that 'in the evolution of the labor contract, the union becomes part of the "control system of management" . . . The union often takes over the task of disciplining the men, when managements cannot' (Bell 1961 : 214–5). At the societal level, British trade unions have been described as 'an essential part of the mechanism of social control' (Fox and Flanders 1969 : 156).

The total incorporation of trade unions into the external structure of social and economic power – their subversion into agencies exclusively of power over employees – is an extreme situation, never attainable in practice however strenuous the efforts of employers or state officials. Yet the fact that evidence of the *partial* achievement of this objective is readily available is of immense importance : it underlines the fact that trade unions, as organisations of the relatively powerless in an environment of power, can achieve any meaningful internal democracy only against external resistance and considerable odds. For this very reason, the role of trade unionism as a medium of control over work relations is inherently ambiguous. 'Job-control rights, and demands for them, may serve the union as an organization, particularly a bureaucratic leadership, or they may be geared to benefit specific strata of workers, or the working class in general' (Herding 1972 : 16). Hence it is always necessary to raise the questions : *whose* power and interests are advanced by a particular measure of job control; who initiates the trade union's involvement in job control; and who is the prime beneficiary?

Such questions can be answered only on the basis of close

analysis of the control relations *within* trade unionism. And as the study of decision-making and control within individual unions indicates, the nature and degree of internal democracy vary considerably. For this very reason, there is a temptation for the student of industrial relations to approach the question of union democracy merely as an internal problém of trade unionism : to treat the specific patterns of a union's membership composition, the contents of its rulebook, and its organisational traditions, as a sufficient explanation of the nature of its internal power relations. Clearly such factors are of considerable importance. But to approach trade union government and administration as a self-contained area of analysis, to treat unions as 'formal organisations' wrenched from their social context, is to ignore the impact of the environing institutions of power with which trade unions constantly interact. Neglecting the significance of broader structural determinants, it is then only too easy to attribute failings in democracy to the personal characteristics of members or leaders : 'apathy' on the one hand, 'corruption' or 'careerism' on the other. To remain at this level of analysis, however, is to moralise rather than to explain.

So long as these considerations are borne in mind, the detail of internal decision-making in the various unions can illuminate many of the problems of union democracy. At first sight, the multiplicity of governmental forms parallels the complexity of British union structure. But patterns are readily discernible; and as in the case of union structure, a *historical* perspective makes these comprehensible.

The earliest organisations – small, localised and exclusive – arose naturally out of the occupational community of the craft. Unionism was rooted in a complex of spontaneous and informal social relationships; the creation of a formal union organisation merely institutionalised this pre-existing basis for collective action. The long period of apprenticeship served not only to train the incipient craftsman in a range of work skills, but also to inculcate a set of beliefs and values revolving round the worth, dignity, traditions and solidarity of the trade. To a lesser degree, occupational factors of this kind provided the foundation for non-craft but industry-specific unionism (in coal and cotton, for example). Here, as Turner puts it, the early unions were often 'simple formalizations of certain natural links between the workers . . . the habit of association between workers of a settled occupational group' (1962 : 86).

Because such unionism was created *from below*, decisions were as far as possible taken through the methods of what the Webbs termed 'primitive democracy'. Government was by all the members 'in general meeting assembled', and this meeting 'strove itself to transact all the business, and grudgingly delegated any of its functions either to officers or to committees'. The principle of regular rotation of officers was commonly enforced, so that no member developed an entrenched position of influence (1897 : 3, 8). This structure of control was increasingly undermined as unions grew in size, as local societies merged nationally, as job control came to involve collective bargaining as well as the autonomous enforcement of union standards in the workplace. Yet such developments as the centralisation of financial control and policy determination, and dependence on a group of professional administrators, occurred only slowly and against considerable resistance. They had, moreover, to be accommodated in many respects to the traditional forms of grass-roots democracy : the rules were as far as possible designed to ensure that the central executive and the local and national full-time officials were subject to rank-and-file control.

These traditional forms remain evident in several of the major craft or ex-craft unions. In the AEU (now the Engineering Section of the AUEW),[3] powerful District Committees continue many of the old traditions of local autonomy; both local and national full-time officials are elected by the members and subject to re-election; the national delegate conference is exceptional among major unions in its power and its *initiating* role in policy formulation.[4] Elements of this pattern occur in some industrial-type unions, with a relatively cohesive occupational composition of membership – or with a tradition of the domi-

---

[3] Each section of the AUEW, at the time of writing, functions largely autonomously on the basis of its own former rulebook.

[4] Traditionally, the ETU operated on a similar basis, but the powers of the central executive were radically increased in the 1960s. Craft-based unions in printing and shipbuilding share many of the traditional forms derived from the spirit of primitive democracy.

nation of participation and decision-making by a skilled or otherwise privileged occupational minority.[5] In both the mineworkers' and railwaymens' unions, for example, all full-time officials are elected but are not subject to re-election.[6]

The course of development of those unions which are horizontally as well as vertically open has been quite different. While spontaneous activity and militancy among rank-and-file workers was an essential part of the explosion of 'new unionism', the formalisation of this upsurge was carried through largely *from above*; and the machinery of government was shaped from above by the original leaders. In most cases, the centralisation and professionalisation of policy and administration met little serious resistance from below, for there were no powerful traditions of rank-and-file autonomy.[7] From the outset, the professional organiser had a key role in the general unions, carrying out functions of recruitment and representation which in the closed unions were largely performed by rank-and-file members. Moreover, the open character of these unions' recruitment gave rise to a range of seemingly divergent interests and loyalties within the membership, and to great variations in strength and militancy between different groups. Sectional strains and pressures thus constituted an ever-present threat to the integrity of the union (and indeed, breakaway movements were not uncommon); and the most obvious solution (at least as it appeared to the leaders themselves) was strong leadership control and only limited scope for rank-and-file autonomy.[8]

[5] Turner (1962) has categorised the closed unions as 'exclusive democracies', and those dominated by a skilled group as 'aristocracies'. For a critical examination of Turner's classification see Hughes 1968.

[6] In cotton, by contrast, the tradition is for officials to be appointed on the basis of a mathematical examination (since the negotiation of complex piecework price-lists is one of their main functions).

[7] There were some exceptions to this generalisation. The dockers, for example, possessed strong traditions of local independence (their local solidarity perhaps reinforced by concentration in a tight-knit geographical community); and they have always been resistant to strong centralised control in the TGWU. See Allen 1957; Lovell 1969.

[8] This comment must be interpreted in *relative* terms. The 'new unions' were far more dependent on full-time officials than were previous unions, and this was reflected in the high proportion of their income which was spent on administration. Even so, by comparison with a business organis-

The government of such unions has been given the colourful label 'popular bossdom' (Turner 1962 : 291): the power of the key leaders within the formal machinery of union decision-making is firmly entrenched, and this dominance they seek to legitimise by cultivating the personal identification and loyalty of the members. This tradition has persisted within the general unions. The ratio of full-time officials to members is high, and (with the exception of the General Secretary) they are appointed rather than elected.[9] Mechanisms of upwards control are limited in significance. National conferences are too large and too short to provide any systematic initiation of policy; in general their proceedings can be readily manipulated by the leadership platform. Elections are confined to the choice of the General Secretary and lay officers and committee members at the various levels of union government. In practice the lay Executive of the TGWU, in principle the sovereign body, is normally dominated by the General Secretary. Moreover, he can virtually appoint his own successor, since the tradition has become established that his deputy becomes the generally recognised heir-apparent. In the GMWU, the General Secretary shares the domination of policy with a virtual oligarchy of full-time Regional Secretaries (who hold half the seats on the National Executive).

Among white-collar unions there exist considerable variations in traditions of participation and control by rank-and-file members. But in the case of most of the larger bodies, organisation has been primarily from above, and this is usually reflected in the powerful position of the centralised leadership. A significant exception is AUEW–TASS (formerly DATA), which has many affinities with craft unionism both in its patterns of membership development and in its current relations of internal control. In certain white-collar organisations is found a problem of internal democracy which has no parallel in manual unionism. Unions with a wide vertical range of membership cover not only sub-

ation or government department the degree of bureaucracy and centralised control was extremely limited; much scope for rank-and-file initiative remained, though largely *outside* the formal union framework.

[9] In the GMWU, officers are required to submit to election two years *after* their appointment. This provides ample opportunity to make themselves familiar with their constituency; moreover, the leadership has the power to veto rival candidates as unsuitable. Not surprisingly, the defeat of an incumbent is unknown. See Clegg 1954: 75–6.

ordinate employees but also those in top managerial positions (obvious examples are senior local government officers in NALGO and head teachers in the NUT); and these groups have tended to dominate key positions in union government at both local and national level. Hence in conflicts involving questions of job control, the union's official position may reflect the managerial viewpoint as against the interests of the bulk of the membership.

It is obvious that the nature and extent of democratic practice vary considerably between unions, along lines which reflect both historical traditions and contemporary problems and practices.[10] The significance of these variations will be considered further below. The points already considered make it possible however to discuss some general issues surrounding the question of union democracy. The most obvious implication of the experience of the different British unions is that *all* forms of governmental arrangement reflect some recognition of the principle of democratic control. This formally democratic character of trade unionism derives from its basic rationale as a medium of *power for* workers to exert control over their jobs. The corollary of members' surrender of their individual autonomy to the collective organisation is that they should possess opportunities to determine – or at least to influence – the application of union strength. Hence trade unions are distinct from most other organisations (factories, hospitals, government departments) in that they explicitly incorporate *a two-way system of control.* Union officials are accorded specific powers of leadership and of discipline; in appropriate situations they are legitimately entitled to exert control over the members. But at the same time they are the employees and the servants of the members, who are thus in appropriate situations entitled to exert control over *them.* The precise

[10] This is made even clearer by international comparison. In the United States, for example, 'popular bossdom' is far more extensively the norm than in Britain. Most major unions derive their existence from organisation from above; and in general the ratio of officials to members is high. The basic unit of organisation – the 'local' – is normally run by a full-time official, often appointed and controlled by the national leadership, whereas British union branches are usually managed by elected lay officials. The extensive patronage at the disposal of the national leadership in America – as well as the collaborative relationship often enjoyed with employers – is a source of considerable power over the rank and file.

character of these 'appropriate situations' is often ambiguous and controversial, and hence the relationship between officials and rank and file involves many contradictions and conflicts. But no union can escape the profound influence of its democratic rationale, even if practice often diverges considerably from the democratic ideal.

One of the sources of this divergence is the focus of a pervasive theme in the literature on union government: the role of the leaders and other full-time officers as *guardians of organisational efficiency*. This role, it is commonly suggested, is liable to be inhibited and obstructed by democratic controls from below. The argument – powerfully developed by the Webbs in their classic *Industrial Democracy* – is that most rank-and-file members lack the skill, knowledge, experience and probably the interest to exercise constructive control over trade union affairs. Coherent and consistent policy, they insisted, was impossible within the framework of 'primitive democracy'. 'The custody and remittance of the funds . . . , the mysteries of bookkeeping, and the intricacies of audit all demanded a new body of officers specially selected for and exclusively engaged in this work' (1920: 203–4). Not merely is this argument applied to administrative technicalities: it is commonly extended to central policy issues. 'Trade union wage policy', insists a typical commentator, 'is inevitably a leadership function. The reason is not that the leadership has wrested dictatorial power from the rank and file, but that it alone is in possession of the necessary knowledge, experience, and skill to perform the function adequately' (Ross 1948: 39). At times the implications of this approach are carried even further. The machinery of democratic control, the various processes of rank-and-file involvement in decision-making, deter officials from initiatives which might provoke opposition; thus they constitute 'obstacles to effective leadership' (Clegg 1970: 112–8). Some draw the conclusion that 'the hazards of the electoral system' must be as far as possible eliminated 'in order to strengthen the powers of decision-making in unions' (Hooberman 1974: 29); or that 'the unions are going to have to attract careerists as well as idealists if they are to survive' (Shanks 1961: 100).

The 'efficiency-versus-democracy' perspective also underlies some analyses of variations in rank-and-file control of union decision-making. A relatively closed pattern of membership, it has been seen, tends to be associated with a relatively high degree of democracy. Two explanatory factors are commonly suggested. First, because of the natural cohesion of an occupationally homogenous membership it is possible for vigorous internal debate and opposition to occur without endangering the integrity of the union. Second, the level of skill, education and social status often associated with the membership of a closed union makes them unusually qualified to participate in union government.[11] Yet it is rash to conclude from this that it is only in organisations with a narrow and restrictive membership composition that democracy and organisational efficiency can be combined. The notion of 'exclusive democracy', as Hughes comments, 'stresses somewhat too pessimistically the nexus between union exclusiveness and a participating democracy in the government of the union' (1968 : 13). It is unnecessarily fatalistic to assume that a heterogeneous membership creates *irresoluble* tendencies to sectionalism and fragmentation, which can be contained only by the suppression of democracy; or that a lower-skilled membership is constitutionally incapable of effective participation and control in key union decision-making. The tendencies revealed by sociological analysis may be regarded as problems to be overcome rather than as insuperable obstacles to union democracy.[12]

A fatalistic assumption of the opposition between efficiency and democracy underlies most academic discussion of trade union government, and often inspires proposals for further limitations on the scope for rank-and-file control over the leadership. Yet such analysis and such proposals are commonly developed with a certain degree of embarrassment. For they seem to contradict the almost unquestioned ethic of trade unionism : the axiom that 'the members are the union', that officials are servants as well as

[11] This factor was stressed by Lipset *et al.* (1956), who argued that the exceptional characteristics of the membership made possible the high degree of democracy within the American printers' union.

[12] The AUEW manages to sustain a more extensive range of rank-and-file controls than in most unions, despite an extremely heterogeneous membership, yet shows no sign of disintegration. Dockers, miners and non-craft printing workers are occupational groups with strong traditions of union activism; yet this is not rooted in exclusive skills. Lessons could be learned from such examples if a serious attempt were to be made to combine rank-and-file control with union solidarity and effectiveness.

leaders, and that procedures *must* therefore function in a democratic manner.

The most common solution to this embarrassment is to *redefine*
– explicitly or implicitly – the very notion of democracy, in such
a way that connotations of serious rank-and-file control are eliminated. Such a strategy is made easier by the ambiguity and controversy surrounding the meaning of any concept which carries a
heavy evaluative load; for in the whole vocabulary of politics, the
concept of democracy is the most value-laden. Yet its traditional
meaning is clear : *popular power*, the active involvement in
decision-making of the ordinary members of a community or institution or organisation. By derivation, the existence of positive control by the rank and file is inherent in the language of democracy.

Yet a far more dilute interpretation has long been customary
among theorists anxious to consign legitimacy on power relationships from which popular control was clearly absent. The
revisionist approach (which in British political theory dates back
to John Locke and other seventeenth-century writers) replaces
active control by passive consent as the key criterion of democracy. The premise of this approach is commonly that most
people are either incompetent or unwilling to exercise active
control over the processes of government; and the machinery of
popular initiative (such as general meetings) tends therefore to be
dominated by vocal minorities or manipulated by demagogic
leaders. The alternative which is proposed (commonly termed
'liberal pluralism') involves reducing popular involvement to the
periodic participation in elections, in which a choice is possible
between rival candidates. In the long intervals between these
episodes of popular involvement, democracy is in cold storage :
'the voters outside of parliament must respect the division of
labor between themselves and the politicians they elect' (Schumpeter 1943 : 295).[13] The arguments against participative demo-

---

[13] The contradictions in the classical revisionist political theories, and
their persistence in current conceptions of democracy, are brilliantly
analysed by Macpherson (1962). Modern pluralist theories of democracy
are criticised by Pateman (1970). (It is interesting to note, in passing, that
contemporary notions of parliamentary democracy incorporate arguments
by such writers as Burke which, in their time, were intended to be
explicitly *anti*-democratic.) Lenin's *State and Revolution*, written at
the time of the Russian Revolution, remains one of the most vivid Marxist
discussions of democracy. But see also Draper 1974.

cracy in trade unions follow closely (though not always consciously) in this same tradition. Arguments which stress the incompetence of the rank and file to control have already been cited. Likewise, it is claimed that most members are apathetic about union government; unionism is only one, usually minor, interest among many. Thus attendance at union meetings is usually extremely low; and those who do participate in meetings and conferences, and hence determine the decisions taken in the name of the union, may be unrepresentative of the membership generally.[14]

From the perspective of liberal pluralism, then, the notion of union democracy is readily defined so as to exclude regular rank-and-file involvement in decision-making: increased power and prerogatives in the hands of the leadership need not be regarded as undemocratic. Yet revisionism cannot stop here. For the liberal pluralist conception of democracy requires, firstly, meaningful elections; and secondly, rights of organised opposition. Yet open and organised opposition, in any way analogous to the party confrontations in parliamentary politics, is virtually unknown among trade unions; often, indeed, it is explicitly forbidden.[15] Moreover, those processes which make union meetings unreliable indicators of membership opinion extend to union elections themselves. In both cases, participation by 10 per cent of the membership would be above average in most unions. In the AEU, branch voting attracted a turnout normally around 7 per cent in elections for major office; in most non-craft unions the figure is even lower. The ETU, using a postal ballot, drew a

[14] For a review of such arguments see Hyman 1971a: Ch. 7.

[15] In the GMWU, for example, 'one of the worst offences a branch or its officers can commit is to form an "unofficial" movement within the union and undermine government through the district. Consequently, branches are prohibited from intercommunication, except through the district secretary, and from divulging business or information to unauthorised bodies or to the press. Members . . . must not associate themselves with any attack on the union or its officials, nor act "singly or in conjunction with any other member or persons" in opposition to the declared policy of the union' (Clegg 1954: 47). In many unions a degree of opposition is permitted, or at least tolerated, and loose factions of left and right systematically contest elections in a few cases. But a fully-fledged party-system, discovered by Lipset *et al.* in their study of the American printers and put forward as the prerequisite of genuine union democracy, is unknown in Britain (and unique even in the USA).

15 per cent poll in an election for General Secretary; while the AEU, which has now adopted the same system, recently drew a 29 per cent vote. The NUM, which uses pit-head ballots, is exceptional, claiming participation of around 60 per cent in elections for officials (Hughes 1968).

Thus in most unions, the mechanics of elections diverge considerably from the liberal-democratic model; and this is reflected in their outcome. The Webbs, writing at the turn of the century, noted that 'with every increase in the society's membership, with every extension or elaboration of its financial system or trade policy, the position of the salaried official became . . . more and more secure'. The chief officers, in particular, enjoyed 'permanence of tenure exceeding even that of the English civil servant'. They added that 'the paramount necessity of efficient administration has cooperated with this permanence in producing a progressive differentiation of an official governing class, more and more marked off by character, training and duties from the bulk of the members' (1897 : 16). The trade unionist who becomes a full-time official enters a new world. His job revolves around an office and a briefcase : in most cases a total contrast to the old tools of his trade.[16] His circle of social relations, both within work and outside, often alters radically; his style and standard of living tend to reflect what he has become – a man with a career.[17] The attractions should not be exaggerated : the hours of work are often long, the pressures considerable, the pay (for junior officials at least) rarely much above the earnings of the higher-paid sections of the membership. What the job does bring, however, is a position of influence, a wide area of autonomy, a sense of meaning and importance, a status in the community, which few trade unionists can expect from their ordinary employment. Once accustomed to this new world, as Michels recognised half a century ago, manual workers in particular 'have lost aptitude for their former occupation. For them, the loss of

[16] The use of the masculine here scarcely needs qualification. While women make up a quarter of all British trade unionists, the number appointed or elected as officials is minute; a sample of almost 200 officials examined by the Government Social Survey (1968) disclosed only one woman. Even in unions with a majority of women members, they normally form only a small proportion of officials and executive members.

[17] For a graphic account of the situation of the full-time official see Lane 1974 : 235ff.

their positions would be a financial disaster, and in most cases it would be altogether impossible for them to return to their old way of life' (1915 : 208).

To a strong incentive to retain office is added a considerable ability to influence the electoral process. Established officials are better known among the membership thàn are lay rivals; indeed top leaders can deliberately cultivate their own image through control over internal union communications. A necessary part of the leadership position centres around the development of *political* skills and experience : how to make speeches, handle meetings, cultivate contacts, perform favours which attract due repayment; and these are of crucial importance in union elections, where a small number of officials and lay activists can exert a crucial influence on voting patterns. Perhaps most important of all, the sitting official can rely on trade unionists' sentiments of loyalty and fairness : 'to defeat the incumbent is to sack him from his job, perhaps to rob him of his pension' (Clegg 1970 : 82). This naturally goes against the grain of the trade union principle of security of employment.[18]

Hence defeat of sitting officials is comparatively rare. A study of the experience in unions where periodic election is the rule showed that, up to 1958, 12 per cent of officials who left office did so because of defeat in a ballot (Clegg *et al.* 1961 : 80). It is plausible to assume that such turnover is more common among newer and less firmly established officers. In elections for lay officials at branch, district and national level, turnover is often significantly greater than among full-time officials; nevertheless the same advantages accrue to incumbents, albeit in a weaker form. The considerable variation in the internal arrangements of different unions is evident in the specific case of the functioning of elections. Interest in the formal democratic processes of trade unionism tends to be enhanced by particular membership characteristics : skill, education, strong occupational identity, cohesion and homogeneity (though as insisted earlier : this does *not* entail that other categories of employee are disqualified from effective union democracy). Many unions – particularly those

---

[18] Though trade unionists have never been in favour of security of office for *politicians* – and much of the official's work is political (i.e. it involves processes of control and policy-making). This is another weakness in applying the liberal pluralist model to trade unions.

with craft origins – have powerful *traditions* of active internal democracy. In the AEU, for example, active competition in elections is normal, and close contests are common.[19] Among full-time officials, defeat of the incumbent seems more frequent than in any other British union. Yet even here, as was seen earlier, active participation in the electoral process involves only a small minority of the membership.

It is clear, then, that the decision-making processes in most trade unions fall far short even of the weak conception of democracy contained in the theory of liberal pluralism. But the conclusions drawn by different commentators conflict considerably. According to Michels' classic analysis, the entrenched position of union leaders and the lack of involvement of most members were interconnected, and stemmed from an 'iron law of oligarchy' which operated in all institutions of the labour movement. Goldstein's study of the TGWU in the 1950s echoes this interpretation. The low level of participation, he argues, renders the outcome of the electoral process unrepresentative of the general membership; and for this reason, full-time officials can often safely disregard the union's constitutional machinery. The result is 'oligarchy parading in democracy's trappings' (1952 : 269).

Yet the notion of a sinister concentration of power among the union leadership is far too crude a characterisation of the actual processes of control.[20] If the official channels of decision-making alone are considered, as Clegg comments, the impression might easily be drawn

> that power in most British unions is highly centralised in the hands of an oligarchy of leaders, or even of a single autocrat. In fact this inference is so wide of the mark, so inconsistent with the facts of trade union life, as to be laughable. The error lies in supposing that there is nothing else to restrain trade union leaders in the exercise of power but the votes of the members. In fact leaders are subject to many other checks (1970 : 92–3).

Among the factors mentioned by Clegg are the factions which operate in many unions, the elements of autonomy allocated to

[19] For discussions of some of the factors underlying the experience of the AEU/AUEW see Edelstein 1965 and Martin 1968.

[20] For a critical discussion of Michels' analysis see Hyman 1971b.

official committees at different levels of union government, the (often unofficial) power of shop-floor organisations, and the influence which can be wielded collectively by junior full-time officials. Lane's argument has very similar implications.

> The form that the union took and the way that it adapted to its political and economic environment was not merely an extension of the leader's personality. The leader was caught up in a whole set of social processes that preceded his arrival and over which he, as an individual, had little influence. He may have been a key figure in some of those processes but he was more their creature than their creator (1974 : 249).

This is a further reason why 'the union' cannot be simply identified with its leaders: it represents a set of more or less stable relationships, a network of positions of greater and lesser power and influence. The top leader(s), in favourable circumstances, may wield far greater power and influence than any other individual in the union, and may be able to adapt organisational relationships to add further to this power and influence. But there is always an important element of organisational inertia, an important degree of diffusion of organisational power, which sets limits to leadership autonomy.

But if their leaders are neither autocrats nor oligarchs, does this mean that unions are therefore democratic? The managing director of a company faces constraints, both internal and external, which are very similar in some respects to those affecting union officials. But it would be unsafe to conclude from this that companies are by nature democratic. A system of checks and balances, while ensuring that control is not too concentrated in the hands of key individuals, does not guarantee that it is widely distributed. Such a system, indeed, normally entails that it is easier to block change than to initiate it; and thus entrenched positions of power are well protected against change.[21] For this reason, descriptions of union government in terms of 'polyarchy' (Van de Vall 1970; Banks 1974) are also somewhat misleading.

---

[21] As an example: there has been much discussion of organisational reform in the GMWU in recent years, partly stimulated by the shock of the Pilkington strike of 1970. But the regional secretaries, who exert a powerful constraint on the union's national officials, can effectively veto any change which would threaten their own control.

Thus it seems odd to suggest that unions are democratic when the power of their leaders is subject to checks, if these do not include the votes of the members. Certainly this is to redefine the notion of democracy even more narrowly than in the liberal pluralist conception. Such a redefinition is explicitly proposed by Turner :

> One of the most significant indices of a union's inner democracy is clearly the extent to which its members not merely are *able* to take a hand in what it does on their behalf, but in fact do so. On the same analysis, however, a large proportion of trade unionists will not wish an active participation in their organization's management. So that a second test of union democracy would well be the degree to which such 'passive' members are also able to identify their leadership's policy and actions with their own interest (1962 : 303).

This argument has an obvious surface plausibility. The inadequacies in the functioning of the machinery of union decision-making do not entail that union policies and actions necessarily conflict with the wishes or interests of the majority of the membership. And indeed, repeated studies have shown that most members *do* express approval of what is done on their behalf. Yet the significance of such findings is put in question by the fact that even a union which is on almost any definition corrupt and undemocratic can win similar expressions of support.[22] Somewhat similarly, survey after survey shows that workers overwhelmingly declare themselves satisfied with their jobs – however unpleasant and stultifying these may in fact be. Blauner, commenting on such findings, remarks that 'there is a natural tendency for people to identify with, or at least to be somewhat positively oriented toward, those social arrangements in which they are implicated' (1960 : 341). Even dictatorships are sometimes benevolent (though less often than is sometimes supposed); but it would be absurd to define them as democracies if the citizens declare themselves satisfied with their conditions. Yet precisely this absurdity is implied, once the concept of democracy

[22] Bell (1961: 204–6) describes the gangster-controlled dockers' union in New York, which won majority endorsement in three separate government-organised elections in 1953–6.

is so diluted as to require merely the tacit consent of the governed.[23]

This issue can be related back to an earlier theme in this chapter : the widespread preoccupation with efficiency as the main touchstone of control relations in trade unions. The common argument is, in essence, that leaders who are relatively free to exercise their own judgment can conduct union business most efficiently and hence provide their members with the best service. These may then be expected to approve the *outcome* of union decision-making, even though they exercise little or no control over the actual *process*. Allen once put this viewpoint bluntly : 'trade-union organization is not based on theoretical concepts prior to it, that is on some concept of democracy, but on the end it serves. In other words, the end of trade-union activity is to protect and improve the general living standards of its members and not to provide workers with an exercise in self-government' (1954 : 15).[24] It is uncommon for advocates of the efficiency argument to go so far as to deny the relevance of democracy to trade unionism;[25] nevertheless the existence of rank-and-file *control* over policy is rarely treated as a serious issue, and the very concept of union democracy is often studiously avoided.[26]

A basic weakness of this approach is that the *meaning* of efficiency is rarely explicitly considered. The concept of efficiency is properly applicable only to the consideration of methods or techniques, of the relative costs and benefits of different means of achieving a given goal or objective. But it follows that nothing

[23] This bizarre approach to democracy can be traced back to Locke, who insisted that the consent of the governed could alone make government legitimate, but added that 'every man that hath any possession or enjoyment of any part of the dominions of any government doth hereby give his tacit consent'.

[24] Allen has since disavowed this viewpoint.

[25] Allen in fact based his argument against union democracy on the presupposition that membership should be voluntary; thus he strongly attacked the closed shop. But as many critics have argued, the closed shop is in fact widespread and can be justified in the same manner as any other trade union rule: some restriction on individual autonomy is the necessary condition of *collective* strength and control.

[26] The fact that the policy-making process in trade unions is commonly discussed under the heading 'union government and administration' makes it easy to adopt a simple empiricist approach, and to suppress the whole issue of the contradiction between power for and power over the membership.

sensible can be said about the efficiency of any procedure until the objective is specified, and it is known what are to count as costs and benefits. (What is the most efficient way of travelling to London? The question is meaningless until it is known whether the traveller wants speed, cheapness, comfort, exercise, or scenery.) What then are the objectives of trade unionism? If unions are agencies of *power* for the working class, elements in a strategy for exerting control over a hostile work environment, it follows that their purposes must be defined *in terms of the members' own aspirations*. Whether or not union democracy is an efficient method of achieving union objectives, it is subversive of the very rationale of unionism to divorce democracy from the formulation of these objectives.[27]

It is common for opponents of democracy to blur this distinction between means and ends. At the level of national politics, for instance, it is often suggested that decision-making should be handed to managers, technocrats and other 'experts' in the interests of increased efficiency. This is in fact to suggest that there is no need to debate fundamental questions of policy; that the objectives of government are already uncontroversially defined. What this really means is that the main drift of capitalist political economy is taken for granted: the priorities and power structure of the established order must form the unquestioned framework of decision-making.[28] And if this is the case, the business of government is indeed primarily technical.

[27] A similar point is made, a little obscurely, by Child *et al.* (1973: 77–8). They distinguish between 'administrative rationality' – the principles governing the implementation of policy – and 'representative rationality' – the principles of goal and policy formulation. They argue that 'administrative rationality speaks for a unified and coordinated system of control, in which the prime source of authority is located at the top of the organizational hierarchy. Representative rationality speaks for a division of power and control, for the opportunity of action taken by one party to be revised by that of another group. It implies a system in which the prime source of authority lies at the grass roots of the institutional hierarchy'.

[28] Such an assumption is encouraged by the fact that these priorities and this power structure are not in fact seriously questioned in the mainstream of British politics; the charade of party conflict conceals a broad consensus that the survival of capitalism is the *overriding* political goal. The ability of the political system to suppress the expression of serious anti-capitalist objectives is one indication that the notion of democracy

In similar fashion, those who treat union democracy as an issue of limited moment often regard the goals of trade unionism as unproblematic. The conception of industrial relations in the narrow terms of job regulation encourages the assumption that union objectives are relatively uncontroversial. Thus Flanders insists that collective bargaining must be recognised as the invariable central purpose. 'All the other activities which the trade unions have undertaken and all the other purposes they have acquired must be regarded as a by-product and auxiliary to this their major activity and purpose, since success in it has been the condition for their survival and the basis of their growth' (1968 : 75). Yet if the sole important function of unionism is to join with employers in negotiating and administering rules governing wages and working conditions,[29] then the business of union decision-making is indeed largely technical. If unions have to accept the capitalist arrangements of industry – the structure of ownership, of economic priorities and of managerial authority – then they can be expected to provide no more than a limited range of improvements in the worker's situation. The reasonable member, in turn, will view his union as no more than a fairly narrow service agency; so long as it delivers the goods he has no cause to worry about its internal government. It would be as pointless to tell his full-time official how he should go about his job as it would be to tell his greengrocer.[30]

Such a definition of trade union purposes is sometimes presented as a simple description of – or deduction from – what trade unions actually *do*.[31] But in fact it incorporates assumptions which are intensely political in character. What is involved is a restrictive specification of the *legitimate* functions of trade unions :

is highly misleading. In fact, popular power is systematically prevented. The character of contemporary 'democracy' is discussed further in Chapter 5.

[29] In fact, Flanders recognised a wider social and political purpose for trade unionism; but this could not be comfortably accommodated within the theoretical framework of 'job regulation'.

[30] The American economist Hoxie, who classified trade unions according to their objectives, noted a connection between the narrow aims of 'business' unionism and a lack of democracy in government (1923: 47).

[31] This was the fervent claim of Perlman (1928) in his famous discussion of trade union objectives.

functions which exclude any serious challenge to the existing social order and the structure of control in industry. This moralising standpoint is made explicit in the recent comments of an eminent labour lawyer :

> Management can legitimately expect that labour will be available at a price which permits a reasonable margin for investment, and labour can equally legitimately expect that the level of real wages will not only be maintained but steadily increased. Management can claim a legitimate interest in obtaining for each job the most qualified worker available; labour can claim a legitimate interest in obtaining a job for each worker who is unemployed. Management can and must always expect that the arrangements of society (through law or otherwise) ensure that labour is as mobile as possible in the geographical as well as in the occupational sense; labour must always insist that workers enjoy a reasonable measure of job security so as to be able to plan their own and their families' lives. Management expects to plan the production and distribution of goods or supply of services on a basis of calculated costs and calculated risks, and requires society to guarantee the feasibility of such planning by protecting it against interruption of these processes; labour well realises that without the power to stop work collectively it is impotent, and expects to be able to interrupt the economic process if this is necessary in order to exercise the necessary pressure. Management's interest in planning production and in being protected against its interruption is the exact equivalent to the worker's interest in planning his and his family's life and in being protected against an interruption in his mode of existence, either through a fall of his real income or through the loss of his job. All this is palpably obvious, except for a person blinded by class hatred either way (Kahn-Freund 1972 : 52–3).

What is taken for granted in this catalogue of 'legitimate expectations' is the existence of a society in which capital dominates over labour. Briefly translated, the argument is that the pursuit of profit by the owners of capital (though remarkably, profit is not explicitly mentioned) is 'the exact equivalent' of workers' dependence on wages. Employers have a natural right to exploit workers and disrupt their lives; workers have a highly qualified right not to be *excessively* exploited or disrupted. Hence the legitimate functions of trade unions extend no further than the protection of their members against the more extreme consequences of their subordination to capital; the *fact* of this subordination they are not entitled to challenge.

However self-evident such assumptions may appear to employers and establishment politicians, it is *not* inevitable that unions objectives should be so narrowly defined. Trade unionists have often proclaimed far more radical aims : the reconstruction of the social order; the abolition of the dominating role of profit; the establishment of workers' control of industry; the reorganisation of the economy to serve directly the needs of the producers and the general members of the society; the humanisation of work; the elimination of gross inequalities in standards of living and conditions of life; the transformation of cultural richness from the privilege of a minority to the property of all. Time and again, the case for these broader social goals has been argued within the trade union movement; and the cogency of the argument is reflected in the rulebooks of many unions (including the TGWU and AEU), which prescribe objects ranging far beyond the narrow confines of collective bargaining.

If the objectives which are in practice pursued by trade unions are confined to the negotiation of limited improvements within the framework of capitalist work relations, this represents a restrictive *policy* which is in turn the outcome of a specific set of power relationships both inside and outside the unions. The effect of powerful external pressures on the definition of trade union objectives is too rarely considered in the study of industrial relations. It is obvious that those with positions of power and privilege in industry and society have a strong interest in the goals espoused by trade unions. Their purely economic objectives, if ambitious, conflict with the capitalist's desire to minimise costs of production; involvement in a struggle for control challenges his managerial prerogatives; while any connection with socialist politics is a potential threat to his very existence. Governments, having as their major priority the stability and success of the prevailing economic system, have a similar interest in the goals of trade unionism. It is not surprising, then, that socialising influences (in Allen's terms) bear heavily on the selection of union policy.

D

The actual behaviour of unions results from the action of a
complex of secondary processes which modify and distort the
basic economic features of union activity and bring it to terms
with society at large. This is what is called socialization. It is
not possible for unions which arose in opposition to the dominant effects of capitalism to operate within the system as permanent bodies without taking on some of the characteristics of
the system itself (1966 : 24).

Some of these pressures are ideological. The terms of discussion
in the media and in everyday political debate – both of which
are profoundly affected by the power of capital – encourage trade
unionists to disavow as 'subversive', 'irresponsible' or 'economically disastrous' any but the most modest of objectives. To embrace more ambitious aims is to challenge everyday language and
assumptions, which presuppose that capitalist economic relations
are natural, permanent, and morally unassailable; and this
requires a highly developed consciousness and determination.[32]
Reinforcing such ideological pressures are more material forces.
The cruellest of the contradictions facing trade unionists is that
those in positions of economic and social dominance – resistance
to whom is the fundamental purpose of collective action – can
readily apply their power to threaten the very security and survival of union organisation. Historically, judges and legislators
have regularly combined to impose the most rigorous restrictions
on employee combination and union action. Employers have
used an armoury of weapons, including victimisation, lockouts,
and outright physical violence, to undermine or destroy unionism.
The possibility of repression can never be wholly ignored, therefore, when trade unionists formulate their objectives.

Faced with such massive external power, the pressures are
intense for unions to engage in a tacit – indeed sometimes explicit
– trade-off. When Flanders writes that collective bargaining 'has
been the condition for their survival and the basis of their growth'
he underlines (perhaps unintentionally) these pressures. For the
more ambitious and extensive a union's objectives, the more likely
are the politically and socially powerful to express their hostility
through acts of repression. Conversely, if it curbs those objec-

[32] The role of ideological pressures is discussed in more detail in Chapter
5.

tives which seriously threaten the *status quo* it may be able to win the acquiescence and even goodwill of employers and the state. Historically, unions which have become firmly established have been drawn inexorably towards policies which are relatively acceptable to these significant others. Thus it is rare indeed for trade union commitment to major social change to be an operational one, in the sense of influencing day-to-day industrial tactics or serious long-term strategies: the socialist attachments of British unions are in general confined to the rhetoric of rule-book preambles and conference speeches. Similar pressures normally affect industrial policies in such manner that interference with managerial control does not go 'too far', while economic demands are characterised by 'moderation'. Evidently, then, the central role of collective bargaining in union policy should be interpreted as an *accommodation to external power*.

Where unions are willing to confine their aims within these comparatively innocuous limits, far-sighted managements have little reason to resist, and some reason to welcome, the unionisation of their employees. By making explicit the many discontents which work in capitalist industry generates, unions help to make workers' behaviour more predictable and manageable. Resentment is not permitted to accumulate explosively, but is processed in a manner which facilitates at least temporary solution; and union involvement in any settlement increases the likelihood that the members will feel committed to the agreed terms. At the level of government, similar considerations apply. The legalisation of unions may in itself mute some of the radicalism associated with their former 'outlaw' status. Involvement in various consultative and administrative committees generates a degree of identification with government economic policy on the part of union leaders, and encourages them to tailor their own strategies accordingly. More generally, once trade unions acquire a recognised social status they tend 'to integrate their members into the larger body politic and give them a basis for loyalty to the system' (Lipset 1959 : 113).

The process involved in this domestication of union goals is often viewed as a reflection of 'institutional needs'. The tendencies just described may be attributed to unions' institutional interest in establishing stable bargaining relationships with those controlling significant reserves of social power, and in avoiding aims and actions which might arouse strong hostility and hence jeopardise organisational security. Such institutional concerns affect not only the basic orientation towards collective bargaining, but also the content of what is collectively agreed. Thus Ross has called attention to what he terms 'union-oriented provisions in agreements. These, he suggests, 'are intended to define the status of the union in the enterprise' and 'cover such crucial matters as union security and managerial prerogatives, and such minor matters as the use of bulletin boards. They often provide for the checkoff of union dues, the right to participate in all grievance negotiations . . . ' (1948 : 23). As another American author comments, 'the union shop, or other forms of compulsion, are highly important to the strength and stability of labor unions. It is the union as an organisation, not the worker directly, that needs the "job control" ' (Olson 1965 : 87). Conceding terms which consolidate a union's membership and reinforce its organisational security may involve little direct cost to the employer; but such concessions may be traded against more material improvements in workers' conditions, and more crucially they are usually dependent on the adoption of conciliatory and accommodative policies on the part of the union.

The notion of 'institutional needs' is a useful piece of shorthand; but it is highly misleading if it conceals the fact that what is at issue is not merely a set of pressures *internal* to trade unionism, but more importantly the impact of *external* agencies with which unions are engaged in continuing power relations. Both pressures are particularly salient for the full-time official, who is specifically concerned with the union's internal strength and integrity, and is also engaged in day-to-day relations with the representatives of capital. Hence commitment to stable and cordial bargaining relationships is particularly strong at the level of the full-time official.

This concern with externally-generated institutional needs is a potent influence on the relationship within trade unionism between power for and power over. This subtle point was grasped succinctly half a century ago by Gramsci, the profound Italian theorist and revolutionary. The essence of trade union achievement, he argued, is the winning of a form of 'industrial legality' which guarantees certain concessions by capitalists to their employees. Such concessions represent 'a great victory for the working class'; yet they do not end the domination over workers and their organisations by employer power. 'Industrial legality has improved the working class's material living conditions, but it is no more than a compromise – a compromise which has to be made and must be supported until the balance of forces favours the working class.' The development of cohesive and aggressive organisation at the point of production is a precondition of a significant shift in the balance of forces and a serious challenge to the power of capital. But the attitude of the official to such a development, Gramsci argued, is ambivalent or even hostile. 'The union bureaucrat conceives industrial legality as a permanent state of affairs. He too often defends it from the same viewpoint as the proprietor . . . He does not perceive the worker's act of rebellion against capitalist discipline as a rebellion; he perceives only the physical act, which may in itself and for itself be trivial' (1969 : 15–7).

The union official, in other words, experiences a natural commitment to the existing bargaining arrangements and the terms of existing collective agreements. This commitment, moreover, is attributable less to any personal characteristics of the official than to his *function* : the negotiation and renegotiation of order within constraints set by a capitalist economy and a capitalist state.[33] Yet if the union official sees orderly industrial relations as essential for stable bargaining relationships with employers and ultimately for union security, his viewpoint in many respects parallels that of management. The union leader, wrote Wright Mills in an often quoted passage, 'is a manager of discontent. He makes regular what might otherwise be disruptive, both within the industrial routine and within the union which he seeks to establish and maintain' (1948 : 9). Job control, as it primarily concerns the 'union-as-an-organisation' (and hence the official as the main guardian of 'organisational interests') is therefore concerned more with stabilising the detail of the relationship between labour and capital than with conducting a struggle *against* the domination of capital. Such control may thus involve the *suppression* of irregular and disruptive activities by the rank and file which challenge managerial control. In this way, *union*

[33] For further discussion of the need to discuss union officials' actions and attitudes in *structural* as well as personal terms see Lane 1974; Hyman 1974b.

control and *workers'* control may face in opposite directions, and
the element of power over the members inherent in union organisation be turned against them.

CONCLUSION

External constraints – the power of employers and the state –
impose forceful limits on the purposes adopted by trade unions.
They find themselves accorded legitimacy, recognised and even
encouraged, only when their aims and actions do not seriously
challenge the continuation of capitalism. Union officials, directly
concerned with organisational stability, are particularly susceptible to these pressures; but the membership at large is also subject to ideological influences which narrowly define the legitimate
goals of unionism. The possibility of the democratic determination, by trade unionists collectively, of objectives best serving their own interests in the struggle against capital is subverted
or suppressed.

The institutionalisation of trade union functions has historically accompanied a more general attenuation of internal democracy; and the two processes are indeed intimately related. For
the more limited the objectives pursued, the less central to the
worker's life interests is his union; and the less, therefore, his
incentive to become actively involved in the machinery of internal decision-making. The more exclusive the focus on collective
bargaining, then, the less likely it is that most members will seek
to control either the means or the ends of union action. At the
same time, the pressures on the official to maintain control *over*
the rank and file in order to support stable and orderly industrial
relations are further corrosive of internal democracy.

Thus the historical development of trade unionism has revealed
strong and mutually reinforcing obstacles to democratic control.
Yet it would be over-simple to conclude that an irresistible and
irreversible 'iron law of oligarchy' is involved in this process.
The variations between organisations in terms of both policy and
internal democracy demonstrate that counter-pressures can in
some circumstances prove significant. And most crucial among
these is the *practice* of workers themselves. The deprivations and
aspirations which drive workers to create collective organisations,
to seek to exert control over work relations, lead them naturally

to react forcibly when their unions appear to retreat from their original purposes. The 'rank-and-file revolt', experienced in almost every industrialised nation in recent years, is clear evidence of this. Its significance is explored further in the concluding chapters of this book.

# 4 Capital and Industrial Relations

It is no accident that *Capital* was the work to which Marx devoted the bulk of his mature life. After his early grounding in classical and German philosophy, the young Marx immersed himself in the study of economic history and political economy. This intellectual reorientation both reflected and reinforced a conviction that theories and philosophies cannot be seriously discussed or understood in the abstract, but must be treated as products of the social conditions in which they arise. 'The production of ideas, of conceptions, of consciousness, is at first directly interwoven with the material activity and the material intercourse of men, the language of real life' (Marx and Engels 1970 : 47). Social life in turn is shaped by the most basic of human activities : the organisation of work, the manner in which men act upon the material world and satisfy their material needs. 'By producing their means of subsistence, men are indirectly producing their actual material life . . . The "history of humanity" must always be treated in relation to the history of industry and exchange' (ibid. : 42, 50).

The core of this approach, which was to guide his work for the remaining four decades of his life, Marx set out succinctly in a letter written in his late twenties.

What is society, whatever its form may be? The product of men's reciprocal action. Are men free to choose this or that form of society? By no means. Assume a particular state of development in the productive faculties of man and you will get a corresponding form of commerce and consumption. Assume particular degrees of development of production, commerce and consumption and you will have a corresponding form of social constitution, a corresponding organisation of the family, of orders or of classes, in a word, a corresponding civil society. Assume a particular civil society and you will get a particular political system . . . It is superfluous to add that men are not free arbiters *of their productive forces* – which are the basis of all their history – for every productive force is an acquired force, the product of former activity. The productive forces are, therefore, the result of practical human energy; but this energy is itself circumscribed by the conditions in which men find themselves, by the productive forces already acquired, by the social form which exists before they do, which they do not create, which is the product of the preceding generation.[1]

This analytical approach – sometimes referred to as 'historical materialism' – was conceived as a *general* theory of social development; and Marx indicated how it could be applied to earlier types of society. But his main concern was with understanding his own society – a society which as he wrote was undergoing fundamental technical, economic and political transformations. This focus on current reality was essentially *practical* : the aim was to understand in order to *change*; to unravel the meaning of social processes which were manifestly out of human control, and thus to enable men and women to subordinate these processes to their own needs and aspirations. This goal of changing the world underlies all Marx's monumental work of research, analysis and

[1] To P. V. Annenkov, 28 December 1846. A later but similar summary of Marx's general approach is contained in the Preface to *A Contribution to the Critique of Political Economy* (1859). There is considerable debate as to the rigour of the determinism which Marx attributed to the productive system. In *The Poverty of Philosophy* (1847) Marx wrote that 'in acquiring new productive forces men change their mode of production; and in changing their mode of production, in changing their way of earning their living, they change all their social relations. The handmill gives you society with the feudal lord; the steam-mill, society with the industrial capitalist.' But Engels later wrote that 'according to the materialist conception of history, the *ultimately* determining element in history is the production and reproduction of real life. More than this neither Marx nor I have ever asserted' (to J. Bloch, 21–2 September 1890). To argue that technological factors mechanically determine all other aspects of social life would be to negate the Marxian emphasis on *practice*: a point which is developed later in this chapter.

theorising which seeks to lay bare the nature and inner workings of capital.

What then is capital? At first sight it might seem sufficient to say that capital (fixed capital, productive capital, forces of production) consists of such physical assets as machinery, buildings and railways which are used in the production of goods and services. In a sense this definition is accurate; and yet, Marx insisted, it is highly misleading. 'A cotton-spinning jenny is a machine for spinning cotton. It becomes *capital* only in certain relations. Torn from these relationships it is no more capital than gold in itself is *money* or sugar the price of sugar' (1958 : 89). Capital, in other words, is not merely a physical object; it is the hardware of production located within specific *social relations* of production; it is an *economic* category. 'Machinery', Marx commented cryptically, 'is no more an economic category than the ox which draws the plough'. A piece of machinery becomes capital only when it has the status of a commodity, owned and controlled by one or a small number of individuals, who can thus oblige others to work for them; when it is an integral part of a social relationship in which some men and women were subordinated in their work to the dominance of others. Just as a man is a slave only within the social context of slavery, so productive assets are capital only within the social context of capitalism.

A brief account of the meaning of capitalism has already been given in an earlier chapter. Key features are the ownership and/or control of the means of production by a small minority, the domination of profit as the fundamental determinant of economic activity, and the obligation on most of society to sell their productive abilities on the market as a commodity. A number of consequences follow naturally. The worker surrenders control over his labour (both are, literally, 'alienated' : a vital concept in Marxian analysis which is today often used extremely loosely). The relationship between the employee and his employment is thus inherently unstable and conflictual. Moreover, wages and salaries represent only a portion of the value of what workers collectively produce; the remainder is appropriated as a natural element in the unequal economic relationship with the employer (they are thus, literally, 'exploited'; and this gives industrial conflict a *class* character). Capitalism, in short, represents a complex of work relations and of social relations of production, of which 'industrial relations' forms one aspect. From a Marxist perspective, obviously, no serious analysis of industrial relations is possible without a central emphasis on the determining role of capital.

In the orthodox study of industrial relations, however, it is customary to neglect the significance of this capitalist context. Certainly any systematic analysis of its implications is virtually unknown.[2] In this chapter, a brief outline is given of some of the main aspects of the impact on industrial relations of capital and capitalism. Attention is focused on the basic character of capitalism – those features of contemporary economic relations which *define* them as capitalist; and also on aspects of their structure and dynamics, some of which may be regarded as empirically and historically contingent rather than as uniquely and necessarily associated with capitalism.

The basic character of capitalism exerts a pervasive influence on the nature of industrial relations, most crucially through the way in which it shapes the structure, actions and objectives of trade unionism. Under normal conditions, trade union action has two fundamental features which are mutually reinforcing : it tends to react rather than to initiate, and it is oriented less towards workers' general predicament than to their particular and sectional grievances.

Trade unionism is primarily reactive because of the right accorded to management in capitalism to direct production and to command the labour force. Unions can win some improvements in workers' conditions, protest successfully at individual decisions, and impose certain general limits on managerial prerogative. But as long as they maintain a primary commitment to collective bargaining, they cannot openly attack the predominant right of the employer to exercise control and initiate change. 'Management would never agree to that' : what unions demand in collective bargaining is necessarily constrained by what is con-

[2] The most obvious exception is Moore's *Industrial Relations and the Social Order*, published as long ago as 1946. But Moore defines capitalism solely in terms of "free labour" and a "free market", and takes little account of contradictory social forces and interests. This severely limits the value of his analysis.

sidered realistic, and what is realistic is defined in terms of what the employer can be persuaded to concede in a negotiated settlement. This clearly does not extend to any radical alteration in the balance of power in industry. 'Hence the power and durability of the notion of "two sides of industry" as the immutable framework of trade union action . . . As institutions, trade unions do not *challenge* the existence of society based on a division of classes, they merely *express* it' (Anderson 1967 : 264).

Because trade unions are predominantly reactive, they normally respond to discrete manifestations of the opposition between labour and capital. An explicit concern with the *general* questions of the structure of control, the distribution of income and other material advantages, and the priorities of industrial policy is foreign to the everyday preoccupations of industrial relations. The function of collective bargaining is to relieve or suppress symptoms rather than to cure the underlying malady. As Marx put it :

> Trades Unions work well as centres of resistance against the encroachments of capital. They fail partially from an injudicious use of their power. They fail generally from limiting themselves to a guerilla war against the effects of the existing system, instead of simultaneously trying to change it, instead of using their organised forces as a lever for the final emancipation of the working class, that is to say, the abolition of the wages system (1958 : 447).

Consciousness of capitalism *as a system* is thus remote from normal trade union perspectives; and the influence of the broader framework, *because not consciously appreciated*, is all the more powerful.

These twin features of spontaneous trade union action (to use a term made familiar by Lenin) have several important consequences. One is implicit in the previous analysis : what Lenin termed 'economism', a narrow focus on wages and conditions rather than on more fundamental characteristics of the social relations of production. Restricting their activities in this way, Lenin argued, trade unions posed no serious threat to the stability of

the society within which they operated; the challenge to capitalism implicit in their very existence was effectively absorbed.[3] The
very concept of collective bargaining, it might be argued, entails
that the relationship between unions and employers is presented
as a merely economic one: they appear as partners in a market
transaction, rather than as antagonists in a struggle for control.[4]
Hence the opposition of class interests is concealed.

Reacting to specific grievances within the unchallenged framework of the employer–employee relationship, trade unions are
quite naturally beset by the problems of sectionalism discussed in
a previous chapter. For the opposition between labour and
capital, in its multiple individual manifestations, is experienced
in contrasting ways by different groups of employees: here as
low wages, there as unsafe working conditions, or an increase in
track speeds, or a challenge to traditional areas of job autonomy,
or a threat to a cherished symbol of status. If these fragmented
issues are seen as the be-all and end-all of trade union action,
then sectional organisation (which permits 'specialised' attention
to the contrasting immediate problems of each occupational and
industrial group) is eminently sensible. It is only when the varied
problems and struggles of different groups are related to a
*common* source, in capitalist work relations themselves, that the
need for unity and solidarity becomes blindingly obvious.

The spontaneous development of trade union structure, it
would appear, follows naturally the lines of the capitalist division
of labour. This same principle, moreover, influences their internal
organisation. Division of labour within capitalism entails, not
merely that different workers specialise in performing distinct
tasks, but that their right to exercise control over the organisation of production *either individually or collectively* is denied.[5]

[3] See the discussion in *What Is To Be Done?* in Lenin 1961; for a critical
examination of this argument see Hyman 1971b.
[4] On slightly similar grounds, Flanders (1970: 213ff.) criticises the
Webbs, who devised the term 'collective bargaining'. But his own focus
on 'job regulation' conceals the extent to which the power relations mediated by the labour market are a form of domination and hence radically
oppositional.
[5] Whereas pre-capitalist specialist producers had considerable autonomy
over the work process; while *collective* control by workers would be per-
fectly compatible with modern technology.

As Marx insisted, 'what is lost by the detail labourers, is concentrated in the capital that employs them . . . Division of labour within the workshop implies the undisputed authority of the capitalist over men, that are but parts of a mechanism that belongs to him' (1959 : 361, 356). To the extent that employees become habituated to the subordinate role required by capitalist work relations, however, there is a natural tendency to acquiesce in a similar role in their trade union. The type of relationship between members and leader castigated by the South Wales miners in 1912 – in which 'the sum of *their* initiative, *their* responsibility, *their* self-respect becomes his' – can thus be explicitly resisted only on the basis of a conception of democratic control which runs counter to the experience of 'normal' work relations.

Arguably, the pervasive influence of capitalist principles and assumptions also underlies the economism of trade unionism. The commodity status of labour is reflected in the prevailing attitude to work as simply a means of 'earning a living' : the implication being that men and women do not genuinely *live* while they are at work, that work serves no purpose apart from the ulterior ends of the employer, and as far as the employee is concerned is merely a pain and a burden necessary in order to live *outside* working hours. The 'instrumental' or 'privatised' worker, who neither finds nor expects intrinsic satisfaction in his job, has his attitudes represented and reinforced by 'business' unionism which seeks nothing beyond a higher price for labour power. There is an inherent contradiction in such an approach : for the social structure which creates employment drained of meaning and control, and the deprivations which this inflicts on the employee, impose severe limits on the chances of meaningful and creative life *outside* work.[6] 'Capitalism civilises consumption and leisure to avoid having to civilize social relationships, productive and work relationships. Alienating men in their work, it is better equipped to alienate them as consumers; and conversely, it alienates them as consumers the better to alienate them in work' (Gorz 1965 : 349). This contradiction generates conflict over conditions and control even among 'instrumental' workers and 'business' unions : neither exists in a pure form, despite the

[6] For an interesting empirical demonstration of this point see Meissner 1971.

somewhat simplistic arguments of some theorists. Nevertheless, powerful cultural pressures (advertising, the media and other socialising agencies) all add weight to the economistic pressures within trade unionism.

A further important consequence of the capitalist environment of union action is to be seen in the characteristic forms of pressure and struggle against the employer. The normal arsenal of sanctions employed by unions is essentially *negative* : a *reduction* of effort in a work-to-rule or go-slow; a *refusal* to work overtime; a *withdrawal* of labour in a strike. A *positive* challenge to the employer, involving the assertion of different relationships of control, is very much out of the ordinary (though recent developments in the use of sit-ins and occupations contain elements of such a positive challenge). The nature of ordinary strike action, moreover, in attacking merely the individual employer or group of employers, maintains the sectionalism and fragmentation of normal union organisation. (Hence workers whose jobs are affected by a dispute in an interdependent firm or industry, or who suffer as consumers from a stoppage in a public service, may react antagonistically to the strikers rather than to their employers.) Even in the extreme case of common action by all trade unionists in a general strike, the challenge to the capitalist class remains only partial : they attack their economic, but not their cultural and political, domination. (This explains why the leaders of the British general strike of 1926 were defeated from the outset, and knew themselves to be so.)

The *structure* of contemporary capitalism has important implications for industrial relations, involving as it does the existence of numerous sectors displaying highly uneven patterns of development. Capital-intensive industries coexist with labour-intensive; small employers with giant corporations; traditional and personalised employer-worker relations with bureaucratic and impersonal employment systems; while international comparisons provide similar contrasts. In 1851, when British capitalists proudly claimed to preside over the 'workshop of the world', only 27 per cent of the occupied population was employed in factory trades. 'Even in the cotton manufacture, with over three-fifths of its working force of over half a million (of a total of almost sixteen millions), in mills, almost two-thirds of the units making returns employed less than fifty men' (Landes 1969 :

120). Well into the present century, the largest single occupational group was that of domestic servants.

Capitalist development has thus involved the superimposition of new patterns of productive relations upon old. At the same time, the general trends have been unmistakeable: towards larger-scale employment; an increasing ratio of capital to labour; the dilution or displacement of traditional crafts, with the growth first of the category of semi-skilled machine operatives, then more recently of white-collar occupations. Both the structure and the patterns of expansion of trade unionism reflect these trends. As Allen comments,

> Developments in the trade union movement were always, inevitably, responses to changes in the environment of unions. When markets for commodities, including labour, were small and localized, so were trade unions. As industrial units grew and became more complex in their organization, so the tasks of unions became more complicated and onerous and demanded organizational adjustments. The changes in the democratic structure of unions, involving the rejection of a rotating head office, the locally based executive committee, the rotation of officials and the decentralization of funds, were all responses to alterations in market structures which enabled firms to expand (1971 : 122).

If the basic character of capitalism encourages trade union sectionalism, its structure shapes the directions of this sectionalism. Trade unionism, wrote Gramsci, 'organises workers, not as producers but as wage-earners, that is as creations of the capitalist system of private property, as sellers of their labour power. Unionism unites workers according to the tools of their trade or the nature of their product, that is according to the contours imposed on them by the capitalist system' (quoted in Hyman 1971b: 12). The strength of the craft tradition in British unionism clearly reflects the uneven development of the formative stages of capitalism. The growth of capitalist employment relations in many traditional trades provided a sufficient incentive to unionise, but in most cases the changes were not sufficiently drastic to undermine the material basis for stable sectional organisation. Later changes in the structure of British capitalism stimulated new organisational forms which, as Chapter

3 indicated, helped create the unique complexity of trade union structure. Differing degrees of employment concentration, differing intensities of exploitation of labour, differing levels of profitability, all help explain the variations in strength of unionisation and the lines of organisational demarcation.

An integral feature of capitalist economic relations is their *dynamic* character. 'The bourgeoisie cannot exist without constantly revolutionising the instruments of production, and thereby the relations of production, and with them the whole relations of society' (Marx and Engels 1958 : 37). This dynamism stems from the profit-oriented character of capitalism. The competitive pursuit of profit spurs each employer to seek new and cheaper methods of production; and, most crucially, to increase the productivity of labour. This generates a two-fold pressure : to organise and exploit labour as intensively as possible; and to introduce constant innovation in the means of production. As one employer increases his productivity in this way, so others must follow suit in order to survive – must carry out the necessary investment, and must extract the necessary level of profit in order to finance this.

Two key sets of consequences emerge. The first involves endemic instability in employment relationships. At a *general* level, the accumulation of constantly increasing amounts of capital of accelerating technical sophistication represents an expansion in productive capacity with which existing social institutions of distribution are ill suited to cope. Historically, this was reflected in regular cycles of economic expansion and severe recession. These necessarily affected the relative power of capital and labour. A 'reserve army of unemployed', as Marx called it, led to declining wages and often caused the collapse of union organisation; whereas relatively full employment brought union growth and movements for improvements in wages and conditions. Unemployment also brought a fall in the number of strikes, though those which did occur were often unusually bitter. (Recent experience, though, has upset many of the traditional patterns : within limits at least, rising unemployment has not destroyed worker solidarity and may have *increased* militancy.)

In recent decades, the extremes of the trade cycle have been cushioned by government efforts at economic stabilisation; while arms production has absorbed such immense resources that traditional 'crises of overproduction' have been avoided. But governments have only been able to apply crude regulation; hence the recurrence of recessions which though comparatively minor are increasing in intensity (on a world scale, technical change appears inexorably to be generating higher levels of unemployment in each recession). Recently even periods of expansion have brought only sluggish growth; while the whole cycle is beset by escalating problems of price inflation. The other traditional resort to relieve 'overproduction' has been the expansion of markets: a process which has historically often served as the motor of international conflict. In recent years, the growing integration of the world market has exposed the international unevenness of capitalist development; any economy which falls behind in the sophistication of its technology and its industrial structure (as is patently true of Britain today) is highly vulnerable.

The *specific* features of employment instability are manifest in the displacement of established industries and occupations. The obsolescence of traditional skills (which eventually undermined the viability of exclusive craft unionism) is a case in point. Another is the drastic decline of such staple industries of early British capitalism as cotton, coal, and the railways (trade unionists from these three industries affiliated to the TUC fell from 1,424,000 in 1949 to 634,000 in 1973). Redundancy has become an everyday feature of contemporary British capitalism; so have speed-up and other forms of work intensification for workers who do retain their jobs. Thus despite the pressures towards trade union economism, conflict is inevitably generated over questions of conditions and control. Indeed, as the most basic element of job control – whether a particular job is to exist at all – assumes central importance, so the viability of purely fragmented struggle is eroded; it is impossible successfully to combat the employer at the point of production, if his intention is in fact to *cease* production altogether. A campaign for the 'right to work' can only be effectively developed as a *general* demand, with explicitly political and not merely economic implications.[7]

[7] Over a century ago Marx wrote that 'the right to work is, in the bourgeois sense, an absurdity, a miserable, pious wish. But behind the

The second key consequence of capitalist development is the concentration and centralisation of capital. In technologically advanced industries, the cost and complexity of capital, and the resources required for research and development, are beyond the reach of any but the largest companies. The biggest firms grow fastest (financing much of their growth out of profits), and in the process take over their smaller competitors. 'In Britain, 180 firms employing one third of the labour force in manufacturing accounted for one half of net capital expenditure in 1963; seventy-four of these, with 10,000 or more workers each, for two fifths. Two hundred firms produce half manufacturing exports; a dozen as much as a fifth' (Kidron 1970 : 26–7). In recent years, mergers have involved the creation of 'conglomerate' companies straddling a range of industries. Even more significant is the growth of the multinational company. The majority of these are American : a reflection of the outward thrust of capital from the world's major economic power since the Second World War. Roughly a quarter of all investment by United States companies takes place outside the USA, in particular in Canada and Western Europe. About a third of total production in the Western world, *excluding* the USA, is today accounted for by American-owned or associated companies. The global role of such firms is particularly crucial in industries dependent on complex and expensive technology, such as chemicals and oil-refining, electronics and computers, and motor vehicles. The British economy is deeply penetrated by such enterprises; British-owned multinationals play a more modest global role. British industry is also extensively involved in relationships of European inter-dependence, reinforced by membership of the Common Market.

In the short term, the process of mergers and take-overs involves 'rationalisations' which are often merely euphemisms for closures and redundancies. The long-term consequence is the creation of concentrations of capitalist power out of all proportion to previous trade union experience. Giant multinationals

right to work stands the power over capital, the appropriation of the means of production, their subjection to the associated working class and, therefore, the abolition of wage labour, of capital and of their mutual relations' (1958: 171). The right to work is a contradiction of the dynamics of capitalist development; the demand is futile except as a challenge to the totality of capitalist political economy.

such as General Motors, Esso and Ford control resources which exceed those of many nation-states. Decisions on the location of production, new investment, plant closures, as well as the more routine elements of industrial relations, may be wholly external to the territorial boundaries within which the relevant unions operate. (The threat of Henry Ford, during the company-wide strike of British workers in 1971, to divert investment to other countries is a clear example of the use to which such control may be put.) Multinationals can readily manipulate their internal accounting (largely for purposes of tax avoidance) so as to disguise the profit position of any national operation; the formulation of union strategy can then be seriously inhibited. Such factors exacerbate the already serious underlying problem : the massive and increasing size and resources of the major adversaries of the unions.

Some trade unionists are clearly conscious of the enormity of these new problems. For over a decade, resolutions concerning multinationals have been passed at the TUC, and in 1970 a special conference was convened to discuss the issue. Links between individual unions and the various international trade union federations have recently been strengthened. Recent amalgamations may be seen in part as a response to the growing concentration of capital, both nationally and internationally. Nevertheless, the problems of sectionalism and fragmentation which have already been discussed in the national context remain even more severe at international level.[8] The difficulties of adapting existing union structure and policies to the unprecedented power of contemporary capital are immense; and adaptation can only be expected to remain slow – at least until the urgency of the problem is forcibly and dramatically demonstrated by the employers themselves.

This points to a factor which requires emphasis after the preceding discussion in this chapter. 'Capital' is an economic category, a term denoting forces and relationships which exert a

---

[8] International trade union action is handicapped by problems of language, the costs of translation, travel and research (all of which are far more easily borne by employers), quite apart from sectional jealousies. Understandably, sentiments of class solidarity are even weaker at international than at national level.

profound influence on the nature of social life in general and work relations in particular. But the impact of capital is expressed through the decisions which are taken – and through those which are not – [9] by real people : most crucially, those who own and control the means of production, entrepreneurs and top managers. It is therefore necessary to consider their *policies* as a major influence on industrial relations.

Trade unions are organisations which consolidate and mobilise the collective power of workers; and they apply this power largely to influence the programmes and decisions of employers. A *power relationship* is thus central to industrial relations : each party pursues strategies which are in part affected by the initiatives and responses of others. The power of capital, represented and mediated by management, cannot fail to influence the character of industrial relations. For this reason, the actions of trade unions cannot be adequately comprehended without reference to the policies of employers. On these grounds, Flanders has criticised the pioneer interpreters of British labour : 'there is', he writes, 'hardly any consideration in the whole of the Webbs' writing of an employer's interest in collective bargaining . . . Today, with advantage of hindsight, it is easy to appreciate the inadequacy of any theory of either the nature or the growth of collective bargaining which sees it only as a method of trade unionism and overlooks in its development the role of employers and their associations' (1970 : 214–5).

Historically, in many industries (more specifically, those domi-

---

[9] At first sight, the notion that a decision which is not taken – a non-decision – can be of any social significance might appear bizarre. But the actions and decisions of different individuals and groups taken in isolation can have *cumulative* consequences which are unintended and perhaps not even recognised. Anderson gives a clear example: 'How many businessmen resolutely decide that they must leave schools and hospitals to rot, and press on with doubling their TV commercials and lacquering their reception rooms with the money saved? Do any at all? On the contrary, how many mightn't even feel a stealthy susurrus of dismay if they learnt that this was the end outcome of their harmless, familiar routines? . . . These decisions are not taken in the board room or the bank manager's suite or even the exclusive club or the pleasure yacht. They are taken *nowhere*. They are *not taken*, they are not decisions . . .' (quoted in Blackburn 1965: 118). Within capitalism, such non-decisions exert a profound social influence: this is what Marxists mean when they refer to the *anarchy* of capitalism.

nated by craft unionism) collective bargaining was initiated not by unions but by employers. The explicit intention was to exert some limitation on the rules and practices imposed unilaterally by trade unionists; and for this reason the process was often bitterly resisted by workers themselves.[10] In engineering, the bargaining procedure which was to operate until the 1970s was accepted by the unions only after a six-month lockout in 1897–8. The resentment of some trade unionists is keenly expressed in the following complaint, written in 1910 :

> It surprises me when I hear 'collective bargaining' spoken of . . . as the 'first principle' of trade unionism. You may search the 'objects' of the older unions for this precious 'first principle', but you will not find it. The object of trade unionism used to be to uphold the price of labour *against* the encroachments of the employers, not in agreement with them. 'Collective bargaining' is an afterthought, forced on Capital and Labour alike because of this straining after industrial peace . . . We are under the guns of the enemy. We 'make peace' with him because he has us by the throat (Coates and Topham 1970 : 24–6).

This is a vivid expression of one aspect of the argument developed in the previous chapter : the power of employers can be so deployed as to modify and contain the oppositional thrust of trade unionism. Union leaders, as was seen, are particularly susceptible to such pressures; historically, it was common for the national leaders to become quickly committed to the new bargaining machinery – even when, as in engineering, they had so strongly fought against its introduction. In part this reflected a desire to secure the union's position through ensuring stable and accommodative bargaining relationships; in part an appreciation that such relationships consolidated their *own* role as mediators between employers and the membership, and hence reinforced their own authority within the union.

For this very reason, lay activists have often shown themselves hostile to the institutionalisation of industrial conflict. Neverthe-

---

[10] For details see Clegg *et al.* 1964. Non-craft unions, lacking a similar capacity for autonomous control, by contrast often took the initiative in introducing collective bargaining in their industries – commonly against strong employer resistance.

less, employers can apply pressures at shop-floor level which closely parallel those which are familiar at the level of the official leadership. A top manager comments as follows :

> It's difficult to say what type of steward does best for his members. A militant may well force a few concessions, but we'll always be waiting to get them back or to make life difficult for him. While a quiet, more reasonable bloke may be less dramatic he'll probably get more for his members because if he's in any trouble we'll help him out. We make concessions to him that we wouldn't make to the other bloke (Beynon 1973 : 158).

The policy of rewarding 'reasonable' stewards (and their members) and punishing 'militants' is pursued, with greater or lesser sophistication, by many managements; and it clearly subjects those affected to intense pressure to conform to accommodative relationships. This is increasingly true the more the steward's preoccupations centre around the routine problems and day-to-day issues of industrial relations; for it is in this context that the *personal* relationship between management and union representatives can exert a major influence on the outcome of negotiations. But when strategic interests of workers and employers are at stake, the *mobilisation of power* becomes of critical importance; and union representatives who are accustomed to rely on a 'reasonable' relationship with management may find themselves disarmed.[11] The fact that trade union concern is so commonly concentrated on the detail of negotiation rather than the underlying realities of power means however that employers' attempts to institutionalise shop-floor action normally achieve considerable success.[12]

[11] Fox (1965) describes the case of a highly collaborative convenor who found himself powerless when management decided to close his plant. By contrast, recent examples of successful resistance to closures have normally involved plants with a tradition of shop-steward militancy and rank-and-file mobilisation.

[12] The success of such strategies normally depends on playing off one representative against another: 'moderation' and 'militancy' are essentially relative, and an employer normally 'helps' one steward only to discourage others or for fear that another more militant may take his place. A strong collective organisation of stewards themselves is the most effective means of inhibiting such tactics.

Policies designed to curb the oppositional basis of trade unionism and encourage a collaborative orientation shape the *general* character of industrial relations. In addition, employer initiative structures many of the details of industrial relations, and differences in management policy explain many of the variations in practices and conditions in different contexts.

Employer policy has normally proved a key factor in the development of the structure of collective bargaining: which means, in brief, who negotiates about what and at which level. For negotiations to take place, an employer must *recognise* a union as the representative of his employees. In the formative stages of union organisation, such recognition has commonly been vehemently withheld; workers have had to fight for the right to collective representation. Yet sophisticated managements have come to recognise that by conceding recognition *before* organisation is firmly established they can influence from the outset the nature of the unionism with which they have to deal. For example, by recognising a single body as appropriate for the whole labour force an employer may avoid the possibility of problems associated with multi-unionism;[13] more crucially, a union with a 'moderate' reputation may be recognised to the exclusion of another regarded as militant. Such strategies have been of some significance with the recent rapid expansion in white-collar unionisation; and also where new establishments have been set up in development areas.[14]

[13] By contrast, the Ford company, which fiercely resisted union recognition at its Dagenham plant, was faced with numerous sectional organisations possessing membership when it was finally forced to concede. (Ironically, the unions themselves were commonly blamed for this situation in subsequent years.)

[14] Some unions may consciously exploit a reputation for moderation. Thus in one region of the GMWU, new employers were invited to give exclusive recognition; they were assured that 'the aim of this Union is to create a cordial atmosphere and thus prevent any serious unrest in the many industrial concerns in which we have members. Our Full Time officers and shop stewards are thoroughly schooled in all the modern techniques of production and we instil into them a policy which has as its permanent aim the peaceful co-existence of Management and workpeople in the factory'. For an example of such an agreement when Ford opened its Halewood plant see Beynon 1973: 66. This practice is particularly common in the United States.

The policy of selective recognition may be used to determine the *scope* of collective bargaining. An employer will naturally favour a union – indeed this may well be a central part of his definition of 'moderation' – which has no inclination to challenge seriously the right of management to control production. Even without such selectivity, the terms on which a firm recognises a union may include restrictions on its right to pursue certain sensitive issues in negotiation. And even where no explicit restrictions exist, union representatives will normally feel inhibited from raising demands against which management reacts so strongly that the bargaining relationship is jeopardised.

The *level* of negotiation is also strongly influenced by employer policy. Phelps Brown describes how cotton manufacturers came to see that uniform arrangements covering a whole district would serve their own interests, and encouraged this development.

The unionists were at least strong enough to bring a number of mills out together, and would go back only when a common settlement had been made for them all. If the employers had begun by feeling that the wider the combination was, the greater the threat to them, they soon found it was really the other way round : except where they were pinned down by foreign competition they might have little to fear from a wage settlement if only it was enforced on all of them alike, and a strong union was their guarantee that it would be. Not a few reached the conclusion that it was a positive advantage to them to have a floor put under price competition in this way. Those who had little love for the union were still willing to meet it to negotiate a rate, because of all union activities this interfered with them least. They would resent hotly any encroachment on their prerogatives as managers of their own businesses, but collective bargaining only meant that they were paying the same price as their competitors for one factor of production, just as they did when they bought a raw material in the same market. By the same token, in one way or another they would victimize one of their own men who came forward as a union spokesman with some demand in their own works, but neither pride nor policy gave them any objection to meet-

ing the officers of the union as equals in a district wage negotiation (1959 : 123–4).

Centralisation of bargaining at industry-wide level owed even
more to management policy : 'the initiative came in nearly every
instance from a recently formed employers' federation, more
often than not after a national lockout' (Clegg 1970 : 201).[15]
Paradoxically, employer policy has also contributed much to the
strength of shop-floor bargaining in manufacturing industries in
recent years – most particularly in engineering. Historically, the
preference for national bargaining reflected a desire to confine
union influence to the most general issues of standard wages and
conditions, preserving the autonomy of management in the
organisation of production. But the growth of collective organisation on the shop floor itself obliged managements to negotiate
over a range of workplace issues. It became normal, however, for
such negotiation to occur informally, with shop stewards, because most managers were reluctant to bring in the outside union
official to deal with domestic matters; the motive was often a
belief that the firm's own employees would prove more amenable
in negotiations than a full-time official, but the reverse has proved
more typically the case. Most employers, however, maintain
their traditional preference;[16] and as Clegg argues, 'this evidence
suggests that the informality of much domestic bargaining in
Britain is primarily due to the attitudes and wishes of managers'
(1970 : 292).

A number of more specific employer influences on industrial
relations have frequently been noted. A firm's technology – which
reflects a specific managerial *decision* on how to carry out pro-

[15] The degree of centralisation of industrial relations also owes much to
the direct influence of the structure of capital itself. Ingham argues that
variations in industrial concentration, technical and organisational complexity and the degree of product specialisation explain the greater
centralisation of industrial relations in Scandinavia than in Britain. His
general conclusion is that 'each of these closely related dimensions sets a
framework on the nature of the power relations between the respective
organisations of capital and labour which, in turn, determine to a large
extent a society's capacity for developing centralised institutions for the
regulation of conflict' (1973 : 40–2).

[16] Faced with a choice of negotiating with a steward or a full-time
official, 70 per cent of managers would choose the steward (Government
Social Survey 1968 : 86).

duction – has often been recognised as an important factor. Dunlop (1958), in his schematic account of industrial relations processes, identifies this as one of three key contextual influences; and taking the examples of coalmining and construction, he analyses the effect of technology on the content and obduracy of the subjects of collective bargaining. A comparison by Woodward of different manufacturing technologies led to the conclusion that assembly-line work gave rise to more grievances than either unit and small batch or process production. She explains this finding by such factors as 'the relaxation of pressure, the smaller working groups, the increasing ratio of supervisors to operators, and the reduced need for labour economy' in the less conflict-prone technologies (1958 : 18). However, a different interpretation might be in terms of the implications for *control* inherent in different production technologies.[17] Where technology is relatively unsophisticated, the worker possesses relative autonomy in performing his or her tasks. Assembly-line work is far more oppressive : and the employer, who determines track speeds, manning levels, job allocations and hence the amount of pressure on the worker, is *visibly* responsible. The process operator remains tied to his or her work, but is not subject to the same continuous pressure of physical activity or overt personal supervision. Discipline is still imposed, but management control is largely exercised *through the technical process itself*; to the worker it therefore tends to appear impersonal, inevitable and hence not obtrusively coercive.[18] Technology can also exert a significant influence on the relative *power* of management and workers. Some work processes bring employees together naturally into cohesive groups, or provide a strategic position in the flow of production which makes management highly vulnerable to strike action. Other processes fragment workers, or reduce the strategic impact of militant action (Sayles 1958; Kuhn 1961; Hill 1974). At times, an employer may deliberately initiate technical changes in order to

[17] In later publications, Woodward has emphasised the notion of management control – but in a somewhat different sense to that employed here.

[18] It is necessary to emphasise that process production does not, as some writers have assumed, transform the nature of *all* work tasks. Heavy and often routine and machine-paced work commonly remains in many occupations.

undermine the position of a powerful and militant occupational group.

As well as installing specific production machinery, managements also take a variety of decisions on the *organisation* of work and men which impinge on industrial relations. The rigidity of task specialisation is not wholly determined by the technology, and – as is today widely recognised – this can influence the extent and type of industrial conflict.[19] The extent to which different occupations form a hierarchy through which promotion is possible is also an important factor. In the steel industry, for example, recruitment to each production grade above the lowest is by promotion, according to seniority, from the grade below. This system tends to engender a sense of commitment among production workers to the industry and the employer; it also gives managements and the union a powerful sanction against potential dissidents. This system does not apply to maintenance craftsmen in the industry, who display a far higher level of militancy.

An aspect of work organisation which has received particular emphasis from students of industrial relations is the payment system, and in particular the operation of payment by results (often loosely termed piecework). Systems of payment by results were often introduced by employers against strong union resistance, as a means of intensifying the pace of work and at the same time forcing employees to agree a rate for the job as individuals rather than collectively. But in engineering and other manufacturing industries, piecework was turned against its makers. The spread of such methods of payment stimulated the growth of workplace union organisation, bringing the piecework bargain under collective control through the mediation of the shop steward. Often, rate-setting became a battle between the operator or his steward and the rate-fixer : a battle in which first-line management is willing to make concessions rather than risk a stoppage by a small group which could disrupt production sche-

[19] This recognition has led to much publicised schemes for the alteration of work tasks, misleadingly entitled 'job enrichment'. Such schemes aim to increase employee productivity and reduce industrial conflict by giving the *appearance* of more autonomous and meaningful work, but without removing the coercive and oppressive character of wage-labour.

dules over a whole section. Where regular changes occur in jobs or production methods, frequent bargaining opportunities arise; and the consequences are twofold. First, bonus earnings are achieved often far in excess of the formally negotiated basic wage rate;[20] second, a strong, confident and assertive shop steward organisation can develop with an influence over the labour force based on concrete bargaining achievements. Piecework bargaining can have disadvantages for workers: customary earnings levels are often vulnerable to fluctuations in production which are outside their control; and anomalous earnings differentials can arise which provoke friction between different worker groups. Both factors can constitute a serious source of conflict; indeed they have been identified as the primary source of the high strike incidence of the British car industry (Turner *et al,* 1967). But a well co-ordinated plant union organisation can at times press successfully for earnings guarantees, and also ensure coherence in the internal earnings structure.

The opportunity for workers to turn piecework to their own advantage is closely related to the existence of weaknesses in management's *internal control system*. Managers, as individuals, have interests and objectives which may diverge considerably from the aims elaborated by the top management of a company; this is perhaps particularly true of foremen, who are often promoted from the shop floor and have little prospect of further advancement. Moreover, the *functions* of line management – ensuring that production targets are met within specified deadlines – may conflict with the attempts of staff departments to apply costing procedures or standardised industrial relations policies. In many companies, first-line supervisors have the authority to override rate-study or personnel department recommendations and make concessions to their workers, rather than run the risk of a stoppage. This makes it relatively easy for trade unionists to win improvements in conditions and to establish precedents applicable in subsequent negotiations (Brown 1973). A wide

[20] For most of the 1960s, for example, average earnings in engineering were double the nationally negotiated basic rate, earnings in car firms being higher still; much of the difference was attributable to payment by results. This upward movement of earnings is often termed 'wage drift'. As Cliff comments, this is somewhat misleading: 'it would be much better called wage *drive,* since it is the result of pressure from workers ...' (1970:40).

range of the gains achieved by shop-floor organisation are negotiated in this manner at the point of production, without the involvement or at times even the knowledge of senior management : controls over manning and workloads, recruitment practices (sometimes including the closed shop), the amount and distribution of overtime, special payments for difficult or unpleasant jobs, rules governing the payment of average earnings (or a specified proportion) in certain contingencies which interfere with production.

By contrast, firms with relatively sophisticated systems of internal information and control can limit the autonomy of first-line management and hence the ability of workers to apply pressure in a fragmented manner. The past decade in British industrial relations has seen growing efforts by managements to introduce such a situation : such developments as productivity bargaining, measured daywork, and the reinforcement of work study as the basis of payment by results[21] all share among their objectives the elaboration of management cost controls and consistently applied industrial relations policies. Employers thus aim to present their workers with a more uniform front, centralising negotiations over all but the most trivial and routine issues at the level of senior management. The decision between obduracy or concession, whether and when to 'take' a strike, can thus be made within the framework of a conscious long-run strategy. In this way managements aim both to increase their control over labour costs and labour utilisation, and to reduce the effectiveness of shop stewards and thus weaken their influence over their members.

Employers can, moreover – either consciously or by default – affect the balance of power *within* the unions with which they deal. A recent study concludes that

> many of the resources commonly enjoyed by independent workplace organisations – facilities for shop stewards' meetings and mass meetings, time off for shop stewards, sinecures for senior stewards or convenors, an office, a telephone – are concessions which managers can make or try to withhold.

[21] These developments were strongly encouraged, for this very reason, by the National Board for Prices and Incomes and the Donovan Commission.

Besides that, union [i.e. union *officials*] and management can cooperate in developing and sustaining a style of bargaining in the workplace which fosters independence, or they can adopt a style of bargaining designed to keep a workplace organisation in subjection . . . Trade unions can influence the scope for workplace bargaining only by agreement with the managers with whom they negotiate and only within the limits imposed by the structure of managerial organisation (Boraston *et al.* 1975 : 187–8).

This points to a key implication of much that has been argued in previous chapters. Industrial relations involves the intersection of *two sets of control processes* – those internal and those external to trade unions – and from this intersection stems much of the character of the total pattern. The ability to negotiate with the employer(s) over a significant range of issues represents a source of power within trade unionism : centralised bargaining over the main substantive conditions of employment normally consolidates the control of the central negotiators over the union membership; where substantial decentralised bargaining occurs, there exist important sources of countervailing power towards the union leadership. Whether a company cedes the principal negotiating power to an employers' association, retains it at the level of its own senior management, or diffuses it (deliberately or otherwise) to first-line supervision can thus be of crucial significance for union democracy.

In analysing the impact of capital on trade unionism and industrial relations, it is necessary to avoid crude determinism or fatalism. Capitalism, wrote Engels, is based on 'a natural law that is founded on the unconsciousness of those involved in it' (quoted in Lukacs 1971 : 133). When Marx developed his famous analysis of the 'fetishism of commodities' he argued that the workings of the market system led men to *misconceive* its nature. 'A definite social relation between men . . . assumes, in their eyes, the fantastic form of a relation between things' (1959 : 72). The prices of commodities derive from the social relations of men as producers and consumers; yet men regard the structure of commodity exchange as natural and immutable, and hence assume that prices are determined by the objects of exchange themselves. It is thus assumed that men's economic relationships are naturally and inevitably remote from their conscious control. Yet the Marxian notion of *practice* presupposes that there is no inescapable logic to this process. Men's domination by a particular set of economic relationships is socially and historically contingent; if men become conscious that the processes to which they are subject are the unintended products of their own activity, the possibility becomes open of liberating themselves. At the very least, the *attempt* can be made (for objective conditions set limits to the possibilities for human freedom); whereas if consciousness is distorted, men are doubly the captives of their circumstances.

This is of great relevance to the study of industrial relations. There are no 'iron laws' of industrial relations : there are merely regularities and associations which are attributable partly to material constraints and power relationships, and partly (and often predominantly) to the force of patterns and habits which are unrecognised or else regarded as inevitable. The objective characteristics of capital, and the policies adopted by managers, create pressures and constraints which set limits to the possibilities of trade union action. But their determining effect depends *also* on the extent to which prevailing patterns of relationships are treated as inevitable by trade unionists themselves. Precisely because the very structure of capitalist control makes it natural for unions to react rather than to initiate, this reinforcing factor is a normal component in industrial relations. Trade union consciousness and ideology, in other words, are of vital importance in maintaining the subordination of workers and of their unions. Yet this ideological subordination is neither watertight nor irremediable : a point which is developed further in the following chapter. With the appropriate forms of consciousness, organisation and strategy, trade unionists *could* take the initiative in challenging patterns of industrial relations which have so far appeared determinate. It would still be necessary to confront the *power* of capital and of the functionaries of capital, in struggles which could be momentous; but a conscious trade union initiative would at least open up the *possibility* of a successful struggle.[22] There are immense obstacles on the route to the situ-

---

[22] The danger of an over-deterministic conception of industrial relations is illustrated by recent developments in Italy. For most of the post-war period the unions have been bitterly divided along ideological lines, and

ation in which 'the associated producers, rationally regulating their interchange with Nature, [bring] it under their common control, instead of being ruled by it as by the blind forces of Nature' (Marx 1962 : 800); but inability even to conceive this objective is the greatest obstacle.[23]

## CONCLUSION

The development of industrial relations has been powerfully influenced by the structure and dynamics of capitalism and by the strategies (or lack of strategy) of employers. The determining impact of capital has been reinforced by the largely reactive character of trade unionism – itself a response to the pressures of the dominant power relations in capitalism. But capitalism is beset by internal contradictions; and today these are manifest in conditions of crisis, both in the British economy and internationally. Production stagnates; firms lack the cash-flow to generate adequate investment (or even, in some cases, to continue operations); inflation escalates even as unemployment mounts; the international trade and monetary systems are in disarray.

The growing instability of capitalism is reflected in industrial relations. The goals of faster investment and stable prices (particularly in export markets) point naturally to the need for a shift

---

total membership has been very small; and learned explanations have been offered of why this weakness was inevitable. But since the 'hot autumn' of 1969, membership has increased (probably to the same level as in Britain), a system of shop-floor delegates has articulated workplace power in a manner which has transformed the structure and content of bargaining, and the unions themselves have been forced into a more militant and more united stance.

[23] Marx argued that the 'realm of freedom' could be constructed as the 'realm of necessity' became conquered. Today, the capacity exists for men's material needs to be satisfied without brutalising labour – if industry and society were differently organised and the structure of control transformed. The forces of production themselves are no longer 'the product of the preceding generation' which narrowly restrict the scope of social choice; the stage of development has been reached when new technical processes can be elaborated with unprecedented speed. For the first time in history, the possibility exists for men to choose their technology to suit their own needs, rather than to be dominated by a technology which is given and unalterable.

E

in the balance of power between capital and labour, between profits and wages and salaries. The necessary strategy for employers involves restraint on workers' incomes, an intensification of work pressure and work discipline, a reinforcement of managerial control at the point of production. Such a strategy is clearly ill-adapted to stable and pacific union–management relations: capital itself engenders new forms and levels of industrial conflict. In this context, the state appears in a crucial role as mediator and as initiator. In contemporary industrial relations, the state cannot escape a central and visible position.

# 5 Ideology and the State

'The executive of the modern State is but a committee for managing the common affairs of the whole bourgeoisie'. This famous remark of Marx and Engels (1958 : 36) is an essential starting point for any analysis of the role of the state in industrial relations; but it is *only* a starting point. Marx insisted on the need to fight for democratic political institutions, but was equally insistent that political democracy could not be properly achieved without economic and social democracy. A class which held economic sway in a society could not coexist with genuine popular control of the state, for if it did not subvert democracy then it would be dispossessed. There is no simple 'Marxist theory of the state'; but central to all that Marx and Engels wrote is the argument that the state has historically always served class interests, and necessarily so.[1] The elaboration of state institutions has been closely associated with the development of antagonistic class interests, and their functions have always included the reinforcement of the system of class rule enshrined in the existing social order by suppressing acts of resistance and revolt by subordinate classes.

In pre-capitalist societies it was common for political power to be *overtly* tied to class rule, political rights being expressly confined to members of economically and socially privileged groups. The industrial revolution was the culmination of a long process of transformation of the traditional processes of class rule both economically and politically. In the economic sphere, the domi-

[1] Marx intended to engage in a systematic study of the state, but was never able to commence this task; his analysis is therefore to be found in a range of diverse writings, many concerned with specific issues of immediate political concern. For useful discussions see Miliband 1965; Draper 1974.

nance of feudal landed property was overcome by the rise of
first mercantile, then industrial capitalism, with the 'free' wage-
labourer replacing the overtly unfree forms of feudal labour.
Politically, the rising capitalist class waged an eventually successful struggle against feudal laws which restricted the accumulation
of capital and against the exclusion of many bourgeois strata
from the franchise. The notable feature of this 'bourgeois revolution' was that in many countries it was expressed in a movement for *universal* political rights; faced by stubborn resistance
from the traditional ruling class, capitalists were forced to enlist
the support of the working class in a campaign for a broadly
democratic constitution.[2]

Democratic *forms* were however fully compatible with the
continuance of class rule. As Engels put it,

> the democratic republic officially knows nothing any more of
> property distinctions. *In it wealth exercises its power indirectly,
> but all the more surely.* On the one hand, in the form of the
> direct corruption of officials, of which America provides the
> classical example; on the other hand, in the form of an
> alliance between government and Stock Exchange, which
> becomes the easier to achieve the more the public debt in-
> creases and the more joint-stock companies concentrate in
> their hands not only transport but also production itself, using
> the Stock Exchange as their centre (1958: II, 321; emphasis
> added).

[2] In Britain, unlike most continental countries, there was never a clear-
cut 'bourgeois revolution'. Economically, capitalist methods were extensively applied in agriculture, while many members of the aristocracy
participated in the development of industrial capitalism. Politically,
rights were gradually conceded to bourgeois strata without the need for
capitalists to unite with workers in threatening insurrection (the unrest
before the 1832 Reform Act was mild in comparison with continental
experience). Hence democratic procedures were only haltingly introduced;
property qualifications were attached to the franchise, as late as the
present century. A more general consequence is that 'one of the most
striking features of the British State is that some of its most prominent
institutions have an apparently unbroken history stretching far back into
the Middle Ages' (Harvey and Hood 1957: 17). For a discussion of the
implications for the development of the labour movement of this incom-
plete bourgeois revolution see Anderson 1965.

The absence of genuine popular control despite formally democratic political machinery[3] is not due solely to the corruption of public officials or the overt collaboration of governments and capitalists. One crucial factor is the restricted and diluted model of democracy which is represented in electoral and parliamentary procedures. As was seen in Chapter 3, the conception of democracy which prevails in contemporary political discussion (and which underlies most analysis of trade union government) rejects the classical conception of active popular control as a defining characteristic. Instead, the mass of the population is assigned a passive role : its democratic rights consist solely in the occasional opportunity to elect parliamentary representatives, who are then autonomous until the next election.[4] The average citizen has the chance to vote in perhaps a dozen parliamentary elections. Allowing a generous five minutes to complete the process on each occasion, this is an hour of democracy in a lifetime. This, it would appear, is the literal meaning of parliamentary democracy.

From this political structure stem a number of important consequences. The constituencies from which parliamentary representatives are elected are defined by more or less arbitrary lines on the map; they contain no necessary internal homogeneity, no patterns of internal relationships which are a source of organic unity (as is to some extent the case, say, of the workforce of the factory). A constituency composed of employers and workers, housewives and shopkeepers, landlords and tenants, is not a meaningful entity outside the election period itself. When the MP sits in parliament he has no organic relationship with his constituency : he is *not* the representative of any coherent unit. As far as democracy is concerned he is, quite literally, irresponsible.

The legislative process thus parallels closely the managerial structure of control in the capitalist enterprise. Outside the brief moments of electoral 'activism', the citizen is subject to the deci-

[3] Even the formalities of democratic rights are subject to limitations. Laws of sedition and conspiracy, various 'special powers', and simple harassment without specific legal sanction, are extensively applied on occasions when the established social order is seriously challenged.

[4] The argument that parliamentary representatives must, between elections, be immune from popular control was originally explicitly *anti*-democratic. It is ironical that this should now be a central proposition of 'parliamentary democracy'.

sions of legislators whom he or she cannot expect to influence. The parallel is reinforced by the bureaucratic processes of state administration, which reaffirm the role of the citizen as object rather than subject of government. Yet the institutionalised passivity which is the normal requirement of the mass of the population undermines the potential of elections as a genuine means of popular control. Knowledge and understanding are fired by action : a normally inactive electorate cannot be expected to acquire political consciousness and sophistication. The long period when democracy is effectively in cold storage creates an apathy which remains apparent during elections themselves. Moreover, the personalisation and trivialisation of contemporary politics indicate that a passive citizenry is particularly vulnerable to the ideological pressures discussed below : the simplistic formulations of 'issue politics' have in common a failure to question the basic structure of capitalist industry and society, and hence are naturally conservative in orientation.

Paradoxically, the passivity of the electorate also disarms the legislator. By virtue of his *individual* autonomy, the MP is susceptible to a variety of corrupting tendencies – either in the crude form of being 'bought' by private interests, or simply by becoming absorbed by the rituals and ethos of 'the best club in the world'. More seriously, the legislature as a *collective* entity has no reservoir of power. The power of trade unionism (which, as has been argued, can be double-edged : 'power for' and 'power over' the membership) derives from the organic relationship between unions and workers, and from the possibility that union members can be *mobilised* in collective action. But the MP, as has been seen, has no such organic relationship with his constituents; there is no tradition or mechanism of mobilising the electorate as a collective force. This demobilisation of the mass of the population affects equally the power of the government, which in theory derives from the legislature, to deploy the various agencies of the state in accordance with the popular will. Against the entrenched social and economic power of capital, parliamentary institutions provide *no effective means* of exerting countervailing power.

The impact of external power on the state in capitalist society is all-pervading.[5] In its detail it takes such forms as the expensive

[5] For a detailed discussion see Miliband 1969.

lobbying activities of major companies, the close relationships of industrialists with politicians and civil servants, the accepted role of businessmen within many of the decision-making institutions of the state. More fundamentally, it is evident in the policy constraints which stem necessarily from the capitalist context of political life. 'Economic stability' is the precondition of all the other goals which governments pursue, whatever their political complexion; yet (in the absence of mobilisation to overturn capitalist economic relations) this inevitably entails the stability of a *capitalist* economy. Hence private profit – the barometer of economic 'health', and the source of new investment – has to be encouraged; and with it, intentionally or not, the associated inequalities of power and material advantage. More generally, policies must be pursued which maintain what is termed 'the confidence of industry' (which means, not the majority who work in industry but the minority who own and control industry); and this sets rigid limits to permissible radicalism. Thus political controversy focuses on issues which are marginal to the functioning and survival of capitalist relations of production, and the privileges of the capitalist class; and in the process, the very possibility of serious political debate around the basic structure of society tends to be obscured.

In mediating the power of capital within the state, labour or social-democratic parties play an important role. The internal and external dynamics of the political organisations of the working class show many parallels to those of the industrial organisations, the trade unions. Despite many of the forms of democratic control, decision-making is largely manipulated from above.[6] The commitment to parliamentarism as the sole legitimate focus of political action necessarily affects the distribution of power within the party : thus in Britain, the parliamentary leadership insists on its own autonomy, and hence its right to disregard conference decisions if these should conflict with its own wishes. This autonomy serves in turn to assist an accommodation with the constraints of capital – in the shape of a strategy of modest and piecemeal reform which can always be

[6] In the Labour Party, this is facilitated by the dominant position of the affiliated trade unions; the election of the National Executive Committee, and the disposition of the bulk of conference votes, is determined effectively at the level of union leadership. See Minkin 1974.

pragmatically trimmed and deferred if any aspect provokes powerful and embarrassing opposition. History indicates as a universal principle that social-democratic governments

> have found in the difficult conditions they inevitably faced a ready and convenient excuse for the conciliation of the very economic and social forces they were pledged to oppose, and for the reduction of their own ambitions to the point where these have ceased to hold any kind of threat to conservative forces (Miliband 1969 : 101).[7]

Such facts support the well-known assertion by Marx that parliamentary institutions represent a 'democratic swindle'[8]. Hence the notion of 'bourgeois democracy' as a political form in which the state continues to serve the interests of the economically dominant class. The classic Marxist emphasis has been on the overtly *coercive* functions of the state : its role in guaranteeing social relations of production which are inherently repressive, adding the sanction of law to managerial prerogatives, forcibly resisting working-class challenges to the social order. Thus Engels' emphasis on 'special bodies of armed men, prisons, etc.' : a theme which Lenin made central to his own analysis of the functions of the state.[9] Nor should the importance of this aspect of state activity be underestimated; as Miliband comments,

[7] For a detailed examination of this process in the history of the Labour Party see Miliband 1961.

[8] Letter to Engels, 7 September 1864. These criticisms did not contradict Marx's insistence that bourgeois democracy was preferable to political systems without even the forms of democracy; and that a necessary condition of socialism was that the functions of the state should be brought under genuine democratic control. (Thus, drawing on the experience of the Paris Commune of 1871, he insisted that dependence on professional officials should be eliminated, the legislature should become a working body and not merely a talking shop, public servants should lose their material privileges, and all representatives should be subject to recall by their constituents.) In this, as in many other respects, the claim of the states of Eastern Europe to be founded on Marxian principles is clearly fraudulent.

[9] For this reason, it was assumed that a transformation in social relations of production which eliminated class exploitation would initiate the 'withering away of the state'. 'State interference in social relations becomes, in one domain after another, superfluous, and then dies out of itself; the government of persons is replaced by the administration of

in most capitalist countries, this coercive apparatus constitutes a vast, sprawling and resourceful establishment, whose professional leaders are men of high status and great influence, inside the state system and in society . . . It is probably the case that never before in any capitalist country, save in Fascist Italy and in Nazi Germany, has such a large proportion of people been employed on police and repressive duties of one kind or another (1969 : 52).

The recent example of Chile – where the army overthrew a duly elected government which infringed too far the prerogatives of capital – shows the potential significance of this aspect of state power.

Yet it is possible to adopt a far broader conception of state power, incorporating a perception that the stability of the capitalist social order rests in part on far less overtly coercive processes. From this viewpoint, the state consists not merely in the machinery of government (including its judicial and military arms) but also in the relationship of the latter with the 'civil society' – the network of social, economic and cultural institutions and relations all of which reflect in different ways the predominance of capital and its agents. Gramsci summed up this approach in suggesting that 'one might say that State = political society + civil society, in other words hegemony protected by the armour of coercion' (1971 : 263). By hegemony, Gramsci indicated the social, cultural and ideological dominance of a social group; and, as its converse, 'the "spontaneous" consent given by the great masses of the population to the general direction imposed on social life by the dominant fundamental group; this consent is "historically" caused by the prestige (and consequent confidence) which the dominant group enjoys because of its position and function in the world of production' (1971 : 12).[10]

things . . .' (Engels 1958: ɪɪ, 151). Arguably, Marx, Engels and Lenin all underestimated the problem of the persistence of a state bureaucracy with vested interests even after the elimination of traditional class divisions.

[10] Gramsci's writings were subject to prison censorship, and he avoided certain terminology. 'Fundamental group' was his normal term in referring to a class.

To the extent that such 'consent' is general, the social order is not subject to overt and systematic challenge, and the *need* for explicit reliance on the institutions of coercion is reduced. Such consent (as Gramsci's use of inverted commas indicates) should not be regarded as 'spontaneous' but can be traced to the *material* domination of the economically powerful. There are close affinities with the famous argument of Marx and Engels in *The German Ideology*:

> The ideas of the ruling class are in every epoch the ruling ideas, i.e. the class which is the ruling *material* force of society, is at the same time its ruling *intellectual* force. The class which has the means of material production at its disposal, has control at the same time over the means of mental production, so that thereby, generally speaking, the ideas of those who lack the means of mental production are subject to it. The ruling ideas are nothing more than the ideal expression of the dominant material relationships, the dominant material relationships grasped as ideas; hence of the relationships which make the one class the ruling one, therefore, the ideas of its dominance (1970 : 64).

For example, the beliefs that there is an overriding 'national interest' which transcends the conflict of interests between rich and poor, exploiting and exploited; that economic life represents a system of free exchange between equal individuals; that the function of the state is to protect the weak and powerless just as much as the strong and powerful : all these ideas serve the interests of those in positions of economic and social control by consigning legitimacy on the social order.

Ideological hegemony, as Miliband insists, 'is not simply something which happens, as a mere superstructural derivative of economic and social predominance. It is, in very large part, the result of a permanent and pervasive *effort,* conducted through a multitude of agencies' (1969 : 181). Important examples are the press and other media of communication and persuasion, educational institutions and religious organisations. Control of certain of these agencies is the virtual prerogative of those with economic power, at times enabling their use in an unambiguously propagandist manner. Other institutions are relatively immune from direct manipulation; yet more subtle constraints ensure that their overall effect is to provide solid support for the established order – support which their apparent independence may render all the more effective. From an apparent diversity of sources, capitalist society and the institutions of control which it incorporates are commonly presented as the embodiment of virtue and reason; or at the very least as a fact of life, unquestionable and unalterable. The consequence, as Marx noted, is that 'the advance of capitalist production develops a working-class, which by education, tradition, habit, looks upon the conditions of that mode of production as self-evident laws of Nature' (1959 : 737).

None of this is to suggest a mechanical integration of capital, ideology and the state. The character and functioning of each display an area of autonomy; and each, moreover, contains its own internal contradictions. The cultural heritage of any society contains pre-capitalist and indeed anti-capitalist elements. The ideological legitimation of capitalism itself rests heavily on the image of the small entrepreneur, dependent largely on his own resources and resourcefulness in a competitive market. Such notions lose their plausibility in an era of monopoly capital : hence recent recognition of the existence of an 'unpleasant and unacceptable face of capitalism'. Prevailing ideological formulations clearly do not come to terms with the fact that 'unpleasant and unacceptable' consequences stem naturally from dynamics and principles *universal* to capitalism; they must be presented as marginal and accidental. To this extent, the legitimacy of the basic structure may be reaffirmed; yet at the same time, a basis is provided for more extensive criticism.

The ideology of the independence and autonomy of the state has important practical consequences. In so far as political leaders and administrators accept an obligation to abstain from narrow sectional partiality – and in many cases this view is probably sincerely held – they must be able to justify their actions and decisions in 'impartial' terms. This task is indeed facilitated by the fact that the survival and stability of a capitalist system form the normally unquestioned framework of policy, and that this commitment is regarded at natural and non-political; decisions which are *systematically* class-biased appear within this framework to be neutral and indeed inevitable. Nevertheless, it is certainly true that *some* actions of the state are contrary to specific capitalist interests, or serve the interests of the working class.

Arguably, occasional instances of this kind are essential if the *general* tendency of state policy is not to appear too blatantly subordinate to the power of capital. But two additional factors are important. Firstly, the sectionalism which has already been discussed in the context of the working class is evident also within capital. Those who own and control the means of economic life have a common interest in the perpetuation of an economic system based on the exploitation of labour. But *within* this system they have divergent interests as monopolists or small employers, financiers or industrialists, consumer or investment goods producers, manufacturers in domestic or export markets; and the result is often contradictory pressures on the state. Thus some sectors of capital gain from high interest rates while others lose; some benefit from membership of the Common Market while others suffer. Where the combined power of capital is weakened by internal divisions, the scope for independent action by governments is greatly increased.[11]

A second important factor is the power which the working class may on occasion mobilise in the political arena. Marx hailed as a signal example the Factory Act of 1847 which imposed a limit of ten hours on the daily labour of women and children in textile mills : 'it was the first time that in broad daylight the political economy of the middle class succumbed to the political economy of the working class' (1958 : 383). This success could be attributed to the ability of textile workers to appeal to humanitarian sentiments (the conditions under which women and children were compelled to work was a source of scandal and outrage); *and* to the force of the campaign mounted by the workers; *and* to the existence of divisions between bourgeoisie and aristocracy, which weakened the resistance of the factory-owners.[12] Very similar explanations could be given for the extension of

[11] Thus anti-monopoly legislation in the USA – which reflects the strength of early legitimations of capitalism on competitive principles – was facilitated by the interests of small capitalists which conflicted with those of the monopolists. (Even so, the power of the latter has limited the impact of such legislation.)

[12] Even so, the success was limited: employers (with the goodwill of the courts) constantly discovered loopholes in the Factories Acts which could be remedied only after new working-class campaigns. Even today, the coverage and enforcement of legislation designed to protect workers' health and safety are woefully deficient.

protective legislation in the present century, and also to the development of the various institutions of the 'welfare state'. But at the same time it is also necessary to note that such reforms have involved no central threat to capitalist interests; often, indeed, humanity went hand-in-hand with the long-term interests of capitalists. Many cotton manufacturers forecast ruin if they were prevented from driving six-year-old children fourteen or sixteen hours a day; in fact, as any intelligent slave-owner could have told them, such abuse of labour-power was wildly inefficient. The maintenance of a relatively healthy and well-nourished working class is the essential condition of a productive labour force; hence most employers have come to accept or even welcome the various concessions which have been made to working-class pressure.[13] And in the rare cases in which no direct advantage accrues from legislative encroachments on their prerogatives, capitalists may still reassure themselves that this is part of the ransom to be paid in forestalling serious working-class attack on their *general* rights and privileges.[14]

The ideology of the neutral state derives in part from the historical development of early capitalism. Pre-capitalist economic activity was hedged around with a vast array of controls and duties, statutory regulations on wages and prices, designed essentially to maintain the *stability* of traditional productive relationships. Yet the expansion of capitalism required that 'market forces' alone should hold sway : only by buying in the cheapest and selling in the dearest markets could entrepreneurs carry on the process of accumulation which was central to the dynamism of capitalism. Their insistent demand was therefore

[13] It is significant that the introduction of the British 'welfare state' followed revelations that a high proportion of working-class recruits for the Boer War were rejected by the army as physically unfit; the needs of the state gave force to arguments of social conscience which had previously proved ineffectual. It is, moreover, important to note that from the outset state welfare has been very largely financed by contributions from workers themselves. Despite a very widespread belief to the contrary, 'progressive' taxation and state welfare provisions have involved redistribution of income *within* rather than *between* classes. For details see Kincaid 1973.

[14] The notion of social reform as a 'ransom' which capital must pay for its own security was put forward in 1885 by the (then) Liberal politician and wealthy capitalist Joseph Chamberlain.

that the state should abandon all attempts to control economic activity. *Laissez faire* – let us do as we wish : this slogan was largely realised in the mid-nineteenth century, as the bourgeoisie consolidated its political influence. Yet non-intervention did not mean state neutrality; in withdrawing from an active economic role, the state endorsed the propriety and legitimacy of economic relations in which unequal power prevailed. The triumphant doctrine of the nineteenth century was known as 'liberalism' : but its meaning in practice was the liberty of employers to exploit and of workers to be exploited. The non-intervention of the state was non-intervention *in favour* of capital.

In the present century the situation has altered radically. The state now performs an increasing role as an *active* participant in economic life. As technology develops, and investment becomes ever more complex and costly, and the ownership of capital becomes concentrated in fewer and fewer giant monopolies, so the need for some overall co-ordination of economic activity increases. One response to this need has been apparent since the last war : government 'demand management', manipulating taxation and government expenditure so as to prevent the disastrous economic slumps which were a recurrent feature of previous trade cycles. (This government role is often attributed to the influence of Keynesian theory; but in fact a major cause has been the absorption of productive resources in military spending.) State planning agencies, aiming to provide a predictable framework within which firms can conduct their own planning, have become a feature of most capitalist economies. There has also been a marked trend towards state ownership of sectors of the economy : in particular traditional sectors which have ceased to be profitable (mines, railways) or the most modern sectors requiring heavy investment for unpredictable returns (atomic energy). State-owned enterprises thus often provide materials or services *at a loss*, subsidising private capital at the expense of the ordinary taxpayer.[15] *Direct* state subsidies to private industry

[15] This is one reason to doubt the notion that nationalisation, in itself, is in any way incompatible with capitalism. The *ideology* of nineteenth-century capitalism remains strong enough to provoke considerable opposition to specific acts of nationalisation, but most industrialists accept that the state sector in its present form serves their interests. It is also significant that generous compensation has always been paid when private companies have been nationalised; this is one reason why the size of the

occur in the form of grants of all kinds, tax concessions, and lucrative government contracts (especially in the arms sector). In recent years, as economic crisis has multiplied the numbers of 'lame ducks', the rattling of the 'capitalist begging bowl' has become ever more insistent. As technological development requires increasing expenditure on research and development, so the state takes on growing responsibilities in this area; moreover, education becomes subject to intense pressures to provide knowledge and training advantageous to capital. And as the advanced sectors of industry press constantly to substitute capital for labour in the production process, so much of the burden of supporting the human casualties falls on the state in the form of redundancy payments, unemployment benefits, and other welfare provisions.[16]

The symbiosis of the state and monopoly capital thus involves an almost total reversal of the separation of state and civil society achieved in the last century : and this clearly indicates that government itself has been transformed, from an agency fundamentally hostile to many of the priorities and practices of capitalist industry, to a committed ally. This has led some Marxist writers to use such concepts as 'the capitalist state' or 'state monopoly capitalism'. Arguably, the situation in which the state assumes the role of 'the ideal personification of the total national

public debt is *greater* than the value of state assets. Moreover, the previous managers and management structure are usually retained. The development of nationalisation as a form of 'socialisation of losses' was predicted a century ago by Engels, who foresaw that 'the official representative of capitalist society – the state – will ultimately have to undertake the direction of production'. Yet he insisted that this would be 'in no sense a socialistic measure'. The modern state, he argued,

> is only the organization that bourgeois society takes on in order to support the external conditions of the capitalist mode of production against the encroachments as well of the workers as of individual capitalists. The modern state, no matter what its form, is essentially a capitalist machine, the state of the capitalists, the ideal personification of the total national capital. The more it proceeds to the taking over of productive forces, the more does it actually become the national capitalist, the more citizens does it exploit. The workers remain wageworkers – proletarians. The capitalist relation is not done away with. It is rather brought to a head (1958: 147–9).

[16] For a discussion of these indirect forms of state subsidy to monopoly capital see O'Connor 1973.

capital' is most clearly apparent in Eastern Europe; the term 'state capitalism' is an appropriate characterisation of these societies. But in the West, a number of factors inhibit the extension of the process to this degree. First, the very success of early capitalists in implanting *laissez-faire* doctrines as an accepted component of the culture entails that the growing economic role of the state attracts strong opposition on ideological grounds unrelated to the *current* requirements of capital.[17] Second, the most profitable sectors of monopoly capital, while far from averse to state subsidies, naturally resist the development of state control of their activities. Third, a considerable proportion of the units involved in the production of goods and (particularly) services are small, labour-intensive, and marginal to the main process of capitalist development; individualist ideology thrives in this sector, while there is little practical cause for state involvement. Finally, the *internationalisation* of capital sets limits to the economic role of the state. While the nation-state remains the key unit of political organisation, the transnational enterprise – which, as has already been seen, exerts an ever greater impact in the economic sphere – is likely to regard too close an integration with any national government as an inhibition on its overall priorities.

Nevertheless there remains considerable scope as yet for an enhanced state role in Western capitalist societies; the trend of past decades continues. This same trend is clearly at work in industrial relations.

Trade unionism became established in Britain during the heyday of *laissez-faire* liberalism. Initially, this doctrine was interpreted in a manner extremely hostile to collective action by workers: their combinations were judged to be 'in restraint of trade', interfering with the right of the employer to make a 'free' contract with his employees as individuals. Legal repression of unionism was justified on precisely these grounds. But as influential employers discovered that it was possible to come to terms

[17] Such ideological pressure can in some contexts inhibit the 'logical' direction of capitalist development. In the United States, for example, it is difficult for the state to become *directly* implicated in an extensive manner in the affairs of private capital – though considerable indirect support and involvement occur. In Britain, by contrast, rigid commitment to *laissez-faire* doctrine is confined to the eccentric fringe of conservatism.

with trade unions that were not seriously disadvantageous, so *laissez-faire* was reinterpreted to imply that unions and employers should carry on their relations with the minimum of state interference.[18] In consequence, 'there is, perhaps, no major country in the world in which the law has played a less significant role in shaping these relations than in Great Britain . . . British industrial relations have, in the main, developed by way of industrial autonomy' (Kahn-Freund 1954 : 44). (In most other countries, by contrast, stable industrial relations developed at a time when the state was actively involved in general economic affairs,[19] and this is reflected in more comprehensive intervention in labour relations.) In Britain, 'voluntarism' in industrial relations shared with *laissez-faire* ideology in general an essentially practical basis : the confidence of employers in their own ability to exercise control without outside assistance. This meant in turn that trade unions should lack either the power or the will to interfere excessively with managerial objectives.

In the formative period of British industrial relations, this was indeed the case. As late as the 1880s, less than a million workers out of a labour force of twelve million were in unions; even in the crafts, organisation was often far from comprehensive. The upsurge of new unionism brought no lasting transformation : in 1910, only about one employee in six was in a union. The following decade altered the picture dramatically; but mass unemployment between the wars quickly eroded labour's new-found economic power. During both world wars, when unions were numerically strong, their policies were deliberately adapted to the priorities of employers and the government; and for the two decades following the last war, the national leadership of almost every union remained committed to the same aims of 'moderation' and 'responsibility', and was in general successful in preventing any serious challenge to stable capitalist development.

[18] *Judges*, however, have been far less 'enlightened' in applying the traditional doctrines to industrial relations; to this day, many express in their judgments a strong ideological bias against collective action by workers.

[19] In many countries where industrial development occurred later than and in competition with British capitalism, *laissez-faire* was inappropriate : the rapid accumulation of capital required to close the gap demanded active intervention and sponsorship by the state.

Even in the heyday of 'voluntarism', the role of the state in industrial relations was far from neutral – and not merely because abstention from the detailed processes of collective bargaining allowed the superior power of capital to structure the terms of the relationship with trade unionism. Through a variety of institutional arrangements, the state facilitated the routine exploitation of wage-labour by capital; and on the rare occasions when the routine was seriously disrupted, it could intervene brutally and decisively. As Harvey and Hood comment,

Ever since the birth of capitalism, the State has been more or less openly on the side of the employers in industrial disputes. In earlier days, it did not even trouble to conceal its partisanship. Today, although no less partisan, it has to walk more warily, because of the strength of the working-class movement. Except at times when the class struggle rises to a pitch of great intensity, either generally as in the General Strike of 1926 or over a particular field of industry as in the dock strike of 1949, it affects "impartiality" and pretends to wield nothing more than a "conciliatory" influence. But, in point of fact, its principal objects remain constant : to secure for capitalist industry a regular and flexible labour supply, and to assist employers to maintain or to restore an "industrial peace" which enables them to extract the maximum profit from industry with the minimum of disturbance in the form of strikes, lock-outs, go-slow movements, etc. It has established labour exchanges to help them recruit their "hands", and a Juvenile Employment Service to facilitate the absorption of young people into the jobs where they will be most serviceable. It provides machinery, such as the Industrial Court, the Wages Councils and a host of specialised tribunals, for arbitration and conciliation in industrial disputes, and lays down the conditions upon which such machinery must or may be used. It actively intervenes, through the Industrial Conciliation Service of the Ministry of Labour, whenever a strike occurs or is threatened. In the last resort, it will bring in the police and the Army to coerce and defeat strikers in "essential services", by charging picket lines, breaking up meetings, and providing uniformed blacklegs to maintain the flow of supplies – always, of course, in the "interests of the community". Under the Emergency Powers

Act of 1920, it has provided itself with virtually dictatorial powers to "protect the community" against stoppages in vital sectors of the economy (1957 : 218–9).

The ostensibly neutral functions of mediation and conciliation – most recently embodied in the 'independent' Advisory Conciliation and Arbitration Service – in fact serve the essential purpose, for both employers and the state, of stabilising the existing mode of production. Mediation by the state, moreover, 'occurs in the shadow of its known and declared propensity to invoke its powers of coercion, against one of the parties in the dispute rather than the other, if "conciliation" procedures fail' (Miliband 1969 : 81). This awareness necessarily structures the trade union response.

Thus 'voluntarism' has always been more apparent than real. But in recent years, the development of interventionism in general economic affairs has been accompanied by a similar process in industrial relations – and for the same reasons. The contradictions which so clearly beset contemporary capitalism limit the available options in labour relations : hence more is now required of governments than that they merely stand on the sidelines ready to repel any challenge to the rules of the political economy of capital. In previous phases of capitalist development, periods of expansion allowed a sufficient margin of profitability for employers to conduct without serious difficulty their response to the (modest) aspirations of labour; while in periods of recession, the unions were ill placed to cause trouble. Yet in an era of 'managed' demand, relatively full employment sustains the economic power of labour at the same time as many firms face grave problems of profitability.[20]

In Britain, the synchronisation of the two forms of intervention is remarkable. At the end of 1961 the Conservative

[20] Marx argued that there is a natural tendency for the rate of profit (i.e. the percentage return on the value of capital) to fall, despite a rise in the absolute amount of profit and even in the rate of exploitation (i.e. the proportion of the value created by labour which goes in profits rather than wages and salaries). This tendency can be offset by other factors: for example, government arms spending (Kidron 1974). However, it is possible to regard the 'profit squeeze' as a major determinant of recent crises in industrial relations and general economic relations (Glyn and Sutcliffe 1972; though their interpretation has been challenged). Recent preoccupation with problems of 'cash-flow' is one reflection of this process.

government symbolically buried *laissez-faire* when it established
the National Economic Development Council. Simultaneously,
the creation of the National Incomes Commission signalled the
first serious attempt to impose direct constraints on wage bargaining in 'normal' economic circumstances.[21] The explicit intent
was to keep increases in wages and salaries within the rate of
productivity growth; hence unit labour costs would be stabilised (or even reduced), the competitiveness of British capital
enhanced, and profitability (and in consequence, it was hoped,
investment) increased. Almost identical objectives were written
into the Labour incomes policy of 1964–70, presided over by
the National Board for Prices and Incomes.[22] Subsequent
governmental intervention has involved variations on the same
theme : with the important difference that what was once presented as a policy for the 'planned growth of incomes' implies, in
a period of total stagnation or even decline, a deterioration in the
real earnings of many employees.

Concern with labour costs has inspired not only incomes
policy but also attempts to 'rationalise' labour utilisation by employers. Capitalist development involves a natural trend towards
more intensive exploitation of labour and hence (unless production expands in step) towards displacement of labour. But strong
trade union resistance to redundancy inhibited many employers
from introducing radical changes in production methods or work
arrangements. Constant exhortation to trade unionists not to
'obstruct efficiency', and to accept unemployment under the

[21] Previous exercises in incomes policy occurred in wartime and during
the post-devaluation crisis of 1948–50. For details of the development of
government intervention in wage determination see Clegg 1970 and 1971;
Fels 1972.

[22] The Labour government presented its policy as an instrument of
social justice, not a mechanism of wage restraint; and on these grounds
the TUC, having refused to cooperate with the National Incomes Commission, endorsed the new policy. But the one significant difference from
the Conservative initiative was the emphasis on low pay as a criterion for
exceptional wage increases; and in practice, as the Board's historian has
indicated, the 'NBPI and the prices and incomes policies, both accorded
a lower priority to low pay than to other wage problems' (Fels 1972: 132).
The Board's own statistics indicate that over the whole period of its
existence, the relative position of the lowest paid actually deteriorated.
For a discussion of the misleading nature of arguments in favour of
incomes policy as a means of social justice see Hyman and Brough 1975.

euphemism of 'redeployment', has proved of little value. In this context the Redundancy Payments Act of 1965 has represented an important example of government intervention, undermining the basis of collective resistance to the elimination of jobs.[23] (Though in recent years, with mounting unemployment, this effect has been reduced : as the chances of finding new jobs have shrunk, so workers have strenuously resisted redundancies and closures.) The central emphasis, in Labour's incomes policy, on increased productivity as the major (indeed virtually the sole) justification for pay increases above the norm similarly encouraged union–employer collaboration in increasing the intensity of exploitation. Direct influence was also exerted on employers through the Manpower and Productivity Service of the Department of Employment and Productivity (the title of the reconstructed Ministry of Labour is symptomatic of the policy emphasis of 1964–70).[24] The Service, headed by the manager who forced through the measured daywork system at Chrysler, provided in effect free consultancy, at the taxpayer's expense, on how to increase the control of employers at the expense of their workers. (That this initiative was devised by a Labour government is itself significant.)

A related development has been the pressure for procedural 'reform', initially associated with the Prices and Incomes Board, made the central theme of the report of the Donovan Commission, and given institutional form in the Commission on Industrial Relations.[25] The Donovan Commission's conception of 'reform' followed naturally from its initial definition of industrial relations 'problems' : such features as unofficial strikes, 'wage drift', 'the inefficient use of manpower', the erosion of managerial control over the work process. To promote the desired aim of 'the orderly and effective regulation of industrial relations within companies and factories' it was self-evident that senior management should be more closely involved in defining personnel and labour relations policies; that payment systems and bargaining

[23] For a detailed analysis see Fryer 1973.

[24] Since the Conservative victory of 1970 the Department has lost the 'productivity' from its title; but the management consultancy function (which in a modest form dates back to 1945) survives.

[25] The Advisory Conciliation and Arbitration Service is, presumably, the new vehicle for this pressure.

procedures should be reconstructed to reduce the scope for negotiation at the point of production where management control was weakest; that employers and union officials should unite to 'recognise, define and control the part played by shop stewards in our collective bargaining system'. The logical implication of this aspect of state policy is not always spelled clearly: 'orderly and effective regulation' involves the reinforcement of management control over workers and, in the process, the erosion of the control which workers have themselves asserted.[26]

State control over workers' collective action may also occur far more directly. In most countries where (because of the absence of a strong *laissez-faire* tradition when unionism became established) greater legal control of industrial relations is the norm, the rights of unions – and in particular the right to strike – are closely and restrictively defined. In general, action which seriously challenges the power of capital is expressly outlawed.[27] In Britain, by contrast, unions' legal rights have in the main been *negatively* defined; against the background of principles of 'common law' which are uniformly hostile to collective action by workers, the trade unions have applied political pressure to achieve legislation *excluding* the courts from intervening in their internal affairs or in strikes. Judges in turn have exercised great ingenuity in discovering unexpected loopholes to attack trade unionists; but for a century, direct *legislative* attacks on unionism have been rare. (The Emergency Powers Act of 1920, and the Trade Disputes Act of 1927 – the government's vindictive response to the General Strike, repealed in 1946 – are the two obvious examples.) Employer pressure for comprehensive antiunion legislation however mounted during the 1960s. In evidence to the Donovan Commission, such influential bodies as the Confederation of British Industry, the Engineering Employers' Federation and – in particular – the Motor Manufacturers called for tough penalties against strikers. In its report the Commission largely – though not entirely – resisted this carefully orchestrated campaign. But the Labour government, in its White Paper *In Place of Strife*, made some move towards greater legal control of

[26] For a more detailed critique of the Donovan Report see Hyman and Brough 1975.

[27] For a survey of legal restrictions on strikes see Kahn-Freund and Hepple 1972.

trade unionism; and the process was completed by the Conservative government's Industrial Relations Act of 1971, which sought to police trade unions' internal arrangements and prescribed drastic penalties for strikers and their unions. Trade union resistance forced Labour to withdraw its proposals, and made the Industrial Relations Act largely inoperative; it was repealed after the Conservative defeat in 1974. It is far too early, however, to assume that there will be no future attempt to impose similar legal restraints on effective union action.

The state's role in industrial relations displays important contradictions. It has already been seen that monopoly capital depends increasingly on the state to provide grants, subsidies and services, to train its labour force, and to support its casualties and rejects. The consequence is rising government spending, which is *directly* inflationary in effect and at the same time indirectly so through the increasing burden of taxation which is required.[28] As Wilkinson and Turner have shown, it is *workers* who are bearing the brunt of higher taxation: the percentage of profits taken in taxes has fallen sharply, while that of wages and salaries has risen equally sharply.[29] The same authors show that, because of the structure of taxation and of various social welfare benefits, employees require pay increases larger (and in some cases substantially larger) than the rate of inflation merely to prevent a decline in the value of their take-home pay: 'only by insisting on wage increases which are necessarily inflationary can wage-earners secure a "moderate" gain in real living standards' (in Jackson *et al* 1972 : 98). In this context, and given the small margin available for improvement in the current economic climate, even the most modest trade union wage aspirations have a disruptive potential; indeed even resistance to a *cut* in living standards may threaten economic stability.

Incomes policy may thus be seen as a response to pressures which the state and capital have together generated. It contains,

[28] Some Conservative politicians have correctly identified the inflationary role of government spending; they fail to recognise its inevitability given capitalism's current stage of development.

[29] Between 1949 and 1968 the percentage taxation on corporate profits fell from 36·5 to 19·0 (excluding dividend taxation; if this is included the decline was from 45·6 to 30·9 per cent); that on wages and salaries rose from 9·8 to 15·5 per cent (in Jackson *et al.* 1972: 80). These trends have almost certainly continued.

moreover, its own internal contradictions. The impact of the policy of 1964–70 was uneven. Strongly organised groups could continue to push up earnings through bargaining on the shop floor; pieceworkers in particular were largely immune from the effects of governmental policy. The main victims were thus workers (most notably in the public sector) who were dependent on official, industry-wide negotiations for improvements in wages and salaries. The reluctance of the Prices and Incomes Board to approve increases based on the principle of 'comparability' – a well-established formula in negotiations – breached traditional pay relationships. At the same time, the officially favoured process of productivity bargaining led to a number of much-publicised instances of apparently spectacular pay increases. (The concessions made by the workers concerned were less well publicised.) In consequence, workers who could still bargain freely were given new and more ambitious targets; while those who could not were provoked into militancy. In particular, the government's veto on 'excessive' pay settlements in the public sector – at times flouting established principles of pay determination – mobilised traditionally passive groups of trade unionists. Eminently respectable bodies, which had not called a strike in half a century or more – the Miners, the Teachers, the Postal Workers – were forced into confrontations with the state. The defeat of the Conservative government in early 1974 was the culmination of this process. This helps explain the recent oscillations in government policy : the contradictory force of the economic pressures to contain incomes, and the fear of dramatically damaging disputes.

A more general contradiction underlies relations between trade unions and the state. Put simply, recent governments have been trapped by the tension between the opposing strategies of incorporation and repression. What is at issue here is the 'trade-off' discussed in Chapter 3 : the accommodation between trade unionism and the external power of the state. Governments have come to appreciate that if union organisation is outside the law but cannot be suppressed – and in modern times, only the brutalities of fascism have succeeded in this –[30] its policies are

[30] Fascist regimes have often risen to power on the basis of quasi-socialist rhetoric; but once in power they assiduously served the interests of capital. Nevertheless, it would seem that fascism is not as yet widely seen as the solution to the problems of British capitalism. In part this

likely to be militant and disruptive, perhaps involving an explicit challenge to the political regime. Conversely, if unions are assigned legitimacy – through legal protection, consultation, representation on governmental committees, 'honours' for individual leaders – they are likely to form a means of integrating the working class into capitalist society, thus serving as a mechanism of social control. The state has come to *depend* on collaborative relations with trade unionism; and this dependence is particularly great when the working class is strongly organised yet is adversely affected by government economic policies. This was the case in both world wars, when trade union representatives were drawn closely into the processes of state; it is true today. It was thus natural that the Donovan Commission placed primary emphasis on the extension of the process of incorporation : particularly at shop-floor level, where the source of 'anarchy and disorder' (i.e. control by workers) was identified. Shop stewards were to be integrated into the 'responsible' patterns of national union–employer relations by a more formalised relationship with senior management and a clearly defined role within official trade unionism. The 'voluntarism' of Labour's initial formulation of its incomes policy (echoed by the 'social contract' of 1974) similarly presupposed that by involving the unions as junior partners in the exercise they would willingly constrain their own objectives.

In both these latter cases, the strategy of incorporation foundered on the rock of rank-and-file resistance (analysis of which must await the following chapter). The Donovan Commission greatly overestimated the willingness of shop-floor trade unionists to cooperate in their own emasculation; voluntary incomes policy faced the problem that union leaders who accepted government restraint might yet be unable to 'deliver' the compliance of their own members. In consequence, overtly coercive measures appear attractive to governments. Thus in 1966, the

reflects the genuine strength of liberal-democratic ideology; but no doubt it also owes something to recognition of the immense disruption which would be caused by an attempt to destroy the organised power of the labour movement. Moreover, the *arbitrary* character of fascist regimes is undoubtedly uncongenial to those who own and control capital; few would willingly create such a hostage to fortune unless all other avenues seemed closed. For a brief discussion of the relationship between fascism and capitalism see Miliband 1969: 87–96.

Labour government resorted to statutory powers to enforce its incomes policy; and the Conservatives acted similarly in 1972. The coercive approach is generalised in legislative controls on strikes and other union functions. The main thrust of the Industrial Relations Act (which contained many contradictory elements) was designed to transform the *internal* power relations of trade unions through the crude application of *external* power. Unions which failed to impose strict discipline on their members were exposed to swingeing financial penalties; both the main unions suffered heavily on being held responsible for 'unfair industrial practices' committed by their members.

Yet overt coercion is double-edged. Labour's pay freeze of 1966 was effective in the short run, but may well have contributed to subsequent union disillusion with the whole policy and its rapid disintegration. The compulsory restraints of the Conservatives likewise had explosive consequences. In the field of general industrial relations legislation, Labour's 'penal clauses' of 1969 were a fiasco : union hostility to these few sections prevented the implementation of the government's whole package, which mainly followed the Donovan recommendations. The Industrial Relations Act also proved little short of a disaster for its creators : the devious strategy to force union officials to curb the rank and file was counterproductive. Whether or not union leaders would have welcomed greater authority over their members, this was scarcely acceptable as the gift of a Conservative government which seemed bent on overturning basic organisational rights and imposing a state licence on their activities.[31] Opposition was unavoidable; and pressure from rank-and-file activists, who rightly appreciated that they were the main target of the legislation, ensured that resistance was more forthright than many leaders probably intended.[32] The final lesson of both 1969 and 1971 was that state action which attacked but did not eliminate rank-and-file power inevitably soured relations

[31] The Act was not altogether without effect in this respect, however. The TGWU attempted to define the authority of its shop stewards more closely.

[32] The legislation was made unworkable by the TUC decision to instruct member unions, on pain of expulsion, not to register under the Act or to cooperate with the various agencies it created. This policy was far more resolute than the majority of unions appeared initially to envisage.

with union leaders, who could scarcely risk the appearance of collaboration; and in the process, their normal restraining role was made more difficult.[33]

The limitations which beset equally the strategies of incorporation and overt coercion explain the curious oscillations in government policy towards the unions in recent years. They also make ideology an increasingly important resource in a period when the state is forced to become more and more actively engaged in industrial relations.

Public discussion of industrial relations is shot through with evaluative and ideological terminology: and in line with the general orientation of the dominant social ideas, its impact is overwhelmingly in favour of capital. The principal ingredients are a notion of 'national interest' which is closely bound up with the interests of employers; and a conception of labour organisation, objectives and action (in so far as these conflict with employer interests) as necessarily sectional and probably selfish, irresponsible, disruptive and subversive. As Miliband notes, 'business demands which are designed to strengthen the position of individual firms or of particular industries, or of capitalist enterprise at large, can always be presented, with a high degree of plausibility, given the capitalist context in which they are made, as congruent with the "national interest" ' (1969 : 162).

In the name of the 'national interest' (which, strangely, is inimical to the interests of the majority of the nation's inhabitants) governments can appeal for public support for their efforts to contain trade unionism. 'Excessive' wage demands must be resisted because they damage, not employers but 'the country as a whole' (indeed the notion of 'wage inflation' clearly identifies labour as the main source of economic ills). Strikes typically reflect the malign influence of 'militants' and 'extremists' within the unions; by no means can employer intransigence be so characterised. When the state intervenes against a trade union, refusal to concede implies a deliberate challenge to law and order, constitutional government and the rule of democracy. Such ideological assaults very commonly succeed in dividing and demoralising trade unionists; 'for labour, as a pressure group, is extremely vulnerable to many internal and external influences

[33] Recent government strategy in industrial relations is analysed in more detail in Hyman 1973.

calculated to erode its will and persistence' (Miliband 1969 : 156).

Ideology is also important in the routine of industrial relations. One of the most popular concepts in the everyday vocabulary of industry is 'fairness', a notion which may at times inspire criticism of practices or relationships which are perceived as inequitable and sustain workers in struggles for redress. Yet in its conventional usage the language of fairness tends on the contrary to contain conflict and reinforce capitalist relations of control. The idea of a 'fair day's work', for example, incorporates the assumption of a moral obligation owed by the worker to the employer : the precise content of this obligation may be disputed, but the conflict is one of detail rather than principle. Conceptions of 'fair wages' are normally structured by the traditional relationships of the labour market,[34] and thus take for granted the prevailing patterns of income inequality and the necessity that labour should receive less than the value which it creates. Institutionalised in the principle of 'fair comparisons', the focus in wage bargaining is on the equalisation of *movements* in wages and salaries so as to preserve the relationship of established differentials the propriety of which is unquestioned. Or, when a case is argued for the alteration of the relative position of a particular group, the demand is typically for an adjustment within, not a transformation of, the structure of inequality of rewards. Thus a concept with potentially radical implications is normally conservative in its application.[35]

Ideological pressures deriving from the broad societal power structure inevitably shape the manner in which workers conceptualise their employment experiences and formulate their aspirations. Subordination, deprivation, monotony, discomfort are presented in a thousand homilies and maxims as unalterable features of the industrial landscape. The 'vocabulary of motives' available to employees – the socially acceptable justifications

[34] Engels stressed this point with the comment that 'social fairness or unfairness is decided by one science alone – the science which deals with the material facts of production and exchange, the science of political economy' (*Labour Standard*, 7 May 1881).

[35] Paradoxically it seems likely that incomes policy, by raising the question of fair pay as a *general* issue, has subjected to critical scrutiny relationships which were traditionally taken for granted. The unintended result has probably been to stimulate increased conflict over relativities.

which can mobilise their own actions and influence the responses of others – imposes serious limitations on their goals and strategies.[36] Class bias is built into everyday thought and language : it is scarcely possible for subordinate employees to present a demand for the control of industry, or for the level of income and associated advantages which are the normal prerogative of higher-status groups, in a form which does not appear outrageous. Similar constraints encourage workers' self-conception in essentially *sectional* terms : the notion of the working class as a group with common interests opposed to those of employers as a class is excluded from everyday language. Fragmented in their presentation, the interests of the majority can thus paradoxically be construed as *minority* interests, to be pursued defensively and apologetically.

The labour movement is handicapped not only by an alien ideology but by the impact of its own history. 'The tradition of all the dead generations weighs like a nightmare on the brain of the living', wrote Marx (1958 : 247). British trade unionism won social acceptance, and consolidated many of its institutions, in the era of mid-Victorian economic expansion. The lessons of the time became deeply ingrained : by piecemeal action, modesty of objectives and respectability of manner it was possible to gain regular if unspectacular improvements in the conditions of the workers. 'Free collective bargaining' gradually acquired the status of trade unionism's central function, valued as a process independently of its achievements. 'The actual technique of bargaining, involving "give and take", making concessions, achieving a compromise solution, is accredited with a virtue. A result reached through compromise is seen as fair, just, equitable and decent, irrespective of the merits of the initial demand or complaint' (Allen 1966 : 30). This commitment to the institution of collective bargaining meshed neatly with the ideological segregation of industrial and political action, each requiring distinctive organisations and strategies. Within this conception, to strike for a 'political' rather than an 'industrial' demand is altogether illegi-

[36] 'Along with the conduct patterns appropriate for various occasions, we learn their appropriate motives, and these are the motives we will use in dealing with others and with ourselves. The motives we use to justify or to criticize an act thus link our conduct with that of significant others . . .' (Gerth and Mills 1954: 118).

timate; the 'political' must be pursued through lobbying, electoral activity and the Labour Party. Today, such traditional assumptions are increasingly inappropriate, whatever their original rationale. In the face of monopoly capital, sectional action spells weakness; in the face of the recurrent crises of late capitalism, the scope for piecemeal reform shrinks; in the face of the integration of state and economic activity, the distinction between the industrial and the political loses all meaning : unions disarm themselves if they continue to respect a demarcation which employers and governments themselves define.[37]

These ideological constraints are not inescapable. The traditions and presuppositions of trade unionism, like more general societal ideologies, contain ambiguities and contradictions. Moreover, the experiences of workers themselves in their relations with capital constantly press against the limitations of established practices and institutions. The interrelation of rank-and-file organisation and action, and the official structures and assumptions of industrial relations, forms the theme of the following chapter.

CONCLUSION

The role of the state in industrial relations has developed in line with the general transformation in its economic functions. The era of *laissez-faire* was associated with the traditional British doctrine of 'voluntarism' : though in industry, as in civil society in general, this implied not neutrality but abstention in favour of the domination of capital. Where this domination was challenged, moreover, direct intervention was prompt. In recent years, a far more active and continuous involvement in relations of production has been necessitated by the intense contradictions of late capitalism; and this has carried with it the need to control and stabilise labour relations. Hence 'voluntarism' has been steadily eroded.

The direct and active governmental role in modern industrial relations requires legitimation if the charge of systematic bias in favour of capital is to be avoided. The ideological identification of the interests of capital with 'the nation as a whole' neatly per-

[37] For a useful critique of the distinction between political and industrial issues see Fox 1974.

forms this function. However, some of the traditional ideological reinforcements of the power of capital over labour are currently under strain: a process clearly revealed in the development of rank-and-file action.

# 6 Rank-and-File Organisation and Action

The previous chapters, commencing with the grievances and aspirations of workers in their immediate work relations, have moved through an analysis of the official organisations of trade unionism to consider the role of the state and the general process of capitalist development. It was seen that the main obstacle to attempts to contain the trade union challenge to capitalism stems from the rank-and-file trade unionists themselves: thus in this chapter, the focus shifts back to the shop and office floor.

It has already been seen that, while practice varies considerably between trade unions, the extent of rank-and-file control of policy and action is in all cases limited. There exists a permanent tension between the institutional distinctness of the union and its democratic rationale. This is by no means a new problem, or one peculiar to any specific national setting; half a century ago, for example, Gramsci wrote that 'the workers feel that the complex of "their" organization, the trade union, has become such an enormous apparatus that it now obeys laws internal to its structure and its complicated functions, but foreign to the masses' (1969: 9). This separation of the mass of the membership from positive control is often analysed pessimistically in terms of 'oligarchy' or optimistically in terms of 'polyarchy'; both approaches are however less than fully illuminating in that their focus on the *internal* processes of control in isolation excludes examination of the impact of *external* power on the possibilities of union democracy.

It is moreover necessary to treat sceptically any attempt to define 'iron laws' of union government: for the *practice* of union members is always liable to test the limits of established relations of control. To cite Gramsci again, 'the trade union is not a pre-determined phenomenon : it *becomes* a determinate institution, that is, it assumes a definite historical form to the extent that the strength and will of the workers who are its members impress a policy and propose an aim that define it' (1969 : 14). Trade unionism is the institutionalised form through which workers can exercise control over employment conditions and the work situation; or the means by which control is wielded, not *by* but *for* and *on behalf of* them; or, because of this differentiation, a source of control *over* them in the interests of officials or external parties. But collective action need not be pursued only through official trade union channels : workers may act independently, or in some circumstances in opposition to the official organisations. Any discussion of control relations in trade unions which refers only to the formal decision-making procedures is therefore inadequate.

The key development in post-war British industrial relations has been what Flanders (1970) has termed 'the challenge from below'. Some aspects of this process have been noted in previous chapters. The traditional institutions of collective bargaining shaped in many industries at the turn of the century and sanctified and extended by the Whitley reports of 1917–8, had the national level as their focus. Previously, the district had represented the exclusive level of formal negotiation and agreement in many industries. The official procedures, in other words, involved *multi-employer* bargaining, above the level of the individual establishment. The two crucial consequences were that wages were prescribed in the form of national or district rates which represented what the least profitable employer was able or willing to pay; and that formal agreements tended to cover only a limited range of terms and conditions which could be precisely specified, in particular excluding detailed reference to the work process itself. The presumption – which naturally reflected the interests of employers, and which union leaders often proved unwilling or unable to contest openly – was that the implementation of district or national agreements would offer little scope for domestic bargaining, and that where the agreements were silent the authority of management would prevail.

From the outset this premise was unrealistic. The craft tradition had always counterposed the principle of worker control

F

to that of management prerogative. Some of the craft rules, as has been seen, were regarded as inescapable foundations of craft status and enforced unilaterally, by withdrawal of labour if necessary. But on many issues the opposition of two claims to authority, craft and managerial, led naturally to processes of compromise and accommodation.

> The 'inner life of the workshop' provided a basis from which bargaining at workshop level was bound to occur. 'Memorials', deputations, shop meetings; the weapons of ca' canny, refusal to teach apprentices or to set up tools for handymen; joint action by members of different sectional societies, and by unionists together with non-unionists – all these forms of workshop bargaining, organization and activity were practised in mid-Victorian times[1] (Hinton 1973 : 78).

From the late nineteenth century, in engineering and ship-building, this process of workplace 'negotiation of order' obtained an institutional link with the official union through the office of shop steward : a representative with the primary function of ensuring the observance of district union standards in the workplace, but who could readily extend this role into that of a domestic negotiator deriving legitimacy from his steward's role. The spread of payment by results, the attack on craft controls by the 'scientific management' movement, and the wholesale transformation in workshop practices during wartime, all stimulated the rapid growth of workplace collective bargaining and the rise in numbers and status of shop stewards.

Exposed to the danger of victimisation by employers, effective shop steward organisation required the existence of relatively full employment. The heavy unemployment which followed the First World War thus had a traumatic effect : as a contemporary observer commented, 'the unofficial shop stewards' movement is at ebb tide, because of the percentage of unemployed in the metal trades. The man at the gate determines the status of the man at the bench' (Gleason 1920 : 184). It was soon a wry joke

---

[1] 'Ca' canny' or 'go canny' was an early name for the go-slow or work-to-rule. 'Handymen' were machine operators without craft experience or training; the term 'semi-skilled' was not widely used before the First World War.

that the shop steward leaders of 1918 had become the un-employed leaders of the 1920s. Conversely the revival of employ-ment with rearmament and the Second World War, and the absence of subsequent recessions of inter-war dimensions, pro-vided the necessary basis in collective employee power to permit a sustained development of the negotiating role of shop stewards.

Recent decades have extended shop steward organisation and action far beyond their craft-based origins, and the process is a continuing one. Initially, stewards were predominantly concen-trated among manual workers in private manufacturing industry; but in recent years there has been a considerable expansion of staff representatives in white-collar unions, and union stewards in local government and the health service. A recent official survey estimated a total of approaching 300,000 stewards and representatives in the United Kingdom, and in addition some 60,000 non-union representatives carrying out some of the func-tions of shop stewards (Commission on Industrial Relations 1973).

The functions and influence of stewards vary considerably, to some extent in parallel with the strength of their historical roots. In much of private industry, with the advantage of a tight labour market, domestic bargaining has raised earnings far above the modest level of the nationally agreed basic rates (the modesty of these rates reinforced by the desire of many union negotiators to display 'moderation' and 'responsibility'). By piecework bargain-ing, control over the level and allocation of overtime, and the negotiation of straightforward increases, stewards have fuelled the motor of 'wage drive' (or 'drift') which has been a key feature of post-war industrial relations. At the same time, the organised erosion of managerial control tends to have developed furthest among private sector manual workers: the extensive involve-ment of stewards in decisions affecting employment, discipline and dismissal; the allocation of workers to jobs and jobs to workers; methods and speeds of production. But in other con-texts, the control which stewards can exercise is far weaker; indeed it would seem that one steward in six never negotiates about anything (McCarthy and Parker 1968 : 21).

These variations are in part a reflection of the objective situ-ation of particular groups of workers. Those carrying out key functions in an integrated production process have a powerful sanction at their disposal – particularly if the product is in some sense perishable, so that the employer cannot recoup strike losses. A tradition of solidarity reinforces such objectively-derived collective strength. Many white-collar groups, by contrast, lack such traditions and also lack ready access to effective sanctions.[2] For strong shop-floor control, bargaining power must be reinforced by bargaining awareness : a sense of grievance, and the consciousness that grievances can be remedied by collective action. Again, workforce tradition can be important, since the efficacy of collective sanctions is learned by experience (though also by example); 'the development of bargaining awareness and the exercise of power . . . reinforce one another' (Brown 1973 : 145).

An additional factor of considerable importance has already been discussed in a previous chapter : the nature of managerial policy and strategy. Flanders has argued that employers have responded to the growth of workshop organisation 'with no clearly defined, long-term, and – above all – consistent, objectives in mind. By making *ad hoc* concessions to pressure, when resistance proved too costly, they have fostered guerrilla warfare over wages and working conditions in the workplace and encouraged aggressive shop-floor tactics by rewarding them' (1970 : 196). Sophisticated and inventive workplace representatives have been able to exploit the discontinuities between the individual firm and its employers' association, play on the internal divisions and weaknesses of management, and generalise concessions won in positions of strength. Among white-collar unionists, the proximity of most employers to senior management permits closer employer control of bargaining; while in the public sector (and to some extent in non-federated private companies) the responsibility of the single employer for determining all aspects of terms and conditions of employment tends to result in greater uniformity and less scope for fragmented bargaining.

[2] *All* employees have sanctions at their disposal if discontented, which oblige managements to take some account of their wishes and interests; but those available to many white-collar groups tend to be of an individual rather than a collective nature (see, for example, Crozier 1964). But this is far from universally true. In Britain, the professions have long exercised a degree of job control far exceeding that wielded by most manual trade unions. Among white-collar trade unionists, the Draughtsmen have pioneered a range of imaginative and effective sanctions: 'Working without enthusiasm', telephone strikes, 'bog-ins', etc.

The extent of workplace bargaining in Britain is virtually unique. As has been seen, employers in many industries sought (by negotiations through external associations) to exclude trade unions from a role within the workplace. But their own internal mechanisms of control did not suffice to prevent workers applying collective sanctions and foremen making concessions. Hence the official collective agreements in these industries became little more than platforms from which stewards could win improved conditions and enhanced control. In the United States, the development of industrial relations was very different. Most large employers fought brutally and successfully, until the late 1930s, to prevent the development of strong trade unionism. When finally obliged to concede recognition, they immediately sought to minimise their loss of control by negotiating, at company and plant level, detailed and comprehensive formal agreements. The explicit aim was to leave little scope for bargaining at the point of production, and union officials often collaborated in preventing the development of independent control by shop stewards.[3] In many European countries, the level of union organisation is considerably less than in Britain, and the movement is further weakened by ideological divisions. In addition, systems of works committees or works councils, on which employees (who may be non-unionists) sit jointly with management, obstruct the development of an effective bargaining process within the plant.

The high degree of domestic negotiation in Britain is linked to a distinctive pattern of strike action. The typical post-war stoppage has been small, short and unofficial (though since the late 1960s there have of course been a number of major official disputes, while the average size and length of strikes in general has risen). The limited size and duration of disputes reflect the fact that they typically involve only sectional issues which can be resolved without great difficulty (indeed the main purpose of the strike may be as a demonstration serving to speed negotiations). They are normally unofficial because the official union has so limited a role in the bargaining process itself. In the motor industry, for example, it has been said that 'there is a state of what might be called "parallel unionism". For the car workers,

---

[3] This did not wholly prevent the development of unofficial and 'fractional' bargaining (Kuhn 1961); but it entailed that 'wildcat' strikes, in contrast to Britain, were typically *anti*-official.

in effect, the unions proper have become mainly a society for
demonstrating class and occupational solidarity by means of
membership . . . Unofficial strikes are not generally "strikes
against the unions" : they are simply conflicts to which the
unions' existence has become . . . largely irrelevant' (Turner *et
al.* 1967 : 222).

The conventional analysis and evaluation of this situation is
exemplified by the Donovan report and its notion of 'two
systems' of industrial relations, formal and informal. 'The informal system undermines the regulative effect of industry-wide
agreements'; it must be condemned because of 'the tendency of
extreme decentralisation and self-government to degenerate into
indecision and anarchy; the propensity to breed inefficiency; and
the reluctance to change' (1968 : 36, 33). Similarly, Flanders has
written of 'this growing anarchy in workplace relations . . . to
be seen : in unofficial strikes and earnings drift; in under-utilisation of labour and resistance to change; . . . in a general decline
in industrial discipline; . . . and in a weakening of control by
trade unions and employers' associations over their members . . .
All the unfortunate consequences of drift in workplace relations
are manifestations of a weakening of control by managements'
(1970 : 196–7). At a different analytical level, the growth of
shop-floor action has been interpreted as a breakdown of the
normative agreement and regulation which is viewed as essential
for stable social relations : a process tending to generate 'cumulative disorder' (Fox and Flanders 1969).

This orthodox interpretation may be criticised both in terms
of its repressive implications and its analytical inadequacy. The
emotive language of 'anarchy and disorder' derives from an un-
compromisingly *managerial* perspective. 'Order', Goldthorpe
comments, 'looks rather different, depending as it were on which
end of it one happens to be' (1972 : 212). 'Unofficial strikes and
earnings drift' reflect the use of workers' power to improve their
situation; 'under-utilisation of labour and resistance to change'
represent self-defence against the priorities of capitalist 'efficiency',
often highly damaging in their impact on employees; 'indiscipline' is the pejorative term for the efforts by workers to be
treated as free human beings. As Eldridge suggests, 'what is
described . . . as a loss of integration could from another perspective be analysed in terms of encroaching control – a response to

inequalities no longer regarded and accepted as legitimate' (1973 : 165). In practice, the existing forms of material inequality and of capitalist control constitute the taken-for-granted framework for conventional industrial relations analysis. Their perpetuation and stabilisation are presupposed in the various proposals for 'reconstruction of normative order' in industry. More specifically, the prescriptions for the reconstruction of control by managements and (in so far as they accept a quasimanagerial role) trade union leaders necessarily assume that the natural condition of the ordinary employee and union member is one of subjection, subordination and passivity.[4]

Not only do conventional analysts uncritically adopt the employer's problems as their own; in interpreting workplace power solely as an 'anarchic' erosion of institutional control they misrepresent the *continuous* role of the rank and file in the processes of industrial relations. For the workplace 'negotiation of order' is both logically and historically prior to the formal institutional relationship between trade unions and employers. Trade unionism is itself constituted out of the 'informal' solidarities, pressures and controls of the workplace. Contemporary shop steward organisations and 'unofficial' movements, like the simple (and often ephemeral) trade societies of the eighteenth and early nineteenth centuries, share an organic relationship with these processes of spontaneous solidarity : 'there is the same basis in the workplace group, which may have informal "friendly" functions as well as trade ones' (Turner 1962 : 85). In modern British industry, as in the Victorian workshop, there is rarely a precise borderline between collective bargaining and 'custom and practice'.

Only against this background can the 'formal system' of industrial relations be adequately evaluated. The processes involved in the formalisation and institutionalisation of collective bargaining have already been discussed in previous chapters : the main initiative was in most industries *managerial*, reflecting the goal of achieving regularity and predictability in labour relations. In particular by raising the level of collective bargaining, defining the subjects of negotiation, and instituting elaborate and protracted procedures 'for the avoidance of disputes', it was inten-

[4] This approach – and in particular the misapplication of the theories of 'normlessness' developed by the sociologist Durkheim – is sharply criticised by Goldthorpe 1974.

ded that management control of labour would be relieved of direct workplace pressures and constraints. The response of trade union representatives, as has been seen, was often ambivalent. They were often conscious of the threat involved in such employer strategies, and at times resisted fiercely. Yet they were also conscious of a common interest with employers in establishing an 'industrial legality', in creating order and regularity : partly because union security seemed dependent on some formal accommodation with the power of capital; partly because they had more faith in employer goodwill than membership combativity as a source of improvements in employment conditions; partly because their own control was consolidated by the new machinery. 'By slow, almost imperceptible degrees, trade union officialdom has become a profession, and its members a social caste. A distinct interest, growing curiously apart from the general interest of the rank and file, and drifting more and more widely away from democratic sentiment and practice, has evolved.'[5] Victims as much as agents of the formalisation of national bargaining, union officials became increasingly detached from the grassroots origins of their own organisations.

It is thus altogether misleading to dismiss as 'anarchy' the inroads made by workers into managerial control (and into that of the union hierarchy). What is involved, rather, is the reassertion, far beyond their original craft context, of prior traditions of autonomous worker control. The real meaning of the 'challenge from below' is a renewed emphasis, in favourable economic conditions, on the grassroots foundations of the institutionalised system of industrial relations. More crucially, it is the necessary basis for the restoration of many of those elements of the workplace power balance smothered by formal procedural arrangements. In the context of the 'rationalisation' of management in modern capitalism, the increasing pace of technical and organisational change, the economic pressures for more intensive exploitation of labour, this process is of necessity deeply conflictual. (For this reason, workers' control today has radically new implications, impinging on the whole social and economic structure as well as the detailed operations of the individual enter-

---

[5] The writer, Frank Rose, was himself an official of the Engineers at the turn of the century. From the pamphlet *Stop the Strike* (1909), quoted in Hinton 1973 : 82–3.

prise; whereas the traditional processes of unilateral worker control over aspects of the work process could often coexist relatively smoothly with the overall strategic priorities of the employer.) Within contemporary capitalism, the exercise of job control by workers is inherently oppositional, and involves a continuous process of struggle. Formal bargaining and disputes procedures, by contrast, disarm and demobilise trade union members : imposing a 'peace obligation' which leaves management the prerogative of initiative. *Only* by a readiness to act 'unofficially' and 'unconstitutionally' can workers maintain a balance of power at all favourable to their own interests, and hence sustain an effective measure of job control.[6]

Workshop organisation necessarily impinges on the internal power relations within trade unionism, for it represents a source of control which is partially but not wholly independent. The development of the shop steward role involved a largely spontaneous process in which workers sought to overcome problems of control at work which the official union machinery proved unable to resolve (particularly as centralisation of bargaining and bureaucratisation of administration proceeded). The *office* of shop steward, as has been seen, was traditional in many unions; but his rights and duties were limited. The elaboration of *bargaining* functions was almost entirely unofficial (though union leaders were obviously aware of the process, and did not necessarily oppose it); only in recent years have the rulebooks of most trade unions even mentioned the steward's role as a negotiator. In relation to managements, a similar situation has applied : some reference to shop stewards has been contained in procedure agreements, but their functions have been narrowly defined. The rights acquired in strongly organised workplaces – mobility within the factory, office or depot without loss of pay; ready access to senior management; the recognition of convenors or senior stewards; facilities for carrying out union activities; payment for time spent on union business; powers of veto over certain managerial decisions – have normally been won autonomously, rarely with the involvement of the outside union. In most cases such rights have been imposed on or tolerated by lower-level supervision as part of the day-to-day negotiation of

[6] This conclusion is vividly demonstrated in the study of American collective bargaining by Herding (1972).

order; senior management may not admit or even realise the powers acquired by the steward organisation in their firms. Until very recently, scarcely any employer was ready to recognise formally the rights in practice accorded to shop-floor representatives.

The spontaneous and autonomous development of workplace organisation relates closely to the character of its *internal* control relations. The 'primitive democracy' typical of early trade unionism remains structurally possible at this level. Sykes, discussing workshop unionism in printing (the 'chapel') emphasises 'the *group-centred* character of its social structure' (1967 : 157). To differing degrees, the same feature applies in any workplace situation : the members are involved in day-to-day interaction, and their relationship with the steward is far more intimate than with the external union official. Hence, as Lane argues,

> The shop steward was not the sort of leader typical of systems of "representative democracy" as manifested in parliaments. He did not, once elected, pack his bags and move off to carry out his representational duties in an institution alien to the experiences of his constituents. Neither was his constituency so large that he could remain personally anonymous to the overwhelming majority of his electors (the average constituency was of the order of sixty people). The steward spent the bulk of his time at work alongside those who had elected him, although some of his constituents were more remote than others since his electorate usually straddled several work groups rather than being based on one. Still, he was highly visible, subject to the same experiences at work as his comrades, and subject to the same group pressures. He would be watched in his dealings with the foreman or supervisor. Not a few stewards took the precaution of having a fellow worker with them when it was necessary to "go upstairs" (1974 : 198).

The shop steward 'machine' is far more rudimentary than the formal organisation of the trade union (though, as suggested below, its role is still important); it provides far less of an institutional basis for sanctions against rank-and-file members. Thus the dilemma of 'power over' as against 'power for' is less radical than in the case of higher levels of trade unionism : the steward's power is largely dependent on the *continuing* support of his members. Shop-floor meetings provide a forum within which all or most members can participate; criticisms can be voiced and explanations demanded, leading in some cases to the recall or resignation of a steward who has lost the confidence of his fellow workers. Through less formal pressures and contacts, upwards control can also be sustained. This does not mean that every steward is at the mercy of the fleeting whim of his members : it is possible to rely on their knowledge of his or her bargaining skills and experience, loyalty won through past achievements, or simply the reluctance of anybody else to take the job. Nevertheless, it is virtually impossible to develop a secure position as a steward in the absence of active support; indeed, any steward faced with serious discontent on his section will be likely to stand down.[7]

While it is essential to stress the autonomous basis of workplace organisation, stemming from workers' immediate collective solidarity, it would be wrong to treat this in isolation from the formal trade union structure. For shop stewards, as the key link between trade unionism and the lay membership, are involved in a two-way relationship of control and dependence with the district official(s) and committee and, more remotely, with the national leadership.

From the outside union the workplace organisation derives a range of specific services and also participation in supportive social networks. Through the various levels of committees and conferences, rank-and-file members can pool information and experiences and in some cases co-ordinate action.[8] Union research and legal departments provide information of use in domestic negotiation and handle industrial injury compensation cases. Full-time officials can provide bargaining assistance on the basis of experience, contacts, or simply the ability as an outsider to get workplace representatives 'off the hook'. More intangibly, the

[7] See Beynon 1973: 197–8. A substantial turnover of stewards does indeed occur: in the two largest unions, for example, two-thirds of all stewards have held office for less than five years.

[8] In general, the members of trade unions' formal representative bodies are elected from the branch rather than the workplace (though in the AUEW, shop stewards are directly represented on District Committees). But stewards normally participate far more actively than other members.

association between shop stewards and 'the union' is often a source of legitimacy in the eyes of membership and management alike: a symbolic prop for power and status which in fact, as has been argued, derive essentially from the members themselves. Moreover, in circumstances when the routine of plant relationships is disrupted, this power itself may require external supplement. In a major dispute, success may depend on support from outside the plant in terms of financial aid, respect for picket lines, or blacking. (External aid is particularly crucial in conflicts over large-scale redundancy or closure, when the workplace organisation alone is in an unusually weak position.) Effective mobilisation of outside support normally requires some organisation through unofficial channels; but it is usually easier to achieve when a stoppage has official union support. Official backing also brings union dispute pay, and may have an important effect in strengthening workers' morale.[9] The official leadership, moreover, can wield significant influence on the basis of reciprocal relationships with representatives of government and employers' organisations; in a serious dispute its intervention (which in some form is eventually almost inevitable), either in support of the workers' demands or to impose an unsatisfactory 'compromise', can be crucial. Since any workplace organisation may at some time find itself in a vulnerable situation, there is a strong incentive to maintain good relations with the external representatives of the union.

Conversely, union officials are dependent on their shop stewards. The latter often recruit members, ensure that their union contributions are in order, in some cases collect subscriptions. They are the main source of information about union activities and decisions for most members (two-thirds of whom never attend branch meetings); even when union leaders seek to communicate with the membership at large through journals and circulars, these are in many cases distributed by the stewards. At the same time, the upwards flow of information depends principally on the stewards. In servicing the membership, dealing with routine (and indeed at times serious) problems, griev-

[9] The importance of dispute pay is often limited; the amount is usually small, and strikers' families have a similar amount deducted from any social security benefit received. The main source of strike finance is in fact workers' own savings.

ances and disputes, trade unions could not function without workplace organisation. (The average first-line full-time official is responsible for a hundred plants, seven to eight thousand members and almost two hundred stewards.) The individual union organiser who enjoys good relations with his stewards can rely on adequate and accurate information, sensitivity to his own problems, and (if he is dependent on re-election) support in 'organising' the vote. Conversely, stewards who are at odds with him can starve him of information, overwhelm him with disputes, and undermine his reputation in the eyes of senior officials.

Thus a relationship of interdependence is the norm. The balance of control and dependence reflects a variety of influences. The degree of autonomy of the workplace organisation is likely to reflect the character of the membership, its self-confidence (reflecting in part past achievements or defeats), bargaining traditions, and the extent to which stewards have won the loyalty of those they represent. The relationship between stewards and full-time officials is affected by the experience and self-assertiveness of each : convenors in large establishments may be effectively full-time negotiators in their own right, perhaps exceeding the local officials in experience, and may successfully assert their autonomy in normal plant industrial relations. National union rules and policies, and the content of national agreements, may also exert some influence by defining the issues appropriate for domestic negotiation and (possibly) prescribing a role for district officials or committees to authorise plant agreements (though such formal requirements can to some extent be evaded in practice). The role of *management*, as suggested in an earlier chapter, can also be crucial : by accident or design it can establish the status of stewards or full-time officials, and enhance or diminish the reputation of particular negotiators.[10]

As in the case of management-worker relations, those between shop stewards and the representatives of the official trade union normally involve a process of 'negotiation of order'. Reciprocal expectations, obligations and understandings develop, and in normal circumstances a stable working relationship (involving the

[10] For further discussion of this relationship see Boraston *et al.* 1975; Hyman and Fryer 1975; and, for a detailed analysis of a single union, Fryer *et al.* 1974.

acceptance of areas of autonomy) is created. Yet on occasion the 'negotiated order' can be disrupted and the power balance inherent in the relationship generate overt conflict. On occasion this may reflect an official trade union initiative which challenges established workplace authority and action. In the docks, for example, the central control of the TGWU was traditionally weak but sectional militancy was widespread, particularly on piecework issues. The report of the Devlin Committee (1965) urged a radical transformation of industrial relations, including the centralisation of management, 'strong and effective trade union leadership', 'greater mobility of labour', 'revision of the wage structure', 'acceptance of firmer discipline', and 'the review of manning scales to take into account increasing mechanisation and changing methods'; and the TGWU accepted changes which followed many of these recommendations. Many rank-and-file activists saw the new system as an attack on customary employee controls over the work process and the earnings opportunities of some dockers; and also feared (correctly) that the greater security of day-to-day employment provided by 'decasualisation' would be offset by large-scale redundancy in the longer term. The consequence in 1967 was a series of bitter disputes, most notably in Liverpool and London, directed in part explicitly against the union leadership.

Overt conflict may also be provoked by intervention by union leaders to end a stoppage involving a section of their membership. In engineering and many other industries, as has been seen, the structure of autonomous domestic bargaining has encouraged the detachment of the official leadership from most disputes. But an obstinate and protracted stoppage may affect the interests of other sections of membership, or indeed lead to powerful pressure from top management or the state; or, if official support is given to the strike, the cost of its continuation may be considered too great. In such circumstances, union leaders have a strong incentive to engineer a settlement, perhaps on terms which the members themselves consider a 'sell-out'. A glaring example was the Ford strike of 1971: after nine weeks the top leaders of the TGWU and AEU (who were not members of the official negotiating body) secretly agreed terms with top management, which were pushed through in a company-sponsored ballot. The result was division and demoralisation: effective organisation at the point of production was undermined (Mathews 1972; Beynon 1973).

The potential for intra-union conflict is increased where only limited scope exists for workplace bargaining. In such industries as engineering, the decentralisation of negotiations is a safety-valve for national negotiators : sections of membership who are dissatisfied with the size of national pay settlements, or develop local grievances, can win improvements for themselves. When most bargaining is centralised, such discontents can have an explosive effect in internal union relations. Two large disputes in early 1970 exemplify this point. In Leeds, workers walked out of most of the major clothing factories in protest against a national agreement, and formed a rank-and-file strike committee. Their objection was to a national agreement which fell far short of the policy laid down by the union conference, and in particular failed to provide equal increases for men and women; their anger was directed against union officials as much as employers. Significant improvements in the agreement were eventually won. In St Helens, a small stoppage over an error in workers' pay packets escalated into a strike of over 10,000 employees at the Pilkington glass works. A confrontation rapidly developed between the strike committee and the GMWU, which ordered a return to work; the union negotiated an increase of £3, which for several weeks the strikers refused to accept. Large numbers of workers tore up their GMWU cards, and an attempt (eventually unsuccessful) was made to form a breakaway union.

Such conflicts have been particularly common in recent years in the public sector, where the scope for domestic bargaining – especially over pay – is usually very restricted. The potential for conflict has been accentuated in an era of government pay restraint, often imposed rigidly by the government on its own employees while earnings in private industry have risen faster (or have appeared to do so). This explains a significant trend of the late 1960s and early 1970s : the growth of rank-and-file organis-ation and action *directly concerned with pressure on the official trade union*. A common sequence (exhibited among such groups as local authority manual workers, hospital ancillary staff, post-men, schoolteachers and civil servants) has been the expression of growing dissatisfaction at the size of national settlements, leading perhaps to unofficial protest strikes; followed by more ambitious demands in subsequent national negotiations, culminating in official strike action – at times, for the first occasion in the union's history. This growing combativity has in part reflected the election of increasing numbers of militantly-inclined conference delegates and executive members; in part the desperate efforts of normally cautious leaders, afraid of losing control to unofficial activists, to *sponsor* and hence contain membership militancy.

The prospects for such conflict are increased by the trend towards bargaining centralisation signalled by the Donovan Report. For most of the post-war period, coalmining was the most strike-prone industry in Britain (at one stage it accounted for *three-quarters* of all recorded stoppages); but until 1972 not one dispute was official. Almost all involved sectional grievances concerning piecework prices or else working conditions which adversely affected piecework earnings. But the power-loading agreement of 1966 eliminated piecework, and hence the scope for fragmented improvements in earnings. This had two consequences : earnings subsequently rose more slowly than in other industries; and militancy was directed towards the national leadership. In 1969 and 1970, major strikes took place in protest against national settlements; in 1972 and 1974 the NUM pursued ambitious pay demands with official strike action. In the docks, the post-Devlin restrictions on sectional pay bargaining provided an impetus to the development of strong rank-and-file organisation, which in turn helped stimulate the official national strikes in 1970 and 1972. In many manufacturing plants, most notably in the car industry, the trend towards centralisation of bargaining at company level and the reinforcement of management control over pay and effort have been reflected in a change in the pattern of strikes : the focus of disputes has widened, larger numbers are involved, and settlement takes far longer.

Changes in bargaining structure thus exert a powerful influence on the patterns of industrial conflict; and in particular, since centralisation of negotiation increases the interdependence of workplace and external union organisations, conflict over control *within* trade unionism is intensified. (Historically, a similar process occurred with the development of national bargaining at the turn of the century. Reform movements and vigilance committees became active in many unions, often mounting vigorous

challenges to the national leadership.) These trends in turn derive
from the structural predicament of British capitalism, discussed
in an earlier chapter. Growing internal and external contradictions necessitate managerial attempts to force back the frontier
of control, to impose stricter limits on both labour costs and
labour utilisation. All this at a time, moreover, when the character of workers' demands provides some evidence of a growing
concern with the *quality* of working life, not merely the immediate issues of wages and workload. Hence the antagonism
between labour and capital becomes increasingly overt; and the
role of trade unionism, as the mediator between the two, increasingly unstable. The control conflicts within trade unions stem
from and also parallel the underlying conflict in work relations.

TABLE 2  British Strike Statistics 1945–74 (annual averages)*

|  | Number of stoppages | Workers involved (000) | Striker days (000) | Average numbers involved | Average duration (days) |
|---|---|---|---|---|---|
| 1945–54 | 1791 | 545 | 2073 | 320 | 3·8 |
| 1955–64 | 2521 | 1116 | 3889 | 423 | 3·5 |
| 1965–68 | 2196 | 1461 | 3207 | 626 | 2·1 |
| 1969 | 3116 | 1654 | 6925 | 531 | 4·2 |
| 1970 | 3906 | 1793 | 10908 | 460 | 6·1 |
| 1971 | 2223 | 1173 | 13558 | 528 | 11·6 |
| 1972 | 2497 | 1722 | 23909 | 690 | 13·9 |
| 1973 | 2873 | 1513 | 7197 | 551 | 4·7 |
| 1974 | 2882 | 1601 | 14740 | 555 | 9·2 |

* Averages can be misleading: a single stoppage, like the miners'strike
of 1972, can dominate a whole year's statistics. Nevertheless, the table
gives a fair impression of recent trends. For a discussion of some of the
problems of official strike statistics see Hyman 1972.

Yet at the same time, pressures to *contain* these conflicts must
be recognised. Institutionalising processes operate at the level of
workplace unionism itself. As the Donovan Commission argued,
'it is often wide of the mark to describe shop stewards as
"trouble-makers". Trouble is thrust upon them . . . Quite commonly they are supporters of order exercising a restraining influence on their members in conditions which promote disorder'
(1968 : 28–9). As the Commission's own research indicated, 'for
the most part the steward is viewed by others, and views himself,

as an accepted, reasonable and even moderating influence; more of a lubricant than an irritant' (McCarthy and Parker 1968 : 56). This reflects the fact that concern with stable bargaining relations affects not merely full-time officials, but impinges on *all* trade union representatives. Shop stewards, indeed, must be particularly conscious that they function against the constant background of employer power. A 'major pressure is the stewards' very real . . . dependence on the management itself. In a sense, the leading stewards are performing a managerial function, of grievance settlement, welfare arrangement and human adjustment, and the steward system's acceptance by managements (and thus, in turn, the facility with which the stewards themselves can satisfy their members' demands and needs) has developed partly because of the increasing effectiveness – and certainly economy – with which this role is fulfilled' (Turner *et al.* 1967 : 214). Both to sustain management's goodwill, and to retain their own sanity (or at least keep their job manageable), stewards have an inevitable interest in 'orderly' industrial relations.

As with the official union, such pressures can be reinforced by the bureaucratisation of workplace organisation. In establishments of any size, a joint shop stewards' committee operates; and in multi-union plants, its co-ordinating functions are of great importance. But within the largest workplace organisations, a distinct hierarchy exists : ordinary stewards, an executive or negotiating committee, and convenors or senior stewards who are often permitted by management to devote their whole time to union functions. For the ordinary steward, the workplace leadership may be far from readily accessible, while the stewards' 'machine' comes to represent an agency of external power. Because of their extensive networks of information, negotiating expertise and influence with management, leading stewards often have at their disposal rewards and sanctions which can be used to discipline and control unruly sections and stewards. As a recent study of the car industry concludes,

In this respect the shop stewards' organization has become the real union – and one with an almost similar degree of elaboration and complexity. And because this organization is now the main agency for the bargaining of actual working conditions – with what amounts to its own full-time negotiators – it has assumed, in relation to managements on the one hand and the rank-and-file of operatives on the other, many of the characteristics that the official unions once displayed under the earlier development of national or industry-wide collective bargaining. The senior stewards, like the full-time union officials before them, are forced to assume something of the role of buffer between the employer and the operatives (Turner *et al.* 1967 : 222).

The restraining role often exercised by the workplace union organisation is paradoxical, for shop stewards (like full-time officials, who are themselves often former stewards) commonly possess more advanced political attitudes than most of their members. In many cases, it is for this very reason that they do the job (which may well be thankless and unrewarding). One reason for their willingness to exert moderating influence is the fact that rank-and-file militancy is so often sectional in inspiration, and centres around narrow material considerations : a 'scramble in the ash heaps of industrialism for piecework and bonuses', as a revolutionary steward of the 1914–18 war described it.[11] A similar perspective underlies the comment of the union leader largely responsible for the abolition of piecework in coalmining : 'the more the wage bargaining system is fragmented, the more numerous the disparities and differentials and the more dominant is the individual and sectional approach to wage problems' (Paynter 1972 : 158). Many stewards would agree : individual and sectional struggles over pay can be corrosive of solidarity, particularly if the issue is framed in terms of differentials as against other groups, and causes lay-offs and resentment. Unity and co-ordination of action, by contrast, tend to be seen as the means of concentrating workers' strength, which should in turn be applied judiciously and not squandered in piecemeal disputes. Moreover, 'in an organized shop individual acts of defiance or "laziness" can threaten the unity and organization achieved by the mass in collective action' (Beynon 1973 : 140).

Yet the irony is that in the (often principled) pursuit of stability, predictability and consistency, workplace unionism

[11] Jack Murphy, quoted in Hinton 1973 : 93.

tends to apply discipline and control of which *management* is the prime beneficiary. Stability, predictability and consistency in the labour force are prerequisites of effective control of production, yet in the face of independent worker power are not *directly* enforceable by management. Hence the shop steward's predicament, neatly captured by Lane :

> while the balance of forces tended to push the stewards in the direction of what management and media defined as "moderation", the typical relationship was one of mutual detachment; a detachment leavened by a joking relationship which provided a brittle veneer of cordiality, but which fooled neither party. The underlying conflicts were too profound to allow widespread practices of self-deception. Each typically regarded the other as more or less fixed features of the landscape. They may or may not have regarded this as regrettable, but they did see it as a fact of life as far as their daily dealings were concerned. The ploys and strategies that were variously set to work were therefore devoted to managing the *status quo* on the most advantageous terms – not to overthrowing it.
>
> This left the shop steward, no matter how tactically brilliant, in an inherently weaker position because it was management that provided the jobs. Labour power was nothing without the instruments to use it – and it was management that owned the instruments and decided whether or not they were to be put to work. All the wiles in the world were powerless in the face of lay-offs or redundancies (1974 : 213–4).

This ultimate impotence stems from the fact that even the most coordinated workplace organisation merely reconstitutes sectionalism at a higher level. The factory, mine, yard or office is the framework of the relationship with the employer : *his* property, *his* concentrated power, *his* underlying authority exists behind every negotiation. Not even politically conscious stewards can escape the implications of their captivity within the *employer's* chosen battleground. 'While they may well agree with the desirability for fundamental political changes they cannot see how to transform this agreement into practical activity. Their equipment is their industrial expertise – the source of their strength and the chink in their armour. Their lives are tied up in the perpetual negotiations with the superintendents of capital on the factory floor. They are all too rarely able to stick their heads above the waters of bargaining with the foreman and the manager . . .' (Beynon 1973 : 318).

There are indeed attempts to break out of this 'factory class-consciousness', which 'understands class relationships in terms of their direct manifestation in conflict between the bosses and the workers within the factory' (Beynon 1973 : 98). Historically, the formation of 'open unionism', and the subsequent ideologies of amalgamation movements and industrial unionism, may be seen as pressures towards broader unity. Trades Councils have traditionally provided a basis for transcending divisions of occupation and workplace at local level; though they have no significant industrial functions, and being composed of delegates from union branches rather than from workshops their links with the rank and file are tenuous. The most extensive of recent innovations is the shop stewards' combine committee, uniting representatives from the various establishments of multi-plant companies. They first became prominent in the motor industry in the 1950s, often being promoted by political activists, and were normally regarded with hostility by union leaderships as a challenge to their own authority. But today, many receive some form of recognition from both union officials and managements. Their purposes vary considerably : from the simple exchange of information to the coordination of mutual support, the formulation of common objectives, and even the joint conduct of negotiations. The actual achievements of combine committees have tended to be fairly modest : ambitious objectives falling victim to sectional tendencies. At times, workplace leaders may be jealous of their own negotiating autonomy, and perhaps participate in combine organisation only as a symbolic gesture to appease political militants in the factory. On other occasions, leading stewards may genuinely desire united action across the combine, but be frustrated by the parochialism of their own members. As Lane suggests, 'as soon as stewards started to reach beyond their base in the workplace they ran the risk of isolation from it – and that could prove fatal' (1974 : 221).

The workplace leader, involved almost continuously in active trade union work, forced by the nature of his position to see immediate issues within a somewhat broader framework which may well accord with his political sympathies, can more readily see the need for the extension of solidarity outside the plant than can the typical employee, immersed in the narrow routines of his everyday work experience. The easy option is to express formal commitments to common action among the minority of enthusiasts in branch or steward meetings, but to fail to fight for this commitment among the members, to shrink from the problems of the constant effort to overcome their natural parochialism. But as Beynon demonstrates, 'if the leadership becomes *isolated* from the masses, its autonomy degenerates into empty talk' (1973 : 178). When commitments must be realised in action, lack of support disarms the shop steward leadership in the face of likely opposition from management *and* the trade union hierarchy.

A central function of some combine committees is less to co-ordinate and facilitate common action at plant level than to exert pressure on *official* union negotiators. This was largely the case with the Ford combine in the 1960s : workers were paid on time rates, negotiated nationally by a committees of full-time officials. This type of organisation closely parallels the rank-and-file movements which have grown up in recent years in a large number of unions and industries in which centralised negotiations are of major importance. As was suggested previously, such movements have achieved considerable success in pressing the official union leaders to adopt more militant demands and action. Yet the paradox of such 'ginger groups' is that success often spells integration. The Ford shop steward leaders won membership of the national negotiating committee; the reform movement in the National Union of Seamen captured leadership positions from a conservative oligarchy entrenched for over half a century; in many public sector unions, rank-and-file groups have won key positions on executive committees. Yet the consequence is that former critics of the previous leadership find themselves subject to the same pressures towards restraint and compromise, and committed to the outcome. A rank-and-file movement with *genuine* links with the mass of membership (rather than with a minority of activists alone) may serve as a continuing means of counter-pressure on the new leadership; nevertheless, the contradictory positions of those directly responsible for what is done in the name of the union, and those sufficiently detached to be able to criticise and if necessary oppose, cannot be adequately transcended.

This problem reflects the more general contradiction inherent in trade union action and trade union consciousness. The priorities and institutions of capitalism, as has already been argued in detail, provide the impetus for workers to organise collectively yet at the same time set the framework of collective action. Even at the national level, the logic of trade unionism precludes serious challenge to the inequalities of power and property on which wage-labour and capital are founded. At the level of rank-and-file consciousness and action, the structure of ownership and control of industry and the dominating role of profit in economic life are even more remote as issues. The strategies of rank-and-file action, however militant, revolve around immediate issues of wages and conditions or (usually less frequently) struggles over immediate job control. The structural location of these strategies is not built into workers' normal perception of their industrial problems and grievances : yet this necessarily limits what can be achieved through collective action, either within or outside official union channels.

The two main reasons for this limitation have been discussed in previous chapters. One is the process of institutionalisation, the impact of the power of capital on the formulation and execution of the collective policies of labour. The other is the ideological hegemony of capital which shapes workers' perceptions of themselves and of their world. The capitalist structure of industry is treated as natural and inevitable; the abstract rights of property and of management are not seriously challenged; the obligation to perform a 'fair day's work' is enshrined in everyday maxims; the rationale of men's subordination to capital is not dismissed as an absurdity.

Yet the hegemony of bourgeois ideology is not absolute. A crucial feature of the convential ideological assumptions regarding industry and industrial relations is their *generality*; yet because they are general and abstract they must be interpreted before they constitute a guide to specific action. A worker may accept the duty to perform a fair day's work, but deny that a particular workload is fair; he may endorse management's right to manage, but challenge a particular instruction; he may assert the sanctity of property, but not when this conflicts with his own assertion of the right to work. This is a natural consequence of the fact that the social values so powerfully and extensively inculcated conflict with workers' obvious interests; the typical response 'is not to reject these values, and thus create an entirely different normative system, but to negotiate or modify them in the light of their own existential conditions' (Parkin 1971 : 92). It is also significant that the dominant ideology is not monolithic : it contains internal contradictions. The prevailing ideology in industrial relations, as Fox has argued, does not 'take the form of a consistent and related body of ideas. Rather does it consist of a ragbag of assorted notions fashioned to suit varying exigencies, sometimes quite incompatible with each other' (1971 : 125). Moreover, ideological notions deemed appropriate in some areas of social life contradict those which prevail in industrial relations : ideas of freedom and humanity, for example, if applied literally in the world of work, would prove highly subversive. The consequence is that *specific actions* disruptive of order and stability in labour relations can normally be legitimised by workers from among the set of beliefs and values which *in general* reflect hostile class interests.

This helps explain the paradoxical character of industrial relations in Britain (and indeed in many other countries) in the last decade. Workplace organisation and action have come to perform an increasingly important role in a growing number of industries; and their *cumulative* effect has been exceedingly corrosive of capitalist order in industry. Workplace controls have undermined managements' power to utilise labour at will as a passive resource; competitive wage bargaining has increased labour costs in a period when their stabilisation (and indeed reduction) has been urgently required; shop-floor militancy has disrupted production schedules and forced an array of unplanned concessions by employers. Thus the challenge from below has been identified by employers, politicians and academics alike as the central 'problem' of current industrial relations. Yet the economic, and to some extent political and social, instability resulting from rank-and-file organisation and action is *intended* by no more than an insignificant fraction of trade unionists. For the vast majority, their piecemeal actions are legitimate within the terms of the political economy of capital; no systematic challenge is envisaged. Hence the profound contradiction inherent in current militancy : objectives are implicit in workers' collective actions (since they cannot prove successful *within* this political economy) which are not explicitly articulated and may well be disavowed. Thus, for example, trade unionists are often at pains to deny the manifest political significance of struggles in which they confront the power of the state. This lack of conscious appreciation of the meanings of their own action is an obvious source of weakness and vulnerability; workers are ill prepared to meet the growing attempt by employers and governments (and to some extent trade union leaderships) to reassert control. Hence the often confused and fragmented response to such developments as productivity bargaining, measured daywork, procedural 'reform' and incomes policy.

At the same time it is important to recognise that not only is capitalist ideology unspecific and contradictory; its hold on the working class is also *uneven*. The 'sub-culture' of the working class contains many elements which oppose the 'official' norms of society. The conventional dichotomy between 'them' and 'us' implies some conception of common class interests hostile to those in positions of control; protestations by the rich and powerful to be concerned solely with the 'national interest' are met with cynicism; the need to act collectively, if necessary by 'deviant' means, in order to survive in a hostile society, is taken for granted. Attitude surveys designed to show workers' lack of radicalism, framed in a manner which invites the conventional responses of the prevailing societal value-system, cannot exclude evidence of such 'deviant' values. Many of the findings 'show the presence, among the bulk of the working class, of a "counter-ideology" critical of the present social order. It is a "quasi-ideology", an ideology at half-cock – not a full-blown radical (let alone revolutionary) ideology – because its elements are contradictory . . .; and because, partly for that reason, its political potential is uncertain, ambivalent and to a considerable extent latent. Social criticism co-exists with attitudes that involve a practical, everyday acceptance of established institutions' (Westergaard 1970 : 123–4).

Among sections of the working class, however, oppositional ideology is far more fully and coherently developed. There is awareness that their grievances and deprivations form a totality, that they are firmly rooted in the basic structure of society, and that the scope for piecemeal and fragmented improvement is therefore limited. But this realisation does not, as with many workers, cause a fatalistic acceptance of their condition : there is a belief in the possibility of an alternative social order. In times of social stability, only a small minority of workers normally possess such an ideology in any articulated form. Yet its perspectives are preserved and sustained by political groups and organisations which deliberately seek their membership from among workers with the most advanced social consciousness; and which enrich Marxist doctrines with lessons drawn from workers' current struggles, victories and defeats – serving, as Lenin put it, as the repository of the historical consciousness of the class. Lenin's conception of the party involved an organisation of conscious and committed revolutionaries, differentiated from workers' mass organisations (the trade unions), seeking to develop an integrated challenge to the *totality* of forms of capitalist domination (economic, political, social, cultural), but at the same time seeking to intervene directly in workers' industrial struggles. For over half a century, Marxists have played an important role in the formation and activity of shop steward organisation, workers' committees, and rank-and-file movements. During the First World War, in Britain, revolutionaries had a leading role in the Shop Stewards' and Workers' Committee Movement, which linked workplace militants at local and national level. In the 1920s, the newly-formed Communist Party sponsored the Minority Movement to frame common demands and co-ordinate action among the rank-and-file organisations in different unions and industries.[12] More recently, members of various left-wing groups (notably the International Socialists) have helped initiate the spread of coordinated rank-and-file action.

In periods of unrest and instability, the presence in positions

[12] For a critical discussion of the experience of the Minority Movement see Hinton and Hyman 1975. In its early years the Communist Party was an explicitly revolutionary organisation, led by industrial militants who had won a considerable reputation in the trade union struggles before 1920. Under the influence of Stalin the emphasis on social revolution was abandoned, and the Party was turned into a left-wing version of Labour, equally committed to parliamentary methods. Some of its rank-and-file activists, however, retain elements of the original beliefs and commitments.

of influence of workers with a developed oppositional ideology can be of immense significance. When engaged in collective struggle, workers are most susceptible to the appeal of new world-views; the 'deviant' elements in working-class attitudes are thrust to the fore, while the conventional assumptions of 'official' society momentarily lose their hold.[13] As the development of capital itself forces more frequent industrial struggles, so the opportunities for a heightening of consciousness are multiplied. Moreover, the possibilities of an escalation of consciousness are increased by the growing involvement in disputes of sections without strong traditions of institutionalised industrial relations : women, black workers, and youth (whose 'indiscipline' has been the subject of much recent comment). Such groups provide a leavening in current industrial conflict, assisting the elaboration of new types of demand and new forms of action. It is important also to recognise the significance of a wide range of challenges, outside the industrial sphere, to established values and the established order. The colonial revolution, feminism, movements for political decentralisation, the environmentalist campaign, student activism, *avant-garde* challenges to conventional culture and morality – all these developments contain profound internal con-tradictions, but their cumulative affect is to shake the aura of *inevitability* which surrounds and protects traditional social rela-tions. In segmented and often margined areas of social life, alternative world-views are extensively canvassed; and this of necessity increases workers' receptiveness to industrial alter-natives.

The principle obstacle to a coherent radicalisation of the objectives of industrial struggle has already been much discussed: the sectionalism inherent in trade union action. The problem of sectionalism is the central theme of Lane's study of trade unionism. Lacking a coherent vision of an alternative social order, it is natural for workers to define their interests not as members of a class but according to the demarcations imposed by the capitalist division of labour. Demands are normally framed in sectional terms and pursued sectionally. Thus patterns of militancy are uneven : within the factory, management can

---

[13] For an example of the impact of collective action on conventional assumptions see the account of the Pilkington strike by Lane and Roberts (1971).

isolate and suppress aggressive sections; within the union, the leadership is strengthened by the fact that, at any normal point of time, active opposition comes only from a few branches or workplaces; at the level of the whole economy, capitalism is protected by the fact that the campaigns of different unions are out of phase and often mutually divisive. 'Sectionalism could only have been held in check if the unions had been capable of generating a programme of a sufficiently broad sweep as to make the differences between workers seem petty and trivial' (Lane 1974 : 268). But sectionalism is incorporated in the organisational structure of trade unionism itself; and so is resistance to the necessarily *political* character of any programme which would articulate common class interests.

Yet it would be wrong to evaluate sectionalism in wholly negative terms. Class consciousness – the recognition that all who sell their labour in order to live, by virtue of that very fact, have common interests in opposition to those who own and control capital – cannot be conjured out of thin air. It must be constituted, if it is to develop at all, out of workers' *direct* experience of the social relations of production : and this experience is necessarily rooted in a particular industry, enterprise, occupation, work group. The immediate context of the world of work is *necessarily* sectional : it is in fragmented contexts that men and women share their hopes and fears, their humour and dejection, as well as the everyday routines of their employment; that they form loyalties and attachments, identify common interests, realise the strength to be gained from collective action. Class consciousness is not an abstraction which *replaces* localised sympathies and face-to-face collaboration : it must be built on and grow out of these, through the imaginative extension of what is directly experienced. Sectional solidarities, in other words, may be integrative *or* divisive. Their implications depend crucially on the manner in which sectional interests are perceived, articulated and enforced : in isolation from, opposition to, or conjunction with those of other groups of workers. The nature of one group's attitudes and actions encourages a reciprocal response from others, thus establishing a pattern of relationships within the class which will contain contradictory pressures and tendencies, but may be predominantly solidaristic or antagonistic. And to note a further dimension of complexity : the effect of some issues tends to be inherently unifying, others the reverse; hence the same groups may be simultaneously allies and opponents.[14]

For many years the predominant tendency in British industrial relations has been for wages issues to be divisive in effect. In the context of sectional bargaining, the natural focus is on *relativities* : the level of one group's earnings, and the size of increase obtained, by comparison with other workers. Thus different sections of trade unionists appear as rivals or even antagonists : the position of the employer as the real enemy, and the common interest of all employees in obtaining the full value of their collective labour, are obscured. Where a common claim can be pursued across a broad group of workers, the effect may well be unifying; but *external* divisiness may still occur (much depends, however, on the pattern of comparisons which has become institutionalised as 'relevant' within different negotiating units). It is important to add that wage bargaining appears to be most corrosive of solidarity in periods of rising prosperity; in times when existing standards are under attack, defensive struggles have often engendered significant displays of class unity – most notably, of course, the General Strike in support of the miners in 1926. At the present time a similar attack is in process : not through the direct action of employers in cutting money wages, but indirectly through price increases. The consequences in terms of consciousness are not readily predictable : there is potential both for intensified sectional efforts to keep pace with inflation, and for combined action to defend the general standards of the working class.

Sectional pay bargaining is normally divisive, in part because the widely propagated notion of a fixed 'wages fund' implies that one group can gain only at the expense of others. This is not the case with demands which relate to conditions of work or control over the production process : here an appreciation of common interests is far more likely to occur. Yet the connection is far

[14] For a sensitive analysis of such contradictory processes among shipbuilders see Brown *et al.* 1972. 'Each worker has a considerable number of possible groupings with which to identify'; in everyday industrial relations (involving issues of differentials and demarcation) narrow sectionalism normally predominates; but changes in the ownership and organisation of the industry make broader solidarities increasingly important.

from straightforward. Traditionally, control in work has often been associated with a relatively privileged status within the working class, and has been regarded by those so advantaged as a sign of their own superiority over other workers. Thus craft control was closely associated with craft exclusiveness; so when engineering craftsmen, at the turn of the century, were faced by the threat of new production methods, the predominant response was to reassert the principle of exclusive control and to identify the new grades of semi-skilled as the immediate enemy. Yet the dimensions of control and exclusiveness *could* be disentangled. For those who recognised that the old ideal of *individual* autonomy on the job could not survive the new technology, 'the tradition of craft control, embodying as it did a tenacious resistance to capitalist rationality' (Hinton 1973 : 99) pointed to a wholly new strategy. Workers' control could retain its meaning only if redefined in *collective* terms : the determination by the whole labour force of the nature, methods and indeed purpose of production; and this required the collaborative effort of all workers, whatever their level of skill or union affiliation. Within this perspective the workers' committees of the First World War, where their effect was greatest, transcended ancient sectionalisms to a remarkable degree.[15]

More recent developments among white-collar employees present interesting parallels. Traditionally, such staff have enjoyed a relatively favourable situation in terms of pay, various 'fringe' benefits, and conditions of work, and have also been comparatively free of continuous supervision. Some of the material advantages are attributable to the market scarcity of literacy and other associated skills (because of the inadequacy of the 'education' inflicted on the bulk of working-class children); others to the ideology which evaluates mental labour (which those who control industry can claim to perform) above manual. Yet such advantages, in the case of the lower grades of non-manual employees, have been reduced in significance. Clerical employment is by no

[15] See Hinton 1973. The unity across craft lines which the shop steward leaders succeeded in creating was always fragile, and shattered in 1918. But it is interesting that the issue which brought a recrudescence of craft sectionalism was not a conventional trade union demand, but the question of exemption from conscription.

means a guarantee of earnings above the level of production workers; manual unions have won many of the 'fringe' benefits[16] and in some cases their members have been assigned 'staff status'; while routine white-collar workers have experienced many of the processes of mechanisation, work measurement and 'rationalised' (i.e. oppressive) control which have traditionally been imposed only on manual occupations. In the extreme situation, the office becomes a factory processing paperwork rather than material products. Less dramatically, increasing numbers of engineers, technicians, clerks, foremen are employed in large-scale organisations and subject to bureaucratic processes of control.

These developments provide the immediate impetus to the growth of white-collar unionism. Yet the motive for collective organisation, it would seem, is often resentment *against* manual workers stemming from the (often exaggerated) perception of the success of the latter in eroding the traditional white-collar advantages. Thus the *methods* identified with manual workers (trade union action) may be adopted in order to restore what are conceived as wholly legitimate privileges over them. Sectional jealousies which were previously latent may thus be made overt and indeed institutionalised. As Lockwood argues in this context, 'it is important to realize from the beginning that action in concert, while obviously an expression of group consciousness, is not necessarily an expression of class consciousness' (1958 : 137). Yet arguably, once unionism becomes established among non-manual groups, the sectionalism of their attitudes and actions on salary and related issues is likely to become routinised in a manner not significantly distinguishable from that of manual trade unionists. And concurrently, concern with *control* issues is likely to point the way to broader solidarities. As capitalist development itself blurs traditional divisions between manual and non-manual labour, so the white-collar response may reflect many of the contradictions of craft reactions over half a century earlier. The situation will create an important potential for the articulation of strategies for collective control which will necessarily implicate all employees, white collar and blue-collar alike. The argument of such French sociologists as Mallet and Touraine is relevant here : the growing involvement of intellectual

[16] Nevertheless, important differences remain. See the survey by Wedderburn (1974).

labour in the production process itself is likely to stimulate explicit concern with the *purposes* of production, and hence a far more fundamental challenge to managerial prerogatives than manual unionism has ever mounted. Though highly tentative, some empirical support can be offered for this analysis.[17]

Such developments should be seen in the context of the growing relevance of control issues in contemporary industrial relations. 'The demand not to be controlled disagreeably', it has been argued, 'runs through all trade union activity' (Goodrich 1975 : 37). Today, with the confidence built on several decades of relatively full employment, resistance to oppressive discipline is a widely noted feature. Yet as the same author insisted, opposition to specific acts of management can in some circumstances spill over into a challenge to managerial authority as such, and from there to the demand that the control of industry be democratised. Structural developments also make explicit the issue of control inherent in industrial relations. The steady rise in technically generated unemployment makes control *over* work a manifest precondition of customary controls *in* work. Some of the consequences can be divisive : white workers are susceptible to racist identifications of black workers as a threat to their jobs; more generally, one group of unionists may be set against another (dockers and cold store workers provide a recent example); or a perception of international competition for jobs may stimulate a parochial nationalist hostility to foreign workers. Yet the most notable of recent developments has been the spate of militant and inventive struggles in defence of employment (work-ins and occupations of which Upper Clyde, Fisher-Bendix and Triumph Meriden are only the most famous among a large number), and the degree of sympathy and solidarity which these have evoked. Just as growing numbers of workers appreciate that the fight for employment cannot be resolved on an individual level (the type of 'solution' which the Redundancy Payments Act was designed to encourage), so there is increasing awareness that sectional competition is also ineffectual : that the issue is a political one which must be pursued at a national level.

Broader solidarity is encouraged, finally, when struggles for control embrace the right of trade union action itself. The fight against the Industrial Relations Act, which put fundamental

[17] For a critical discussion of these theories see Mann 1973.

organisational principles at risk, created an almost unprecedented sense among trade union activists of participation in a common movement. The most dramatic example was initiated by the gaoling of five dockers in 1972. The stewards from the cold store which the dockers had been picketing – and whose own jobs would have been lost had the dockers succeeded in their action – participated in the mass protest which secured the men's release. It was recognised that a legal attack on established forms of trade union action activated the common interests of all workers, transcending divisions which until then had appeared unbridgeable. The subtle dialectic between sectionalism and class unity could scarcely be more starkly demonstrated. Given the increasing involvement of the state in industrial relations, curbing the traditional norms of 'free collective bargaining', the chances of similar confrontations are considerable. Increasingly, then, the question of control is likely to become manifest as a class issue.

CONCLUSION

The spontaneous association of workers on the shop floor, from which the formal institution of trade unionism itself derives, provides the basis for *autonomous* enforcement of control over work relations. At the same time this provides an independent source of power in the relations between union members and their official leaders, counteracting the limitations on the formal democratic processes. Recent trends towards containment of the scope for autonomous workplace bargaining have had the unintended consequence of directing rank-and-file militancy *within* the trade union hierarchy, causing intra-union conflict and stimulating a revival of official militancy.

The development of contemporary capitalism generates increasing volatility in industrial relations, with recurrent conflicts involving workplace union members, the official leaders, employers and the state. A paradoxical feature of this process is that rank-and-file militancy is primarily sectional in character, and unrelated to conscious disruptive intent : whereas its cumulative effect is to create radical instability. Sectionalism and the limitations of consciousness are both most likely to yield if *control* becomes explicitly central as the issue of industrial relations; and there are some signs that this is occurring. Nevertheless, the *routine* processes of 'regulation' remain the most overt aspect of industrial relations at both workplace and national levels. The dialectic between regulation and the struggle for control is the subject of the concluding chapter.

# 7 Conflict and Accommodation: the Dialectics of Industrial Relations

To conclude this introductory discussion of industrial relations from a Marxist perspective, it is now possible to take up again some of the general issues of interpretation which were raised in the first chapter. What is the central character of industrial relations? Academic theorists, it will be recalled, tend to define their subject as a study of the institutions of job regulation. Yet this is far removed from the viewpoint of the average layman, whose immediate understanding of the term would almost certainly involve notions of industrial conflict in general and strikes in particular.

This everyday attitude to industrial relations owes much to the simple-minded treatment it often receives in the media. Strikes can often be described as dramatic or catastrophic, and provide opportunities for moral denunciation of 'subversive' or 'irresponsible' groups of workers. In this way, a convenient scapegoat can be found for the problems of British capitalism, which need not then be traced back to the contradictions of the economic system itself.[1] The impression could easily be gained that trade unionists spend more time on strike than at work : for the more mundane activities of industrial relations often appear as boring as work itself is for most employees, and therefore receive little attention in the press and on television. Hence union officials often complain that their routine functions of conducting negotiations, drawing up agreements and *preventing* strikes –

[1] For a discussion of the ideological treatment of industrial conflict in the media see Hyman 1972.

which occupy the bulk of their time – are not considered news-worthy and therefore not reported.

Yet the popular identification of industrial relations with conflict is not wholly due to the sensationalism of the media. In part it reflects a straightforward recognition of the fact that sophisticated academic discussion often obscures: that work relations (within capitalism) are an inevitable source of dispute. The interests of employees are in large measure opposed to those of employers: hence both parties seek to wield power and mobilise resources in order to ensure the predominance of their own interests. The strategies they adopt inevitably clash, and conflict is the obvious outcome.

'The industrial worker', it has been written, 'for the most part, works harder than he likes at tasks which are frequently arduous, usually monotonous, and sometimes dangerous. On the job he is nearly always subject to the direction of higher authority. His income is seldom sufficient to cover what he thinks his needs demand. The natural state of the industrial worker, therefore, is one of discontent' (Harbison 1954 : 278). Industrial conflict is the natural outcome.

What forms does industrial conflict take? The strike is its most obvious manifestation, but it is useful to define the term more broadly. One well-known textbook argues 'that the general object of study is not the labor dispute, the strike or the lockout, but the total range of behavior and attitudes that express opposition and divergent orientations between industrial owners and managers on the one hand and working people and their organizations on the other' (Kornhauser *et al.* 1954 : 13). The type of activity encompassed by this definition is obviously varied. As Kerr has argued, 'its means of expression are as unlimited as the ingenuity of man'. In addition to a variety of forms of conventional strike action, 'conflict with the employer may also take the form of peaceful bargaining and grievance handling, of boycotts, of political action, of restriction of output, of sabotage, of absenteeism, or of personnel turnover' (1964 : 171). Some of these forms of action may involve large number of workers and be planned and executed by a trade union or workplace shop stewards' organisation; others may occur relatively spontaneously and represent individual rather than collective behaviour.

Is it useful to apply the same label to so wide a range of behaviour? The justification for an all-embracing definition of industrial conflict is that these diverse types of action often appear to reflect similar causes, or to represent alternative responses to similar grievances and deprivations. This is convincingly argued in a sociological study of coalmining in north-west England (Scott *et al.* 1963). The authors draw an important analytical distinction between 'organised' (collective) and 'unorganised' (individual) forms of conflict. Research findings indicated that workers who engaged regularly in organised conflict showed a lower incidence of unorganised conflict than those who rarely pursued collective action. Thus higher-skilled groups of miners tended to monopolise the domestic negotiating procedures and were also predominantly involved in strikes, overtime bans and go-slows; lower-skilled groups by contrast recorded a high rate of absence, accidents and labour turnover.

Behaviour of the latter type is not commonly regarded as a form of conflict, even by those immediately involved. It has, however, been closely analysed in recent years by industrial psychologists who have applied the label 'withdrawal from work'. The evidence indicates that absenteeism, bad time-keeping, turnover, low productivity, and even industrial accidents, can represent conscious or unconscious responses to discontents which derive from identifiable features in the work situation. Collective action in the form of strikes also constitutes a withdrawal from work; but here the action is not merely a means of withdrawal from a stressful and uncongenial situation, it also represents a calculative attempt to apply pressure in order to change the situation. It is interesting to note, however, that some spontaneous strikes display little calculative intent; indeed, concrete demands may be formulated only *after* the walk-out. Such stoppages are akin to mass absenteeism, since the 'withdrawal from work' aspect predominates; they straddle the categories of organised and unorganised conflict.

How plausible is it to view organised and unorganised conflict as alternative outcomes of discontents caused by a given work situation? Scott's study of coalmining, it has been seen, indicated that higher-skilled (and more cohesive) occupational groups tended to react to grievances in a collective and organised manner, whereas in the case of other groups similar grievances found individual and unorganised forms of expression. Closely analogous findings emerge from a detailed study in the United States. Workers with a degree of skill whose occupations gave them a key role in the production process and facilitated the development of cohesive social relationships tended to form 'strategic' work groups, applying collective pressure in a calculative and militant fashion. But in other respects, these were often regarded by managements as model workers. By contrast, unskilled or isolated occupations with little strategic importance often gave rise to 'apathetic' groups which rarely engaged in collective conflict but 'were not trouble-free, only superficially so . . . There was evidence of worker discontent, but often it was not found in terms of specific demands or grievances.' Because of their high level of unorganised conflict, the lack of militancy on the part of such groups did not suffice to endear them to managers (Sayles 1958).

The evidence suggests that the various types of expression of discontent are to some extent interchangeable, and are likely to be affected by the strength, solidarity, traditions and determination of different employee groups. It seems more than fortuitous that women, who are less strongly unionised than men and strike far less, should have a higher record of turnover and absence;[2] whereas turnover in the highly unionised and strike-prone car industry is much lower than in manufacturing generally. Changes over time can often suggest the transfer of conflict from one form to another. In coalmining, the sharp reduction in strikes in the decade following the mid-fifties coincided with a rapid increase in absenteeism. In the car industry, the decision by a number of companies – most notably Ford – in the early sixties to root out shop-floor 'trouble-makers' led to a fall in strike figures but a dramatic rise in absence, accidents and turnover. This suggests that efforts to suppress specific manifestations of conflict, *without removing the underlying causes of unrest*, may merely divert dis-

[2] The lower rate of organisation and collective action is largely attributable to the social ideology which defines 'women's work' as of secondary importance to their domestic role; and to the discriminatory processes which force most women into lower-skilled occupations with limited potential for successful militancy. Despite these obstacles, though, some sections of women workers are strongly unionised and have carried through notable struggles. For an account of the largely neglected history of women's industrial militancy see Rowbotham 1973.

order into different channels. 'We find instead of work disputes, individual actions whose connection with social conflicts is barely recognizable at first sight' (Dahrendorf 1968 : 178). Or strikes may give way to less overt 'cut-price' collective sanctions such as slow-downs.[3] Paradoxically, management attempts to control industrial conflict at the level of the symptom rather than the underlying cause may generate new and less manageable symptoms.

While 'organised' and 'unorganised' conflict may stem from similar objective situations and reflect similar concrete grievances, and both constitute serious problems for employers, their significance for the *workers* concerned involves a considerable contrast. Individual sabotage, 'indiscipline', and the various forms of 'withdrawal from work' typically involve spontaneous individual action – or *reaction* – in the face of uncongenial work relations. Such unorganised conflict is not normally part of a deliberate strategy to remedy the source of grievance; indeed it may well derive from a generalised sense of dissatisfaction rather than consciousness of a specific grievance, and so may not be conceived as industrial conflict at all. Collective action, by contrast, normally involves a deliberate attempt to change the situation which gives rise to conflict; it is purposeful activity designed to achieve some concrete improvement. Organised conflict is thus a form of *practice*, a transformation of labour from the passive and reactive role assigned within capitalist social relations of production to an active and initiating one.

Academic 'experts' have from time to time proposed that collective conflict is withering away, being replaced by peaceful forms of dispute resolution. Such an argument – which recent 'explosions' of strike activity in most industrialised nations have forcefully refuted – is based on a profound misconception of the nature of industrial relations. Collective bargaining is a meaningless ritual if nothing more is involved on the trade union side than the eloquence and statistical finesse of the official negotiators. For the employer can always ignore the union's case, however solidly documented and cogently argued, unless it is backed up by the possibility of sanctions. Serious negotiation involves the overt or implicit threat of collective action, the mobilisation of the

[3] This has been the experience of American companies which imposed tough disciplinary penalties on unofficial strikers: see Kuhn 1961.

power of the membership, if a satisfactory settlement is not achieved.[4] Strikes and related sanctions are a vital *weapon* of the working class in pursuing its industrial objectives. The various forms of *refusal* to continue the normal relations of subordination to management (and the normal production of surplus value for the employer) are a crucial support for any serious aspiration by workers to improve their position. Strikes, and the wide range of other kinds of militant action, are an inescapable demonstration of the antagonism to capital which is the prime source of the trade union function. Hence it is quite correct to treat industrial conflict as the central reality of industrial relations.

Yet this does not mean that overt conflict is typical of the day-to-day processes of industrial relations. The Donovan Commission was told that in 1964, out of a total expenditure of almost £32 million by all the registered unions, less that £½ million went on strike benefits. In 1970 – the year with the largest number of strikes ever recorded in Britain – the TGWU paid out just over £1 million in dispute benefit, out of a total budget of nearly £16 million. In all but two years since the war, the average trade unionist has spent less than a day on strike. Other forms of organised conflict add to the total of militancy; while unorganised conflict multiplies the everyday expression of discontent. Nevertheless, it is clear that most workers spend most of the time performing their assigned roles within capitalist relations of production.

The question obviously arises : why is there so *little* open conflict in industry? One answer is that industrial disputes involve costs to all those concerned. Where a strike lasts any length of time, it is rare for the workers' direct gains to outweigh what is lost in wages. In no way does this mean that their action is futile : *only* because trade unionists are from time to time willing to prove their readiness to endure the costs of militancy can they

[4] At one time a number of unions, especially of white-collar workers and in the public sector, forswore the strike weapon. But their pacifism was supported by the willingness of the employer (directly or through arbitration) to concede pay increases in line with those won by collective bargaining elsewhere. Such unions were in effect the indirect benificiaries of *other* unions' militancy. But recently, as government incomes policies have upset the traditional principle of 'fair comparisons', they have been forced to use militant action themselves.

sustain a position of power in their negotiations with the employer. A union would lose all credibility if it never took a firm stand. For similar reasons, employers are often willing to bear considerable strike losses (though they often try to provoke or manœuvre workers into striking when stocks are high and order books are low). Yet in consequence – and despite the notion often propagated in the press – few trade unionists enter a serious strike with enthusiasm; and if they have recently been involved in costly action, they will normally seek to avoid further stoppages if at all possible. By the nature of things, then, employers and workers alike will usually seek to make open dispute the exception rather than the rule. And where each side has a reasonable appreciation of the balance of forces, and can guess the strength of the other's determination on a particular issue, it is in most cases possible to anticipate the likely outcome if a stoppage were to occur and to negotiate an agreement accordingly.

In elaborating this point, the theorists of job regulation make an obvious contribution towards understanding the causes of industrial peace. The key concept in their explanation is *institutionalisation*. In the words of an American sociologist, 'collective bargaining is the great social invention that has institutionalized industrial conflict . . . Collective bargaining has created a stable means for resolving industrial conflict' (Dubin 1954 : 44). The basic thesis is that while the *causes* of conflict remain inherent in the structure of social and economic relations, its *expression* is contained by a network of institutions and procedures. In particular, the more destructive manifestations of conflict are suppressed, and industrial relations though still conflictual becomes increasingly 'constructive'. Thus it is argued that unions increasingly seek to achieve their objectives along lines not fundamentally at odds with the aims and interests of managements : the relationship between the two parties becomes what has been termed 'antagonistic cooperation'.

Many analysts have asserted the *inevitability* of a trend from hostility to collaboration in union-employer relations. Three reasons are usually given. The first and most obvious is that through collective organisation and action it is possible for workers to win improvements in their conditions. As Marx insisted, it is dangerous to exaggerate these gains : the structure and dynamics of capitalism set narrow limits to what can be achieved, and constantly disrupt established conditions; while the sub-ordination to alien control inherent in wage-labour remains. The exercise of managerial control is indeed rendered less arbitrary – and this is perhaps the most substantial outcome of trade union bargaining activity – but the oppressive consequences of managerial priorities are not radically altered. Yet this is not necessarily how the situation is perceived by workers themselves : their focus may well be on what has been gained rather than on what remains unchanged, and union negotiators naturally encourage such selectivity. As Allen suggests, 'there has developed a myth of achievement whereby unions have an illusion which magnifies fractional changes in wage rates or marginal improvements in employment conditions into resounding successes' (1966 : 30). In the process, collective bargaining 'provides a drainage channel for the specific dissatisfactions and frustrations which workers experience on the job' (Harbison 1954 : 276).

The two other reasons are closely related. Trade unions have acquired an important measure of social legitimacy : their national leaders are consulted by governments, have direct access to ministers and top civil servants, and can expect towards the end of their careers the offer of a peerage or similar badge of upper-class status; their local functionaries obtain parallel though more mundane indications of social acceptance. When unions have been treated as virtual outlaw organisations, the transformation of the established order has often seemed a precondition of their secure existence and effective operation; but once they are treated as legitimate social institutions, the incentive to define their functions within the framework of the existing system becomes strong. The social acceptance of trade unions by those with industrial and political power both reflects the extent to which union policies can be accommodated within capitalism, and encourages continued moderation. At the same time, the external pressures on the official representatives of the unions tend to produce similar results. Concern with organisational security, as already argued, inhibits the adoption of policies which might lead to serious confrontation with employers or governments, for fear of jeopardising unions' established status and relationships. Stable bargaining relations, so the argument runs, though at root conflictual, lead naturally to the development of shared understandings among those involved, and the perception of a growing area of common interest.[5]

Hence the paradox which academic theorists often emphasise: that once industrial conflict is openly articulated, it stimulates institutions of regulation which limit its disruptive manifestations. Most differences are resolved through peaceful negotiation. Bargaining often takes on an 'integrative' or problem-solving character, as both parties seek means of achieving their own interests which impose the minimum of costs on the other. The influence of institutionalisation remains evident even when overt conflict occurs. The *aims* of strikers are normally such as to permit scope for compromise; trade unions do not normally seek to expropriate the employers, or employers to smash the unions. The remarkable fact about most industrial disputes is that, given the wide range of demands which *could* reasonably be raised by workers, union aspirations in bargaining are unambitious and the gap between the disputing parties is thus relatively narrow.

The *methods* of industrial conflict have moreover become largely ritualised. The early stages of labour organisation and action were often marked by riots, arson, sabotage, and widespread physical violence. Today, industrial conflict is subject to unwritten 'Queensberry Rules' which almost wholly exclude such occurrences. ('Picketing violence', a subject of recent controversy, is an exceptional occurrence and is in any case trivial by comparison with the practices of both sides in many historical

[5] The fundamental conflict of interest between employers and employees (with the exception of senior managerial employees possessing many of the privileges and functions of traditional capitalists) is the necessary starting point of any serious analysis of industrial relations. Nevertheless, this does not mean that there is *no* convergence of interest between employers and workers: both may suffer, for example, if companies go bankrupt or factories burn down. At a different level, it is often argued that high profit ratios are 'good' for workers. What this entails is simply that, within capitalism, workers are normally the main victims of economic misfortunes; it does not detract from the fact that the existence and perpetuation of the capitalist system constitutes a permanent and unbridgeable conflict of interest between workers and employers. As Marx commented, 'capital and wage-labour are two sides of one and the same relation . . . As long as the wage-worker is a wage-worker his lot depends upon capital. That is the much-vaunted community of interests between worker and capitalist' (1958: 93).

conflicts.) A dramatic indication of the change was provided by strikes in several major American companies shortly after the Second World War : employers who a decade earlier had hired thugs and assassins to terrorise union organisers now provided pickets with shelter and refreshments. This was doubtless exceptional : but the normal situation where collective bargaining is established is that, at the very least, the employer will refrain from action which strikers might regard as provocative. Unions reciprocate by ensuring that the cessation of production and the conduct of the strike occur in an 'orderly' manner. As Dubin comments, 'collective bargaining tends to produce self-limiting boundaries that distinguish permissible from subversive industrial disorder' (1954 : 45). The assumption underlying this moderation is the mutual understanding of the *temporary* character of disputes : both sides take it for granted that there will eventually be a settlement, the strikers will return to work, and the routine of negotiations will resume.[6] A stoppage of work has become, apart from exceptional cases, the pursuit of negotiations by other means. Hence the aims of strikers are normally negotiable aims (or become so once the official respresentatives of the union are involved); while their methods are normally such as will not embitter ongoing bargaining relationships. Even militant union representatives are subject to the logic of these considerations, and thus assist in regularising industrial disorder : militancy itself is institutionalised.[7]

This illustrates the inherent duality of trade unionism, the subject of much discussion in previous chapters. Collective organisation is the means whereby workers create social power far greater than the sum of that which they possess as individuals, for unity and coordination replace competition and division. This power is a weapon which can be used to win real improve-

[6] The Pilkington strike of 1970 provides an interesting example of this effect; though the company refused to negotiate with the unofficial strike committee, it was careful not to appear provocative in its attitude. For 'Pilkingtons did not want to do anything that could create a reservoir of ill-feeling towards the company and thus inhibit the establishment of faithful co-operation once a return to work had been organised' (Lane and Roberts 1971: 153).

[7] Paradoxically, some sophisticated employers prefer to be faced by a militant rather than a moderate trade union, believing the latter will be more successful in sustaining employee loyalty, cohesion and morale.

ments in their situation: the organisation of conflict gives their discontents direction, and is thus the precondition of any significant remedy. Yet the organisation of conflict also makes their disaffection *manageable* by employers and by governments: for grievances are brought into the open, channelled to the appropriate authorities, expressed in a form which makes compromise possible, and articulated by a bargaining 'partner' with whom an agreement can be reached which employees will feel some commitment to observe. Thus an inescapable function of trade union action is, in Mills' terms, the 'management of discontent'. In the process, there is a persistent tendency for union representatives to allow their role as advocate of the members' own express interests to yield precedence to their role as guardians of organisational interests (that is, as a means of transmitting the pressures of external power on to their own members). As a result of such external pressure, the dimension of 'power over' inherent in trade unionism constantly threatens to predominate over the dimension of 'power for': allowing managements to 'regain control by sharing it' (Flanders 1970: 172).

The management of discontent is the exclusive focus of theorists of job regulation; the emphasis is on collective bargaining 'as a social process . . . that . . . continually transforms disagreements into agreements in an orderly fashion' (Flanders 1973: 369). Yet the argument of this book has been that industrial relations must also be recognised as a process through which agreements are transformed into disagreements, often in a disorderly fashion. Conflict and and disorder cannot be excluded from the most finely regulated industrial relations, and their means of expression are (thanks to workers' ingenuity and creativity) often highly irregular. (Hence the recent development of factory occupations challenges the unquestioned commitment to the 'rights of property'; the elaboration of forms of non-cooperation by white-collar unionists overturns notions of a 'fair day's work' which are a vital support for managerial discipline.) Industrial peace may be 'normal', in the statistical sense that employees spend more time at work than on strike; but it is always precarious.

The conception of industrial relations as a source of order and regularity – conditional only on the existence of appropriate institutional arrangements – derives from a general theoretical approach commonly known as *pluralism*. Pluralists accept that the interests of workers and employers diverge, and that conflict is therefore endemic in industry. Yet the additional assumption is made, usually implicitly, that the 'divergencies between the parties are not so fundamental or so wide as to be unbridgeable by compromises or new syntheses which enable collaboration to continue' (Fox 1973 : 196). The analogy employed to illuminate the character of the industrial enterprise is that of 'a coalition of interests, a miniature democratic state' (Fox 1966 : 2). Conflict is not located in the fundamental structure of capitalist relations of production : the divisions of interest are relatively superficial when contrasted with the common interest and commitment which, it is assumed, are directed to the maintenance of the existing social order. Hence order in industrial relations derives from an underlying consensus, and is not imposed through the superior power of capital; indeed power relations rarely receive systematic attention within the pluralist perspective, for otherwise the fanciful image of the factory as a 'miniature democratic state' would be wholly untenable. Two other devices are used by pluralists to reinforce their distinctive interpretation of industrial relations. First (as was seen in Chapter 3), the *legitimate* interests of workers and the legitimate purposes of trade unions are defined so narrowly as not to conflict with the basic priorities of capitalism. Hence, by a conceptual sleight-of-hand, a stable process of compromise and collaboration is made to appear unproblematic. Second, the structure of group interests is defined purely in sectional terms. Management is thus treated as merely one of many sectional interests, mediating the competing claims of suppliers, customers, shareholders, community interests, and different employee groups. There is no consideration that the constellation of specific sectional interests, particularly in terms of the advantage gained from the perpetuation of capitalist economic relations, involves parallels and convergences which justify analysis in terms of *opposing class interests*.[8] The pluralist faith that industrial conflict is necessarily susceptible to insti-

[8] Pluralism in industrial relations and in political theory share this preoccupation with the surface pattern of multiple group competition, to the neglect of underlying class alignments. They also tend to share a conception of the state as a neutral agency, since no social group is assumed to exert overriding political influence.

tutional regulation thus stems naturally from a restricted conception of the structure of interests within capitalism.

As soon as the structure of interests and work relations is set within a more adequate conceptual framework, it becomes possible to understand industrial relations as a process generating conflict and disorder as well as order and regulation. Within the workplace itself, the wage-labour relationship contains a constant potential for disorder. Management commands, employees are expected to obey; but the *limits* of management authority and worker obedience are imprecise and shifting. The frontier of control over work relations is in principle too fluid and dynamic to achieve stable definition through formally agreed rules : it must be constantly negotiated and renegotiated through a permanent process of pressure and counter-pressure, the mobilisation by both sides of sanctions and resources, at the point of production.

At the higher levels of the 'industrial relations system', internal contradictions similarly pose a persistent threat to stable regulation. An obvious example is provided by the pattern of wages and salaries across the economy which, as the Pay Board commented, 'result from the separate histories of firms, groups and institutions and do not form a consciously designed structure' (1974 : 2). The relative scarcity of different occupational abilities, variations in the prosperity and productivity of particular industries, and generalised social ideologies of occupational worth, all exert an influence on earnings relativities. But just as the total structure of inequality in capitalist society is not open to any coherent justification, so the pattern of relativities among wage and salary-earners owes much to the persistence of more or less arbitrary historical differentials which have become sanctified by custom. But in consequence, one of the main sources of wage aspirations and wage bargaining is the force of 'coercive comparisons' (Ross 1948): 'pay increases negotiated for whatever reasons by employers and trade union representatives become part of the grounds for claims by other groups' (Pay Board 1974 : 3–4). Hence a cumulative process of instability is easily initiated if the relative position of a particular group is altered as a result of labour market pressures, a productivity bargain, changes in bargaining power or bargaining awareness, or a strong feeling that established relationships are inequitable. This last factor – perhaps reflecting greater awareness of the extent of present inequalities, and a widespread decline in readiness to accept traditional social relationships as unquestionably correct – has become an increasingly apparent feature in British industrial relations.[9] In such a situation, the pattern of agreements reached between unions and employers evokes little enthusiasm or commitment from those affected; the maintenance of orderly industrial relations 'is contingent upon the estimate of the parties . . . that they have more to lose than to gain by an overt struggle, and is not the result of their acceptance of any standard of remuneration as an equitable settlement of their claims. Hence it is precarious, insincere and short' (Tawney 1961 : 41).

Disorder is, finally, constantly generated from within the social and economic *context* of industrial relations. 'The real barrier of capitalist production', wrote Marx, 'is capital itself. It is that capital and its self-expansion appear as the starting and closing point, the motive and the purpose of production; that production is only production for capital and not vice versa, the means of production are not mere means for a constant expansion of the living process of the society or producers' (1962 : 245). Technical change, and the decline of old industries and the expansion of new, create instability and insecurity on the one hand while on the other they necessitate processes of social collaboration and social control for which traditional capitalist institutions are inadequate. The need to compete internationally sustains competitive pressures as capital within each economy becomes increasingly monopolised, and indeed the requirement to contain labour costs and accumulate new, more sophisticated and more costly forms of capital becomes ever more imperative. At the same time, the deliberate (and expensive) efforts by consumer-goods industries to manipulate demand inevitably affect employees' pay aspirations. These contradictory forces help generate the inflationary spiral; and, because of their uneven international impact (accentuated by archaic trade and monetary arrangements), contribute to balance of payments crises. It need hardly be added that they disrupt established relations and understandings between workers, employers, unions and the state. Any serious analysis which takes the form of a political economy of industrial relations must necessarily appreciate that

[9] In part, as suggested earlier, this may be an unintended consequence of incomes policy.

the internal contradictions of capitalism tend naturally to create disruption.

Within this framework, recent trends within industrial relations – scarcely explicable by the theorists of job regulation – are readily understood. *The process of institutionalisation is itself beset by contradictions.* The rise in strike activity in most industrialised nations; increasingly ambitious wage demands; the explicit articulation of *non-wage* concerns (control over production, the humanisation of work) traditionally excluded from trade union perspectives; 'indiscipline' on the shop floor, particularly among young workers; challenges to official union policies, agreements and leaders; the revival in official militancy as the only means to maintain leadership authority : all these developments are highly threatening to social and economic stability, even though few trade unionists explicitly intend such a challenge. The explanation is, essentially, that the institutionalisation of industrial conflict does indeed achieve a *provisional* containment of disorder; but where workers' grievances and discontents are not resolved, they give rise eventually to new forms of conflict, perhaps involving new types of demand and new means of action. Is it fanciful to suggest that the breakdown of institutionalised control in so many countries reflects, not merely the international accentuation of the economic contradictions of capitalism, but also a generalised consequence of and reaction to the suppression of workers' discontents through a generation of post-war job regulation?[10]

CONCLUSION

The argument of this chapter – and of the whole book – has been that there is an inherent dialectic in the processes of control over work relations : conflict and accommodation are two contradictory but inescapable aspects of industrial relations. The tension

[10] It is noteworthy that in the United States, where the institutionalisation of industrial relations in the post-war period appeared unshakable, the 'blue-collar revolt' has become a talking-point of recent years. The annual number of strikes, which fell to little more than 3000 in the early 1960s, has been above 5000 in every year since 1968: an unprecedented level of militancy. Most of these disputes are unofficial, and in many cases explicitly anti-official. For a discussion of this rank-and-file revolt see Herding 1972.

between pressures generating regulation and disorder is an inevitable reflection of capitalist social relations of production : the one conditions the other. This tension necessarily sets limits to the functions of trade unionism. On the one hand, the structure of power relations within capitalism constrains the goals and strategies which unions can adopt without provoking a challenge to their security or their very existence. Yet, on the other hand, trade union organisation historically emerged from the antagonism between the interests of wage-labour and capital, and must continue to express this antagonism in order to retain any plausible claim to represent employees. If unions fail to articulate seriously their members' grievances and aspirations the eventual response is either the development of internal challenges to the leadership, membership apathy and organisational disintegration, or the emergence of rival channels for the expression of workers' discontents.

Rank-and-file consciousness and action are often volatile; while the intensity of the pressures from employers and the state vary according to the urgency of the contradictions within capitalism itself. Thus the relative strength of the internal and external forces bearing upon union policy shift and fluctuate. In certain historical epochs, the pressures from below are of overriding effect; in others, external constraints predominate. On occasion, both sets of pressures may be comparatively weak, allowing union representatives a considerable range of freedom in the formulation of policy and initiation of action. At other times, both may be powerful, and the unions appear trapped between irreconcilable forces. Such is the situation today.

Rank-and-file action has been discussed, in this chapter and the preceding one, primarily as a disruptive influence : a force that undermines established forms of regulation in industry, an explosive expression of the antagonisms generated by the institution of wage-labour itself. Yet there is also a *positive* dimension to rank-and-file action : it represents the *practice* of the working class, containing intimations of a different form of social and industrial order in which the character of relations of production would be transformed. Marx himself based his whole life work on the goal of the revolutionary transformation of capitalist society, setting out the essential requirements of a socialist alternative. Foremost is the need for workers collectively (manual, technical, clerical acting together) to control production, and through a structure of delegatory bodies to determine the overall framework of economic policy, rather than to be subject to authoritarian managerial control and the vagaries of the market. From the fact of positive workers' control a number of consequences would follow. The *priorities* of economic life could be directly oriented to the satisfaction of social needs, rather than being subordinated to the dictates of profit. A serious effort could be made to create work compatible with human dignity, building into the design of jobs a concern for safety, decent working conditions, and scope for responsibility and initiative. The more upleasant forms of labour would be retained only if it were clear that they contributed significantly to social welfare – in which case the performance of such work might be made more tolerable by receiving the social recognition due to it; moreover, a serious attempt to reverse the rigid capitalist division of labour could ensure that no individual or group need be permanently condemned to drudgery. And given a transformation of control in industry, and the abolition of private profit, the dynamics of social and economic inequality would be eliminated.[11]

*Consciousness* of socialist objectives among organised workers is extremely limited. Yet working-class sub-culture, and the current practice of trade unionists, contain fragmented elements of such a consciousness. The priority of social needs over profit is at times explicitly asserted – as for example, when health service workers demand the abolition of private practice in public hospitals, or when workers whose factories are faced with closure demand nationalisation and the protection of their jobs. Many of the demands being raised in respect of working conditions and the control of the production process are clearly incompatible with the normal relationship between wage-labour and capital. The organisational forms thrown up in the course of struggle often transcend traditional divisions within the working class. Old inequalities – made more overt by the spread of

[11] Marx did not propose the immediate equalisation of all incomes. 'The abolition of the wages system' was the ultimate objective; but initially, rewards would reflect productive contributions (which would radically narrow existing inequalities and might indeed *reverse* the relative status of some occupations). See 'The Critique of the Gotha Programme' in Marx and Engels 1958 (II).

the mass media – are less automatically accepted as inevitable.

All this is far from constituting a clear and extensive consciousness of common working-class interests, let alone a coherent
vision of an alternative society and a determination to struggle
for its achievement. Nevertheless, there is some basis for the
minority of workers who *do* possess such a consciousness to influence their fellows, for revolutionary organisation to interact
with rank-and-file militancy. If the contradictions within the
political economy of capitalism become more acute, and the
scope for achievements through orthodox trade union action
becomes increasingly limited, growing numbers of workers are
likely to seek an alternative. As bargaining *within* capitalism
comes to yield shrinking gains (and indeed to require a *deterioration* in conditions) trade unionists can be expected to become
more and more susceptible to the idea of its elimination. An explicit and aggressive commitment of trade unionism to socialist
politics would provoke intense and brutal resistance from those
who wield social and economic power; and most of those in positions of authority within trade unionism, fearing such a confrontation, would do their best to prevent any such development.
There is nothing *inevitable* about the growth of socialist consciousness, organisation and action; as Lukacs insisted, 'history
is at its least automatic when it is the consciousness of the prole-
tariat that is at issue' (1971 : 208). Yet what can be asserted with
confidence is that *only* if the implicit meanings of rank-and-file
action are made explicit is there any prospect that the sources
of disorder in industrial relations can be effectively contained.

Conflict in industry would not indeed be eliminated in a society
in which consciously expressed social needs replaced profit as the
main dynamic of economic activity. No social order can provide
perfect and permanent harmony : whatever the institutional
framework, work relations can be expected to generate some
frustration and discontent and thus give rise to antagonism. But
in a socialist society, industrial conflict would not be rooted in
*an antagonistic social structure* : it would not stem from the exercise of control in the interests of a minority class of capitalists, or
by an authoritarian bureaucracy. Industrial conflict would therefore be less irreconcilable, less pervasive. And for this reason the
notion of stable and orderly 'job regulation' – a futile objective

within capitalist relations of production – would acquire greater credibility in the absence of fundamental conflicts of class interest, and in the context of a genuine ability on the part of workers to exert positive control over work itself and its social and economic environment. Conflict would thus be frictional rather than fundamental; there would exist a practical basis for commitment to agreed rules defining economic interrelationships.[12]

A systematic understanding of industrial relations – the processes of control over work relations – points inescapably to a single conclusion. Only a total transformation of the whole *structure* of control, at a level which transcends the conventional narrow definitions of industrial relations, can resolve the current contradictions within the organisation of work and in social and economic life more generally. The obstacles to such a transformation are immense; but until they are overcome, conflict in industrial relations is likely to undermine an increasing area of the foundations of regulation and accommodation.

[12] Given what has been said in previous chapters it should be unnecessary to repeat that those societies, in Eastern Europe and elsewhere, which currently claim to be socialist do so without material justification. Because of the absence of independent union organisations in these countries, the forms of organised conflict which are routine in the West rarely occur; but it would seem that unorganised conflict is rife, while the collective expression of workers' discontents is occasionally explosive.

# Guide to Further Reading

## *Introduction*

Of recent general texts on industrial relations, Clegg (1970) is most useful in providing a wide range of detail which serves to deter any easy generalisation in this complex area. The author's theoretical presuppositions – which reflect the empiricist-pluralist school long predominant in British academic writing on industrial relations – are not explicitly stated. Two Penguin books of readings contain useful items : one edited by Flanders (1969) on collective bargaining, and the other by McCarthy on trade unions (1972). Allen (1971) argues the need for a Marxist approach to industrial relations; some of the essays in this collection, which were written over a number of years, display this approach more clearly than others. For a discussion of American industrial relations, though from a largely managerial perspective, see Chamberlain and Kuhn (1965). Essays in Hunnius *et al.* (1973) give Marxist accounts of some aspects of labour struggles in the United States. Broader international comparisons may be found in Kassalow (1969).

The works of Marx and Engels are widely available, in most cases published by Progress Publishers (formerly the Foreign Languages Publishing House, Moscow) and distributed in Britain by Lawrence & Wishart. The two-volume *Selected Works* (1958), referred to in this book, is no longer in print and has been replaced by a less comprehensive single volume, which is however still a very good introduction. Bottomore and Rubel (1963) provide a useful collection of extracts from a wide range of works. Probably the most lucid of recent discussions of Marxist theory is by Avineri (1968); while Hallas (1971) provides a short, clear introductory discussion.

## Chapter 1

The position of the worker within capitalism is succinctly stated by Marx in his article 'Wage-Labour and Capital', included in the *Selected Works* and also produced as a separate pamphlet. The situation of workers in contemporary Britain is analysed by a variety of Marxist writers in Blackburn and Cockburn (1967); see in particular the articles by Blackburn – 'The Unequal Society' – and Coates – 'Wage Slaves'. A more recent summary of the dimensions of social and economic inequality has been compiled by Field (1974).

For a discussion of the relationship between the structure of capitalism and the sources of industrial conflict see Hyman (1972). [If in a number of cases in this Guide I refer to my own works this is not simply through egotism. I have tried in the text to avoid repeating at length what I have previously written elsewhere, even though this often has an important bearing on the book's main themes.] A classic study of the struggle for control in British industry, now reprinted, is Goodrich (1975).

## Chapter 2

The two historical and analytical studies of British trade unionism by the Webbs (1897 and 1920) have deservedly the reputation of classics. Their treatment, however, reveals throughout their preconceptions as the dominant theorists of British Fabianism : the control exercised by workers through their unions is regarded as a necessary but transitional process before industry is taken over and administered by a bureaucratic state. Cole (1913) offers a divergent interpretation which has equal claim to the status of a classic : though hasty and at times superficial, his study shows a keen appreciation of the subtle interrelation of trade unionism, workers' control, and the possibilities of a socialist society. His criticisms of the existing inadequacies of trade union structure and government are often vitriolic.

Modern analyses of union structure, from a pluralist perspective, are contained in chapters of Flanders (1968) and Clegg (1970). Turner's study of the cotton unions (1962) is a remarkable book, labyrinthine in structure but full of profound insights. He combines historical with contemporary analysis, and seeks to draw general conclusions about trade union development as well as providing great detail on the cotton industry. An extremely detailed account of trade union history during a key period of structural development (but abstracted from any explicit theoretical framework) is contained in Clegg *et al.* (1964). Lane (1974) seeks to relate a brief account of labour history to a general Marxist analysis of trade unionism : his main theme is the persistence of sectionalism (criticised in part in Chapter 6 of this book).

## *Chapter 3*

The pioneer analysis of union democracy by the Webbs (1897) remains an essential starting point : though it is necessary to assess critically their preference for bureaucratic 'efficiency' over rank-and-file control, and their belief that sophisticated constitutional provisions would serve to guarantee leadership responsiveness to membership interests. Turner (1962) again offers stimulating theoretical analysis; some of his arguments are summarised by Hughes (1968). A number of important contributions to the discussion of union democracy are surveyed by Magrath (1959).

Anderson (1967) discusses, at times a little mechanically, the constraints which the capitalist context of union action impose on the formulation of policy. Herding (1972) has written an account of the control processes exercised by and operating within American trade unions; his treatment is by no means easy to follow, but his theoretical arguments are of great importance and are in many cases highly relevant to the British situation. Hyman (1971b) and Hyman and Fryer (1975) discuss a number of issues covered in this chapter from a Marxist point of view.

## *Chapter 4*

The serious student of Marxist economics needs to master all three volumes of *Capital*; Volumes I and III (1959 and 1962) are particularly relevant to industrial relations. So are the rough notes published as the *Grundrisse* (1973), though they often demand considerable pains to follow. A polemical and at times simplified, but still important brief statement of Marx's general analysis of capitalism is contained in the 'Manifesto of the Communist Party' (in the *Selected Works,* also published separately).

Among recent studies of contemporary capitalism from a Marxist perspective are Kidron (1970 and 1974) and Glyn and Sutcliffe (1972). The development of multinational companies, and their implications for trade unionism, is analysed (though not within a Marxist framework) by Levinson (1972). An example of the Marxist conception of capitalist development, and its internal contradictions, used to illuminate labour history can be found in several of the essays in Hobsbawn (1964).

Justifiably famous as an analysis of the limitations of trade union consciousness within capitalism is Lenin's pamphlet *What Is To Be Done?* (1961; also published separately). Written in 1902, as a hasty polemic against a section of his party which insisted that trade union struggles could lead spontaneously to socialism, this pamphlet oversimplifies a number of the issues – as Lenin himself later emphasised. For a critical discussion see Hyman (1971b).

## Chapter 5

Marx and Engels never presented a systematic theory of the state : the most detailed formulation is in Engels' 'Origin of the Family, Private Property and the State' (in the *Selected Works:* II). The most famous interpretation of the various writings of Marx and Engels is Lenin's 'State and Revolution', which is included in the single-volume *Selected Works* (1968). More recent discussions of Marx's writings are by Miliband (1965) and Draper (1974). The problem of ideology in relation to state power is subtly analysed by Gramsci (1971).

Recent Marxist discussions of the general character of the modern state include the primarily empirical analysis by Miliband (1969) and the somewhat ponderous and abstracted theoretical treatment by Poulantzas (1973). For the specific role of the state in industrial relations see Allen (1960 and 1966) and Hyman (1973).

## Chapter 6

There have been many recent studies of shop steward organisation and action, but few of real substance. Goodman and Whittingham (1973) provide an uninspiring general discussion. Cole's early study (1923) remains valuable. Sykes (1967) gives an interesting analytical treatment of the sources of cohesion in the shop-floor organisation in printing; while Turner *et al.* (1967) examine the motor industry and point to the institutionalisation of the shop steward hierarchy. (They devise the notion of 'unofficial unofficial' strikes to cover the growing number of disputes called by rank-and-file workers without the knowledge or against the advice of senior stewards.) Brown *et al.* (1972) analyse with great sensitivity the subtle interplay of divisive and cohesive forces within the yard organisation in shipbuilding. Brown (1973) explores theoretically the operation of piecework bargaining in the Coventry engineering industry; he tends to generalise too readily from the extreme sectionalism of local wage bargaining, and to gloss over the extent to which the introduction of 'order' by shop stewards serves managerial interests and reflects an accommodation to managerial power.

Of Marxist accounts of current shop-floor trade unionism, Beynon's (1973) description of the Ford factory in Liverpool is outstanding : he recounts graphically the constant struggle for control, and also illustrates the limitations of 'factory class-consciousness'. Lane (1974) develops a similar interpretation of rank-and-file action, emphasising the limitations imposed by sectional consciousness and organisation. Against this should be set Hinton (1973), an account of how, in the context of the engineering struggles of 1915–19, the narrow sectionalism of craft unionism nevertheless formed the basis for workshop militancy led for a time by revolutionaries with an explicit commitment to anti-sectional action.

## Chapter 7

Clear presentations of the pluralist conception of industrial relations can be found in Fox (1966), Fox and Flanders (1969) and Flanders (1970). Fox himself (1973 and 1974) has subsequently developed a partial critique, pointing to the neglect of the power imbalance built into the capitalist organisation of industry. For Marxist assessments of pluralism see Hyman and Brough (1975) and Hyman and Fryer (1975).

The character of the socialist *alternative* to capitalist industry is rarely described in detail. This is understandable, for if socialism is to be established by the creativity of workers' own collective action it will not be according to any predetermined blueprint. Marx did however discuss some of the problems of the transition to socialism and its principles of organisation in the 'Critique of the Gotha Programme' (in the *Selected Works:* II). A profound discussion of many of the procedures appropriate for socialist industry is contained in the writings of William Morris, often falsely dismissed as a romantic medievalist totally opposed to machine production. See in particular his essay 'Useful Work Versus Useless Toil' in *Selected Writings* (1962). Later proposals and debates on the question of workers' control can be found in Coates and Topham (1970). A succinct recent discussion of general issues relating to the transition to socialism is provided by Hallas (1971).

# Bibliography

V. L. Allen (1954) *Power in Trade Unions*, Longmans.
—— (1957) *Trade Union Leadership*, Longmans.
—— (1960) *Trade Unions and the Government*, Longmans.
—— (1966) *Militant Trade Unionism*, Merlin.
—— (1971) *The Sociology of Industrial Relations*, Longmans.
P. Anderson (1965) 'Origins of the Present Crisis' in Anderson and Blackburn 1975.
—— (1967) 'The Limits and Possibilities of Trade Union Action' in Blackburn and Cockburn 1967.
P. Anderson and R. Blackburn (1965) *Towards Socialism*, Collins.
A. Aspinall (1948) *The Early English Trade Unions*, Batchworth.
S. Avineri (1968) *Karl Marx: Social and Political Thought*, Cambridge University Press.
G. S. Bain (1970) *The Growth of White-Collar Unionism*, Oxford University Press.
J. Banks (1974) *Trade Unionism*, Collier-Macmillan.
D. Bell (1961) *The End of Ideology*, Free Press.
H. Beynon (1973) *Working for Ford*, Penguin.
R. Blackburn (1965) 'The New Capitalism' in Anderson and Blackburn 1965.
—— (1967) 'The Unequal Society' in Blackburn and Cockburn 1967.
R. Blackburn and A. Cockburn (1967) *The Incompatibles: Trade Union Militancy and the Consensus*, Penguin.
R. Blauner (1960) *Alienation and Freedom*, Chicago University Press.
I. Boraston, H. A. Clegg and M. Rimmer (1975) *Workplace and Union*, Heinemann.
T. Bottomore and M. Rubel (1963) *Karl Marx: Selected Writings on Sociology and Social Philosophy*, Pelican.
R. K. Brown, P. Brannen, J. M. Cousins and M. L. Samphier (1972) 'The Contours of Solidarity', *British Journal of Industrial Relations*, 10, 1.
W. A. Brown (1973) *Piecework Bargaining*, Heinemann.

N. W. Chamberlain and J. W. Kuhn (1965) *Collective Bargaining* (2nd ed.), McGraw-Hill.

J. Child (1973) *Man and Organization*, Allen & Unwin.

J. Child, R. Loveridge and M. Warner (1973) 'Towards an Organizational Study of Trade Unions', *Sociology*, 7, 1.

K. Clark (1964) *Ruskin Today*, Penguin.

H. A. Clegg (1954) *General Union*, Blackwell.

—— (1970) *The System of Industrial Relations in Great Britain*, Blackwell.

—— (1971) *How to Run an Incomes Policy*, Heinemann.

H. A. Clegg, A. Fox and A. F. Thompson, *A History of British Trade Unions*, vol. I, Oxford University Press.

T. Cliff (1970) *The Employers' Offensive*, Pluto Press.

K. Coates (1967) 'Wage Slaves' in Blackburn and Cockburn 1967.

K. Coates and A. Topham (1970) *Workers' Control*, Panther.

G. D. H. Cole (1913) *The World of Labour*, Bell (repr. Harvester Press, 1973).

—— (1923) *Workshop Organisation*, Clarendon Press (repr. Hutchinson, 1973).

Commission on Industrial Relations (1973) Study No. 2, *Industrial Relations at Establishment Level*, HMSO.

M. Crozier (1964) *The Bureaucratic Phenomenon*, Chicago University Press.

R. Dahrendorf (1968) *Society and Democracy in Germany*, Routledge & Kegan Paul.

Lord Devlin (Chairman) (1965) *Final Report of the Committee of Inquiry on the Port Transport Industry*, HMSO.

Lord Donovan (Chairman) (1968) *Report of the Royal Commission on Trade Unions and Employers' Associations*, HMSO.

H. Draper (1974) 'Marx on Democratic Forms of Government', *Socialist Register 1974*.

R. Dubin (1954) 'Constructive Aspects of Industrial Conflict' in Kornhauser *et al.* 1954.

J. T. Dunlop (1958) *Industrial Relations Systems*, Holt.

J. D. Edelstein (1965) 'Democracy in a National Union : the British AEU', *Industrial Relations*, 4, 3.

J. E. T. Eldridge (1973) 'Industrial Conflict : some Problems of Theory and Method' in Child 1973.

F. Engels (1952) *The Condition of the Working Class in Britain in 1844*, Allen & Unwin (first English edition 1892).

—— (1958) Articles in Marx and Engels 1958.

A. Fels (1972) *The British Prices and Incomes Board*, Cambridge University Press.

F. Field (1974) *Unequal Britain*, Arrow.

A. Flanders (1965) *Industrial Relations: What is Wrong with the System?* Faber.

—— (1968) *Trade Unions* (7th ed.), Hutchinson.

—— (1969) *Collective Bargaining*, Penguin.

—— (1970) *Management and Unions*, Faber.

—— (1973) 'Measured Daywork and Collective Bargaining', *British Journal of Industrial Relations, 11*, 3.

A. Flanders and H. A. Clegg (1954) *The System of Industrial Relations in Great Britain*, Blackwell.

A. Fox (1965) *The Milton Plan*, Institute of Personnel Management.

—— (1966) *Industrial Sociology and Industrial Relations*, HMSO.

—— (1971) *A Sociology of Work in Industry*, Collier-Macmillan.

—— (1973) 'Industrial Relations: a Critique of Pluralist Ideology' in Child 1973.

—— (1974) *Man Mismanagement*, Hutchinson.

A. Fox and A. Flanders (1969) 'The Reform of Collective Bargaining: from Donovan to Durkheim', *British Journal of Industrial Relations, 7*, 2.

R. and E. Frow and M. Katanka (1971) *Strikes: a Documentary History*, Charles Knight.

R. H. Fryer (1973) 'Redundancy, Values and Public Policy', *Industrial Relations Journal, 4*, 2.

R. H. Fryer, A. Fairclough and T. Manson (1974) *Organisation and Change in the National Union of Public Employees*, NUPE.

H. H. Gerth and C. W. Mills (1954) *Character and Social Structure*, Routledge & Kegan Paul.

A. Gleason (1920) *What the Workers Want*, Harcourt, Brace & Howe.

A. Glyn and B. Sutcliffe (1972) *British Capitalism, Workers and the Profits Squeeze*, Penguin.

J. Goldstein (1952) *The Government of British Trade Unions*, Allen & Unwin.

J. H. Goldthorpe (1972) 'The Industrial Relations Act in Theory and Practice' in *Problems and Prospects of Socio-Legal Research*, Nuffield College (mimeo).

—— (1974) 'Social Inequality and Social Integration in Modern Britain' in Wedderburn 1974.

J. F. B. Goodman and T. G. Whittingham (1973) *Shop Stewards*, Pan.

C. L. Goodrich (1975) *The Frontier of Control*, Pluto Press (first published 1920).

A. Gorz (1965) 'Work and Consumption' in Anderson and Blackburn 1965.

Government Social Survey (1968) *Workplace Industrial Relations*, HMSO.

A. Gramsci (1969) *Soviets in Italy* (articles written 1919–20), Institute for Workers' Control.

—— (1971) *Selections from the Prison Notebooks*, Lawrence & Wishart.

D. Hallas (1971) *The Meaning of Marxism*, Pluto Press.

J. L. Hammond and B. Hammond (1917) *The Town Labourer*, Longmans.

F. H. Harbison (1954) 'Collective Bargaining and American Capitalism' in Kornhauser *et al.* 1954.

J. Harvey and K. Hood (1957) *The British State*, Lawrence & Wishart.

R. G. Herding (1972) *Job Control and Union Structure*, Rotterdam University Press.

S. Hill (1974) 'Norms, Groups and Power', *British Journal of Industrial Relations, 12, 2.*

J. Hinton (1973) *The First Shop Stewards' Movement*, Allen & Unwin.

J. Hinton and R. Hyman (1975) *Revolutionary Trade Unionism?: the Industrial Politics of the Early British Communist Party*, Pluto Press.

E. J. Hobsbawn (1964) *Labouring Men*, Weidenfeld & Nicolson.

B. Hooberman (1974) *An Introduction to British Trade Unions*, Pelican.

R. F. Hoxie (1923) *Trade Unionism in the United States*, Appleton.

J. Hughes (1968) *Trade Union Structure and Government*, HMSO.

G. Hunnius, G. D. Garson and J. Case (1973) *Workers' Control*, Random House.

R. Hyman (1971a) *The Workers' Union*, Clarendon Press.

—— (1971b) *Marxism and the Sociology of Trade Unionism*, Pluto Press.

—— (1972) *Strikes*, Fontana.

—— (1973) 'Industrial Conflict and the Political Economy', *Socialist Register 1973*.

—— (1974a) 'Inequality, Ideology and Industrial Relations', *British Journal of Industrial Relations, 12, 2.*

—— (1974b) 'Workers' Control and Revolutionary Theory', *Socialist Register 1974.*

R. Hyman and I. Brough (1975) *Social Values and Industrial Relations*, Blackwell.

R. Hyman and R. H. Fryer (1975) 'Trade Unions : Sociology and Political Economy' in J. McKinlay, *Processing People*, Holt, Rinehart & Winston.

G. K. Ingham (1973) *Strikes and Industrial Conflict*, Macmillan.

D. Jackson, H. A. Turner and F. Wilkinson (1972) *Do Trade Unions Cause Inflation?*, Cambridge University Press.

O. Kahn-Freund (1954) 'Legal Framework' in Flanders and Clegg 1954.

—— (1972) *Labour and the Law*, Stevens.

O. Kahn-Freund and B. Hepple (1972) *Laws against Strikes*, Fabian Research Series.

E. M. Kassalow (1969) *Trade Unions and Industrial Relations: an International Comparison*, Random House.

C. Kerr (1964) *Labor and Management in Industrial Society*, Doubleday.

J. M. Keynes (1936) *The General Theory of Employment, Interest and Money*, Macmillan.

M. Kidron (1970) *Western Capitalism since the War*, Pelican.

—— (1974) *Capitalism and Theory*, Pluto Press.

J. C. Kincaid (1973) *Poverty and Equality in Britain*, Pelican.

P. Kinnersly (1973) *The Hazards of Work*, Pluto Press.

A. Kornhauser, R. Dubin and A. M. Ross (1954) *Industrial Conflict*, McGraw-Hill.

J. W. Kuhn (1961) *Bargaining in Grievance Settlement*, Columbia University Press.

D. S. Landes (1969) *The Unbound Prometheus*, Cambridge University Press.

T. Lane (1974) *The Union Makes Us Strong*, Arrow.

T. Lane and K. Roberts (1971) *Strike at Pilkingtons*, Fontana.

V. I. Lenin (1961) *Collected Works*, Vol. V, Foreign Languages Publishing House.

—— (1968) *Selected Works*, Lawrence & Wishart.

C. Levinson (1972) *International Trade Unionism*, Allen & Unwin.

S. M. Lipset (1959) 'Political Sociology' in R. K. Merton *et al.*, *Sociology Today*, Basic Books.

S. M. Lipset, M. A. Trow and J. S. Coleman (1956) *Union Democracy*, Free Press.

D. Lockwood (1958) *The Black-Coated Worker*, Allen & Unwin.

J. Lovell (1969) *Stevedores and Dockers*, Macmillan.

G. Lukacs (1971) *History and Class Consciousness*, Merlin.

S. Lukes (1974) *Power*, Macmillan.

W. E. J. McCarthy (1972) *Unions*, Penguin.

W. E. J. McCarthy and S. R. Parker (1968) *Shop Stewards and Workshop Relations*, HMSO.

C. B. Macpherson (1962) *The Political Theory of Possessive Individualism*, Oxford University Press.

C. P. Magrath (1959) 'Democracy in Overalls', *Industrial and Labor Relations Review*, *12*, 3.

M. Mann (1973) *Consciousness and Action among the Western Working Class*, Macmillan.

A. Marshall (1920) *Principles of Economics* (8th ed.), Macmillan.

R. Martin (1968) 'Union Democracy : an Explanatory Framework', *Sociology*, 2, 2.

K. Marx (1958) Articles in Marx and Engels 1958.

—— (1959) *Capital*, vol. I, Lawrence & Wishart (first English edition 1887).

—— (1962) *Capital*, vol. III, Lawrence & Wishart (first English edition, 1909).

—— (1973) *Grundrisse: Introduction to the Critique of Political Economy*, Pelican.

K. Marx and F. Engels (1958) *Selected Works*, Foreign Languages Publishing House. [References in the text of this book to the first volume merely give the page reference; those to Volume II are thus indicated.]

—— (1970) *The German Ideology*, Lawrence & Wishart (first English edition 1938).

J. Mathews (1972) *Ford Strike*, Panther.

M. Meissner (1971) 'The Long Arm of the Job', *Industrial Relations*, *10*, 3.

R. Michels (1915) *Political Parties*, Hearst's.

R. Miliband (1961) *Parliamentary Socialism*, Merlin.

—— (1965) 'Marx and the State', *Socialist Register 1965*.

—— (1969) *The State in Capitalist Society*, Weidenfeld & Nicolson.

C. W. Mills (1948) *The New Men of Power*, Harcourt, Brace.

L. Minkin (1974) 'The British Labour Party and the Trade Unions', *Industrial and Labor Relations Review*, *28*, 1.

W. E. Moore, *Industrial Relations and the Social Order*, Macmillan.

W. Morris (1962) *Selected Writings and Designs*, Pelican.

J. T. Murphy (1972) *The Workers' Committee*, Pluto Press (first published 1917).

T. Nichols (1969) *Ownership, Control and Ideology*, Allen & Unwin.

J. O'Connor (1973) *The Fiscal Crisis of the State*, St. Martin's Press.

M. Olson (1965) *The Logic of Collective Action*, Harvard University Press.

F. Parkin (1971) *Class Inequality and Political Order*, MacGibbon & Kee.

C. Pateman (1970) *Participation and Democratic Theory*, Cambridge University Press.

Pay Board (1974) *Relativities* (Advisory Report No. 2).

W. Paynter (1972) *My Generation*, Allen & Unwin.

S. Perlman (1928) *A Theory of the Labor Movement*, Macmillan.

E. H. Phelps Brown (1959) *The Growth of British Industrial Relations*, Macmillan.

N. Poulantzas (1973) *Political Power and Social Classes*, New Left Books.

A. M. Ross (1948) *Trade Union Wage Policy*, University of California Press.

S. Rowbotham (1973) *Hidden from History*, Pluto Press.

L. R. Sayles (1958) *The Behavior of Industrial Work Groups*, Wiley.

J. A. Schumpeter (1943) *Capitalism, Socialism and Democracy*, Allen & Unwin.

M. Shanks (1961) *The Stagnant Society*, Pelican.

A. J. M. Sykes (1967) 'The Cohesion of a Trade Union Workshop Organization', *Sociology*, *1*, 2.

R. H. Tawney (1961) *The Acquisitive Society*, Fontana (first published 1921).

H. A. Turner (1962) *Trade Union Growth, Structure and Policy*, Allen & Unwin.

H. A. Turner, G. Clack and G. Roberts (1967) *Labour Relations in the Motor Industry*, Allen & Unwin.

M. van de Vall (1970) *Labor Organizations*, Cambridge University Press.

S. Webb and B. Webb (1897) *Industrial Democracy*, Longmans.

—— (1920) *History of Trade Unions* (2nd ed.), Longmans.

D. Wedderburn (1974) *Poverty, Inequality and Class Structure*, Cambridge University Press.

J. Westergaard (1970) 'The Rediscovery of the Cash Nexus', *Socialist Register 1970*.

J. Woodward (1958) *Management and Technology*, HMSO.

# Index